The Confusion of Realms

Richard Gilman

Vintage Books

A Division of Random House

New York

For my wife,
LYNN,
without whose loving impatience
this book might not have come about.

Contents

Introduction

The pieces in this book are intended to make up a unity. At any rate, they are not intended to constitute a "collection" in the usual sense, since that is a gathering of things one has written at various times with no thought—or am I being naïve?—of their coming to live permanently together. The book began with my recognition that a number of writings of mine that I felt especially pleased with, or at least not displeased by, particularly well exemplified certain continuing preoccupations and lines of thought. These make up somewhat less than half the volume. The rest is comprised of four new long essays, the ones on Norman Mailer and on Ibsen and Strindberg, which have not been published before (except that I incorporated into the Mailer essay fragments of earlier reviews and essays I had done on him; about ten percent of the piece is from this source), and those on "The Living Theatre" and on "Art and History," which in shorter form have appeared in periodicals.

I spoke of my continuing preoccupations and lines of thought. Of course every critic has these; the reason I mention mine is that I suspect I have them in an unusually pressing or noticeable way. This may mean I'm limited and single-minded, or it may simply mean that I don't regard criticism as a broad, humane, cultured, and dispassionate activity, but as a means, like that of any writer, of expressing an attitude and approach to experience. I'll leave this to the reader to decide, of course, just as I'll leave it to him to discover what my ideas and preoccupations are; he'd certainly resent my telling him here.

One matter I would like to mention in this brief note. On a number of social occasions I have met people who didn't know who I was (never any shortage of these) and been asked, cocktail-party fashion, what I *did*. To my reply that I wrote, the question naturally has been "what?" and to the reply "criticism," it's been "what kind?" "On drama, fiction, films, and other things," I've replied, and discovered that a certain blankness, even an unhappiness, has been my reward, a disconsolate response to the evidence of non-specialization. Well, there it is; I know I would never have been able to have gone through my intellectual life this far, the way many other critics do, confined to one subject or field. Perhaps the essays in this book will throw some light on the matter; in any case, I hope an apology isn't expected of me.

A few remarks on the erosions and displacements of time. Although none of the pieces in this book is earlier than 1963 and some of them are as recent as 1969, a number of instances of datedness occur. A mild and amusing one: I have used the term "broad-jump," which every track fan knows has been officially replaced by "long-jump." A bit more serious: Eldridge Cleaver, since I reported on his various activities in San Francisco, fled to Havana and, as I write this, is now in Algiers. Gravest of all: "happenings" is now a word nearly gone out of use; yet what these events began in the theater is still under way and important.

A note on previous publication: the essays and reviews on Updike, Gass, Bartholme, Rechey, McLuhan, Sontag, and Black Writing originally appeared in *The New Re-*

public; "MacBird! and Its Audience" and "The True and Only Crisis of the Theater" in the *New American Review;* "Art and History in the *Partisan Review;* and "The Living Theatre" in *The Atlantic Monthly.* Thanks are due to the editors of these publications for permission to reprint.

Finally, I want to express my gratitude to some friends, for friendship, ideas, interchange, confidence, and support: Richard Poirier, Robert Brustein, Stanley Kauffmann, Robert Evett, James Finn, Anatole Broyard, David and Lore Segal, Theodore Solotaroff, Sherman Drexler, Jack Kroll, and not least, my editor, Alice Mayhew.

Part One

White Standards
and Black Writing

There is a growing body of black writing which is not to be thought of simply as writing by blacks. It is not something susceptible of being democratized and assimilated in the same way that writing by Jews has been. The movement there was, very roughly, from Jewish writing to Jewish-American writing to writing by authors "who happen to be Jews." But the new black writing I am talking about isn't the work of authors who *happen* to be black; it doesn't make up the kind of movement within a broader culture by which minorities, such as the Jews or the Southerners in our own society, contribute from their special cast of mind and imagination and their particular historical and psychic backgrounds something "universal," increments to the literary or intellectual traditions.

These black writers I am speaking of take their blackness not as a starting point for literature or thought and not as a marshaling ground for a position in the parade of national images and forms, but as absolute theme and necessity. They make philosophies and fantasias out of their color, use it as weapon and seat of judgment, as strategy and outcry, source of possible rebirth, data for a future existence and agency of revolutionary change. For such men and women, to write is an almost literal means of survival and attack, a means—more radically than we have known it—to *be*, and their writing owes more, consciously at least, to the embattled historical moment in which black Americans find themselves than to what is ordinarily thought of as literary expression or the ongoing elaboration of ideas.

That universality is not among the incentives and preoccupations of this writing is something that makes for its particular, if sometimes provisional, strength. A book like *The Autobiography of Malcolm X*, the type and highest achievement of the genre (if we have to call it that), forges its own special value and importance partly through its adamant specificity, its inapplicability as a model for many kinds of existence. Its way of looking at the world, its formulation of experience, is not the potential possession—even by imaginative appropriation—of us all; hard, local, intransigent, alien, it remains in some sense unassimilable for those of us who aren't black. And that is why it has become, to an even greater degree than novels like *Native Son* and *Invisible Man*, the special pride and inspiriting book of so many black Americans.

Malcolm's literacy, his capacity to write the book at all, were of course formed by what we have to call white traditions, but the book was not a contribution to those traditions, not another *Education of Henry Adams* or *Apologia Pro Vita Sua*, documents of the white normative Western consciousness and spirit, which blacks in America today have begun to repudiate in ways that are as yet clumsy, painful and confused. The point is that most Western intellectual autobiographies, apart from the writings of revolutionaries in whom the life was subordinate to the action in the world, have been luxury documents. Rising out of an already assured stock of consciousness and technical means, building on a civilization which had thrown up many precedents and models for the extension of the self into memorial and apologetic literature—writing which *takes for granted* the worth, dignity and substantial being of the individual, his right to talk about himself in public—such books could only have provided Malcolm with certain technical or organizational principles of procedure. As for spiritual models, could he have learned from *Up from Slavery*, that book which so many black Americans so fiercely repudiate today as much for its having been written in the borrowed, deferential spirit of imitation of Western sagas of the self as for its explicit Uncle Tomism?

There was a central element of dishonesty in white liberal reactions to Malcolm's book. It should have alarmed them far more radically than it did. But by praising Malcolm for his candor, his "power" or his "salutary indictment of our society," by making a literary compatriot of him, the white cultured community effectively blunted the really unsettling fact about his book: that it was not written for us, it was written for blacks. It is not talking about the human condition (that Western idea which from the battle line looks like a luxury product) but about the condition of black people; it is not, moreover, anything less—although it is other things as well—than a myth of blacks to live by now, as we have our myths of so many kinds.

The black man doesn't feel the way whites do, nor does he think as whites do—at the point, that is, when feeling and thought have moved beyond pure physical sensation or problems in mathematics. "Prick me and I bleed," Shylock rightly said, but the difference begins when the attitude to the blood is in question: black suffering is not of the same kind as ours. Under the great flawless arc of the Greco-Roman and Judeo-Christian traditions we have implicitly believed that all men experience essentially the same things, that birth, love, pain, self, death, are universals; they are in fact what we mean by universal values in literature and consciousness. But the black man has found it almost impossible in America to experience the universal as such; this power, after all, is conferred upon the individual, or rather confirmed for him, by his membership in the community of men. Imagine how it must be to know that you have not the right to feel that your birth, your pain, your joy or your death are proper, natural elements of the human universe, but are, as it were, interlopers, unsanctioned realities, to be experienced on sufferance and without communal acknowledgment.

"We shall have our manhood. We shall have it or the earth will be leveled by our attempts to gain it." So writes Eldridge Cleaver in his book, *Soul on Ice*, a collection of letters, essays, reflections and reports from his life which go to make up a spiritual and intellectual autobiography that stands at the exact resonant center of the new black writing I have been referring to. Cleaver's book is in the tradition—that just-formed current—of Malcolm X's, and the latter is its mentor in the fullest sense. Unsparing, unaccommodating, tough and lyrical by turns, foolish at times, unconvincing in many of its specific ideas but extraordinarily convincing in the energy and hard morale of its thinking, painful, aggressive and undaunted, *Soul on Ice* is a book for which we have to make room, but not on the shelves we have already built.

Cleaver was born in Arkansas in 1935, grew up in the black ghetto of Los Angeles and at eighteen was sent to prison for possessing marijuana. Since then he has spent most of his time in one or another California prison, being at present on parole from the institution at Soledad and living in the Bay area where, the dust jacket quotes him as saying, he works as a "full-time revolutionary in the struggle for black liberation in America." He is a staff writer for *Ramparts*, minister of information for the Black Panther Party for Self-Defense, and at work on a book about "the future direction of the black liberation movement."

The year he first went to prison was the year of the Supreme Court decision overthrowing school segregation, and Cleaver holds the two events in firm, unambiguous relationship. The decision moved him into thought for the first time: "I began to form a concept of what it meant to be black in white America." As his intellect sought materials, he turned to the great white revolutionaries—Marx, Tom Paine, Lenin, Bakunin, Nechayev (most of whom he must have read in periods outside prison)—and later to Negro writers like Richard Wright, W. E. B. Du Bois and, of course, with enormous impact on him, Malcolm X. The last stages of his education seem to have been his reading of white writers like Mailer, Burroughs and Ginsberg, who put him in touch with certain energies and approaches which he badly needed to escape provincialism.

He started to write a few years ago, he says, "to save myself." For from being jailed for possessing pot he had passed to true criminal status. Agonized, furious, blind with vengefulness, he had embarked, after completing his first sentence, on a deliberate career as a rapist, first with black women as victims—"in the black ghetto where dark and vicious deeds appear not as aberrations or deviations from the norm, but as part of the sufficiency of the Evil of a day"—and then with whites. "I had gone astray—astray not so much from the white man's law as from being human, civilized . . ."

This struggle, to be human and civilized without submitting oneself to the *whiteness* of those words, and above all without submitting to fear of the law which embodies them, is at the heart of much passionate activity among blacks in America today. It was Malcolm X's struggle: in that change of heart and mind he underwent before his death, and which was the immediate cause of his death, Malcolm worked himself free of racism, out of the trap of being merely opposed, of being, therefore, fixed in the reduced identity of the opponent. "I have, so to speak,"

Cleaver writes, "washed my hands in the blood of the martyr, Malcolm X, whose retreat from the precipice of madness created new room for others to turn about in, and I am now caught up in that tiny space, attempting a maneuver of my own."

That tiny space: from one perspective it is the space between absolute hatred and repudiation of all whites and Uncle Tomism, from another, wider one the murderously curtailed room any one of us has to remain human and yet to *make something happen*, to change things. For Cleaver, the "maneuver" he carries out is an effort at grace, complexity and faithfulness. It is to *be* black, with no concessions, no adaptations to white expectations, but at the same time to hold back from excess; it is to be able to invent myths and intellectual schemes for containing black experience and providing for a black future, but at the same time to distinguish in the white-controlled present whatever has remained human and might recommend itself as ally.

Cleaver finds the ally among young whites, whose "prostrate souls and tumultuous consciences" are evidence to him of the great split in this country of which the racial war is only one, if major, constituent. "There is in America today," he writes, "a generation of white youth that is truly worthy of a black man's respect," "a rare event" in our "foul history." They are a generation which has lost its heroes, and Cleaver has no hesitation in asserting that the new heroes are black or yellow or Latin, in any case never Anglo-Saxon: Mao, Castro, Che Guevara, Martin Luther King, Ho Chi Minh, Stokely Carmichael, Malcolm. (In the several years since he wrote this, his list of heroes has been reduced by time's erosion of ideality— Nasser, Ben Bella and Kwame Nkrumah have of course lost their revolutionary credentials—but the general truth holds up.)

Yet having made his acknowledgments to white revolutionary youth and having distinguished, as it is crucial to do, the fact that the political conflict in this country is "deeper than race," Cleaver keeps going back to race as his theme and arena. As a self-described "ofay-watcher," he has his eye on a hundred manifestations of American ugliness or depravity or dishonesty, but he is not a social critic for *our* sake: his is a Negro perspective, sight issuing from the "furious psychic stance of the Negro today," and in its victories of understanding, its blindness and incompletions, its clean or inchoate energies, its internal motives and justifications, his writing remains in some profound sense not subject to correction or emendation or, most centrally, approval or rejection by those of us who are not black.

I know this is likely to be misunderstood. We have all considered the chief thing we should be working toward is that state of disinterestedness, of "higher" truth and independent valuation, which would allow us, white and black, to see each other's minds and bodies free of the distortions of race, to recognize each other's gifts and deficiencies as gifts and deficiencies, to be able to quarrel as the members of an (ideal) family do and not as embattled tribes. We want to be able to say without self-consciousness or inverted snobbery that such and such a Negro is a bastard or a lousy writer.

But we are nowhere near that stage and in some ways we are moving farther from it as polarization increases. And my point has been that it would be better for all of us if we recognized that in the present phase of interracial existence in America moral and intellectual "truths" have not the same reality for blacks and whites, and that even to write is, for many blacks, a particular act within the fact of their Negritude, not the independent universal "luxury" work we at least partly and ideally conceive it to be.

Here is Cleaver on a social manifestation of what I am talking about:

One thing that judges, policemen and administrators never seem to have understood, and for which they certainly do not make any allowances, is that Negro convicts, basically, rather than see themselves as criminals and perpetrators of misdeeds, look upon themselves as prisoners of war, the victims of a vicious, dog-eat-dog social system that is so heinous as to cancel out their own malefactions: in the jungle there is no right and wrong.

To turn from this to intellectual creation is to indicate how I myself, a "judge" who passes on writing, must take something into account. Cleaver's book devotes a great deal of space to his elaboration of a structure of thought, a legend really, about the nature of sexuality in America today. Some of it is grand, old-fashioned Lawrentian and Maileresque mythmaking:

> This is the eternal and unwavering motivation of the male and female hemispheres, of man and woman, to transcend the Primeval Mitosis and achieve supreme identity in the Apocalyptic fusion.

Some of it is a Marxist-oriented analysis which ends by creating certain large controlling figures with which to account for experience. These are the white man, the Omnipotent Administrator, the white woman, the Ultrafeminine, the black man, the Supermasculine Menial; and the black woman, the Subfeminine Amazon. Sexually each has been forced into a role, as a result of his or her position in the society, and this frozen typology is what we have to battle against.

I find it unsatisfying intellectually, schematic and unsubtle most of the time. I don't want to hear again that the white man has been cut off from his body or that the black male has been forced back into his, that the black penis is more alive or the white woman's sexuality is artificial and contrived. Yet I don't want to condemn it, and I am not sure

I know how to acknowledge it without seeming patronizing. For Cleaver has composed a myth to try to account for certain realities, black realities more than white ones: the fascination of black men with white standards of female beauty, the painfulness of having one's sexuality imprisoned within class or racial lines, the refusal of the society to credit the black man with a mind, the split between black men and women.

He knows what he is talking *from*, if not fully what he is talking *about*, and it is not my right to compare his thinking with other "classic" ways of grappling with sexual experience and drama; it isn't my right to draw him into the Western academy and subject his findings to the scrutiny of the tradition. A myth, moreover, is not really analyzable and certainly not something which one can call untrue.

But Cleaver gets me off the hook, I think, by providing me with a very beautiful section to quote, a letter "To All Black Women, From All Black Men," in which ideas are subordinated to intense feeling and in which the myth's unassailable usefulness is there to see. In it he addresses the black woman as "Queen-Mother-Daughter of Africa, Sister of My Soul, Black Bride of My Passion, My Eternal Love," and begs forgiveness for having abandoned her and allowed her to lose her sense of womanness. The last lines of the letter, and the book, make up an enormously impressive fusion of Cleaver's various revolutionary strands, his assertion of a black reality, his hunger for sexual fullness and the reintegration of the self, his political critique and program and sense of a devastated society in need of resurrection:

> Black woman, without asking how, just say that we survived
> our forced march and travail through the Valley of Slavery,
> Suffering and Death—there, that Valley there beneath us
> hidden by that drifting mist. Ah, what sights and sounds and
> pain lie beneath that mist. And we had thought that our hard

climb out of that cruel valley led to some cool, green and peaceful, sunlit place—but it's all jungle here, a wild and savage wilderness that's overrun with ruins.

But put on your crown, my Queen, and we will build a New City on these ruins.

The passage is not addressed to me, and though I have called it beautiful and impressive and so on, that is out of the habit of the judge-critic, and I don't wish to continue in this strange and very contemporary form of injustice, that of sanctioning black thought from the standpoint of white criteria. I will go on judging and elucidating novels and plays and poetry by blacks according to what general powers I possess, but the kind of *black writing* I have been talking about, the act of creation of the self in the face of that self's historic denial by our society, seems to me to be at this point beyond my right to intrude on.

Black Writing
and White Criticism

The mail elicited by my review of Eldridge Cleaver's *Soul on Ice* has been heavy enough for me to feel justified in going back to it. The letters were about evenly divided for and against, but the negative ones all made a criticism which I think it important to deal with. The whole issue of black writing and white criticism is enormously significant in its own right and for what it may tell us about some changing conditions of writing, thought and imagination.

I wrote that I knew I was likely to be misunderstood, for I was presenting a quite radical and potentially unsettling idea: that white critics have not the right to make judgments on a certain kind of black writing, which I was careful to distinguish from what might be called "writing by blacks" in the same way that Southern or Jewish writing may be distinguished from writing by Southerners or Jews. In refusing to pass judgment on certain essays and personal statements by Cleaver, a former prisoner and current black power spokesman, I argued that his writing, like that of Malcolm X, was not intended for me, but was an act of creation and definition of the self on the part of a black who, as a measure of the wound and dissociation in our society, was estranged from me and other whites, had some new and different values and impulses, and lived now across an abyss not bridgeable by simple good will or by independent, "disinterested" intellectual criteria.

The misunderstanding on the part of my critics was, just as I had feared, almost complete and took the form in nearly every case of the accusation that I had "subverted the very notion of criticism" itself. This phrase is from a letter by the sociologist Lewis Coser of Brandeis University, who went on to say that by the "standards" I had set up I "could not assess the writings, say, of Jean Genet," since I am "presumably neither a thief nor a homosexual," and that I "could scarcely write about Doris Lessing's *The Golden Notebook*," since I "am not a woman and hence [don't] know what it means to menstruate."

The first thing I want to say to Dr. Coser, whom I will regard as my representative critic, is that, as he riskily assumed, I *am* a nonlarcenous male heterosexual and as such am shut out in certain essential ways from Genet's universe of crime and homosexuality (as from his Frenchness, his status as a famous writer, his being fifty-eight years old and so on) and from Miss Lessing's life as a woman. We are all excluded from one another in ways like these, and criticism (of any kind) has never depended on our not being so. There are several crucial points to make in regard to all this, and I am grateful to Professor Coser for so handsomely setting up the opportunity for me to attempt them.

To begin with, both Genet and Miss Lessing are imaginative writers who produce *fictions*, however autobiographical these may appear, works of literary art whose governing impulses are aesthetic, not psychological or sociological or political. Like other writers, they may and do put to use what they know themselves to be—criminal or invert or woman—but this, if they are true artists, will emerge as data, constituent, ground or presence, never as "subject." When I enter the world of their fictions, I encounter these psychological or social or biological materials, and it is precisely through the work's function as art that I am enabled to overcome much prior separation, to slip past, as though by a ruse, the barriers of exclusion that make up an existential fact.

But I have not overcome physical or ontological separation. For this world of fiction—Genet's, Miss Lessing's or any other writer's—is merely (miraculous understatement) a *possible* world, an artifice, a creation, not a report in an actual state of affairs, not *the truth*, and judgment therefore rests on how successfully the writer has established this possibility, what authority his vision has. I am put by this authority in the presence of the writer's imagination, and it is this movement, a matter of analogical process, by which I draw closer and escape exclusion, at the same time as I am left with no more knowledge in the cognitive sense than I had before.

If Genet's or Miss Lessing's writing works for me as literature, it isn't because I now know more about homosexuality or what it's like to be a woman. Actually I now know less, in a strange, merciful sense. And this is because I have had my otherwise invincible structure of inevitably and inherently wrong ideas about homosexuality or womanness (inevitably wrong precisely because I am not these other persons and my ideas are a means of *warding off* their differences) replaced by the only form of knowledge that truly breaks down barriers, the knowledge of another person's imagination as it refashions the materials of the world in a work of art. This is what we really mean by communication, and when it is happening, it hits against the stupid pride we have in our ostensible knowledge of the world, to which art is forever restoring the strangeness and unexpectedness that the habit of life is always destroying.

Judgment doesn't, then, rest on how accurately the

writer has described or "captured" (a favorite word of
utility-minded and predatory critics) the milieu, or lineaments or significance of the particular condition; in some
final and decisive sense literary works have nothing to do,
as literature, with the particularities of their instigation,
with the places where writers start. Thus Proust's fiction
leaves homosexual love behind, Faulkner's leaves the South,
Conrad's the sea, Joyce's Dublin and Hemingway's
virility or honor—to reveal these scenes or subjects as pretexts. For what is being sought is a fiction, an increment
to the known world and a corrective to it.

Now Genet and Miss Lessing may indeed be evaluated
by homosexuals or thieves or women, but the latter would
not be functioning as literary critics (or even as proper
readers) if they were to address themselves to the pretexts,
to praise or damn, say, *The Miracle of the Rose* or *The
Golden Notebook* on sexual or moral or feminist grounds.
(It goes without saying that we have plenty of purported
literary critics who do just this kind of thing, without even
the justification—on that level—of claiming kinship with
a writer in one or another condition of specific being.)
And by the same token, deprivation of homosexual or
female being is no disqualification when I come to judge,
to respond to, Genet's or Miss Lessing's work any more
than my not being French or English is, although being
American may of course make me lose some nuances and
subtleties.

But *not being black* is, I argued in my Cleaver review,
just such a disqualification when it is a matter of judging
a kind of writing in which one's condition is not a pretext,
not the raw material for art, but the very subject of the
work, and when the work, furthermore, has been instituted
as a reply, a counterstatement, to those ideas of universal
value which we (whites) of the West have for so long been
propagating and into which, for all their radical inversions,
Genet's writings easily fit.

Cleaver's book seemed to me to fall into that category of new objects, books written with obvious and inescapable debts to Western literacy, to the prevailing and, for anyone in the West, only traditions of organizing thought and experience, but also with an almost wholly new morale and subversive intention: to propound new values and new myths for blacks in the face of white monopoly of values and myths. Such books are Malcolm X's autobiography and Frantz Fanon's *The Wretched of the Earth*.

Writing about the colonial world in his introduction to Fanon's book, Jean-Paul Sartre describes a change of consciousness and attitude on the part of black Africans which was the forerunner of what has lately been happening here:

> A new generation came on the scene. . . . With unbelievable patience, its writers and poets tried to explain to us that our values and the true facts of their lives did not hang together, and that they could neither reject them completely nor assimilate them. By and large, what they were saying was this: "You are making us into monstrosities; your humanism claims we are at one with the rest of humanity, but your racist methods set us apart."

Fanon is even more explicit about the sundering that has taken place between white and black consciousness and ways of looking at the world:

> The colonialist bourgeoisie, in its narcissistic dialogue, expounded by the members of its universities, had in fact deeply implanted in the minds of the colonized intellectuals that the essential qualities remain eternal, in spite of all the blunders men may make: the essential qualities of the West, of course. The native intellectual accepted the cogency of these ideas, and deep down in his brain you could always find a vigilant sentinel ready to defend the Greco-Roman pedestal. Now it so happens that during the struggle for

> liberation, at the moment that the native intellectual comes into touch again with his people, this artificial sentinel is turned into dust. All the Mediterranean values—the triumph of the human individual, of clarity and of beauty—become lifeless, colorless knicknacks. All those speeches seem like collections of dead words; those values which seemed to up-lift the soul are revealed as worthless, simply because they have nothing to do with the concrete conflict in which the people is engaged.

In my original essay I argued for a suspension of judgment—more specifically a moratorium on the public act of judgment—in the light of the phenomena Fanon was talking about. And Fanon, who wrote about societies which were literally colonial or had just recently been, so that the colonial mentality was still strong, is extraordinarily relevant. In far more than a metaphorical sense black Americans are a "colonial" people (it is the coherence they find with their own experience that makes Fanon's reflections on Africa so useful and inspiriting a book to the leaders of the black revolution here), and we whites who subscribe to all those Mediterranean values which have become so nearly empty but which we continue to offer all underdogs as though they were immediately convertible into food or housing, or into automatic self-respect, we whites who go on making empty gestures are, vis-à-vis the black, the ruling class, the imperialists.

This is why our vocabularies of rational discourse are so different now from black Americans' (when a subject people finds its voice at last, it has to be different from the masters'). This is why certain books by blacks seem written in a new language and are not therefore for us, why the fact that they are not for us is so threatening to our historical belief in the universality of ideas and values. In all the letters I received from white readers there was evident an anxiety, which mostly expressed itself as anger, over the threat I had posed, or revealed, to tradition, to the ways in which judgments have always been made and so to the very principle of judgment, or criticism, as that which allows us to distinguish for the militant purposes of our culture among the multifarious phenomena that minds and imaginations are constantly throwing up. Beneath the statements about my abandonment of critical procedure, my surrender to . . . what? pressure? guilt? . . . there seemed to me to exist a strong and menaced belief in the powers of critical method, that analytic sword which the West has so actively brandished to keep us from chaos and disaster.

It is a faith I share. If I didn't share it, I wouldn't have taken the risk of seeming to support an anti-intellectual position in order to turn such powers as I possess to the analysis of a situation broader than the problems of style and statement in a particular book. But my belief in the power and necessity of criticism is tempered by my awareness of the constant danger of what Kierkegaard called the "deadlock" which can result from a persistence in the habits of reflection and criticism, which try to turn the world into manageable and categorical realities. The deadlock is reached when the critical mind insists so vehemently on the primacy of its activity that it ends by "transforming the capacity for action into a means of escape from action."

This is what I think is happening, and will go on happening to our deeper injury as long as we refuse to recognize that we can no longer talk to black people, or they to us, in the traditional humanistic ways. The old Mediterranean values—the belief in the sanctity of the individual soul, the importance of logical clarity, brotherhood, reason as arbiter, political order, community—are dead as *useful* frames of reference or pertinent guides to procedure; they are even making some of us sick with a sense of laccrating irony.

To look at each other now in this country, black and

white, across a gulf of separate speeches, gestures, intentions, hopes, is more *reasonable* than to go on insisting that black people or any other group have got to be enrolled under the ancient Western humanist flags so that progress can be guaranteed and chaos averted. Fanon writes:

> The natives' challenge to the colonial world is not a rational confrontation of points of view. It is not a treatise on the universal, but the untidy affirmation of an original idea propounded as an absolute.

When an idea is made into an absolute, we may see it is being fashioned into a myth. The new myths (of which Fanon's own books, which among other things document and describe the process of mythmaking, are themselves examples) may share in Western white literary and intellectual procedures, but are not subject to being brought into the critical arena and there dispatched or pardoned. Such themes or myths as black power, black sexual superiority, white decadence, black eschatology, the white man as devil, the inheritance of the earth not by the meek but by the outraged, have no basis, in *the concrete reality* that faces us, for being analyzed, criticized, turned into abstract, sound or unsound theory. They are "untidy affirmations," and they are to be encountered by us, in all the mysterious and frightening ways this has to happen, without recourse to the moldering Western arsenal of brilliant, clarifying intellectual weapons from which we have always felt ourselves supplied.

The rejoinder may be made that what I have been saying adds up to something very near that kind of fanatically Marxist (or any other type of rigidly sectarian) approach to events by which truth is defined as that which serves the cause. But I am not asking us to subvert truth in this way. I am saying that I don't know what truth for black people is, that I don't wish any longer to presume to know, that I am willing to stand back and listen, *without comment*, to these new and self-justifying voices. And I am also saying that something has happened to our means of gaining access to human truth, of which the black revolution is only one sign and factor, that demands of us an unprecedented effort to get past the deadlock in order for reflection and thought to become again a springboard for action and not an occlusion.

The Doors McLuhan Opens

The first thing we might do in the matter of the state of civilization versus Marshall McLuhan is to stop treating him as a personality or a cult figure and begin manfully to consider what he has been saying. McLuhan is clearly interested in being regarded as a presence, a star, his ego being very much more involved with his work than he would like known. Sometimes, however, he lets the cat out of the bag with a real screech. The last line of this new book, *McLuhan: Hot and Cool,* a collection of previously published reviews and essays on McLuhan, together with his comments on these and some fugitive pieces from his old magazine, *Explorations,* is an answer to a question by the book's editor: "Are you disturbed by the sometimes harsh critical responses your work excites?" "Even Hercules," McLuhan replies, "had to clean the Augean stables but once."

Now anyone who feels himself engaged in *that* line of work isn't likely to be discouraged by adverse comments on his personality or, shifting to a much more respectable plane of discourse, his methodology; he will in fact thrive on it. The more McLuhan is decried, either as a noisome presence or an intellectual muddle, the more strength he takes from his identification with the great misunderstood, the light-bringers who were looked on first as heresiarchs or destroyers. This is the spiritual backing to his intellectual stance; he is squarely in the tradition of the classic Marxist debater for whom the nonacceptance of his arguments is proof of his opponents' imprisonment in an outmoded form of being: you can't understand me because of what you still *are*.

It seems to me that the way to deal with McLuhan is to talk about him but not to him, to pretend that his theories were discovered under a big banyan tree or brought in by a Labrador retriever. He may after all, as Tom Wolfe stridently reminds us in one of the essays of this book, be right; but we are never going to find out, or discover the important ways in which he might be wrong, through head-on assaults.

McLuhan's chief threat has been to our "literate" values, to literacy itself. It is the vested moral interest in literacy, and literature, as indispensable to civilization that is almost always at the center of detractions of his work, crowding out reason and sight, as it crowded them out in the early responses to Freud's propositions and goes on doing still. This is not to say that McLuhan is another Freud, or Darwin or Marx, but that the material he offers is new and revolutionary in a way that requires the full exercise of rationality to deal with. And rationality operates only when moral biases—although not necessarily moral concerns —drop away, which is what gives McLuhan his big edge over his value-minded opponents. It may not be true, as he says in the long interview with which this book ends, that "anybody who spends his time screaming about values in our modern world is not a serious character," but if this is all "anybody" does, he is surely going to be ineffective.

There are actually two species of ineffectiveness on display in this volume, the less instructive being the work of McLuhan's "hottest" or most uncritical admirers—Howard Gossage, Rudolf E. Morris, Walter Ong, S. J., Dean Walker—each of whom has his own way of unconsciously parodying the master. The other is rooted in just that kind of outrage, pained or sneering, which McLuhan inspires in many literary or academic minds as they feel their foundations menaced. For George P. Elliott, Benjamin DeMott, Dwight Macdonald and Christopher Ricks the danger is to individualism, personal choice, literary "beauty," feeling, responsibility, reason itself. All of them catch McLuhan in their sights from time to time (Macdonald, for example, is entirely right on McLuhan's extensive misunderstanding of film art), yet their hits never come close to being mortal or even to slowing down the charging beast.

"I am civilized and maybe I'm foggy," Elliott writes, "but I don't want either myself or my world to be retribalized. He wants, and wants us to want, to turn most of the work of our minds over to the computers." The protest is haplessly misdirected. Apart from the fact that McLuhan has never said he *wants* this to happen, any more than Freud wanted the unconscious to be a source of turmoil and unrest, it isn't even an accurate summary of what he has been describing. Again, when Christopher Ricks deplores McLuhan's "unfelt, unfeeling and nerveless style," the reply has to be that this style isn't at issue, that McLuhan is not trying to convince us through an older mode of verbal beauty or vitality. It may even be, though it does sound rather far-fetched, that as George Steiner remarks elsewhere, "McLuhan's bad writing is almost an illuminative instrument of obsolescence." In another vein, when Benjamin DeMott calls McLuhan "a purveyor of perfect absolution for every genuine kind of modern guilt," he is describing a purchase not a sale; that McLuhan is used this way is undeniable, but it is not a fact that can be used to invalidate his thought.

McLuhan has of course made everything more difficult

by proffering his intuitions and ideas, in his books at any rate, as dogma when they are actually hit-or-miss actions of the mind on safari, "probes," as he himself in a humbler or more defensive mood has called them, stabs into areas of history and experience which have hidden their true natures from us precisely through our having thought our understanding of them was complete. This is why it is so ineffectual to trap him in inconsistencies or local errors, or to complain about his style or manner or his disregard of seemingly contradictory data. If his confusion about the difference between information and knowledge weakens his specific theory of how media work, or if his insistence on the distinguishing qualities and effects of print as a medium flattens out the differences *among* books, the fact remains that he has given us a way of looking at media, and a great many other present phenomena, that we didn't have before.

The best pieces in this book (which has a McLuhanesque "zowie" typography) are by Frank Kermode, Harold Rosenberg and Kenneth E. Boulding. All find him deficient in one way or another, but they use reason to try to illuminate and put in perspective what he has been saying, instead of trying to disqualify him on the grounds of irrationality or antihumanist morale. All three have the kind of historical understanding which allows them to escape being terrorized by what seems to be overthrowing history as we have interpreted it, and at the same time preserves them from the excesses of a history-hating enthusiasm. And all three, in quite different ways, finally see McLuhan as much less impressive as a scientific or systematic thinker than as an artist-philosopher-critic on the order, as Rosenberg lists them, of D. H. Lawrence, Oswald Spengler, T. S. Eliot, F. R. Leavis and Hannah Arendt.

Only Kermode specifically calls him a mythmaker (a "congenial" one), but all agree on McLuhan's value as the creator of what I would call (since nobody has offered anything better) a structure of "attention," a perverse, disorderly, repetitive and frequently ugly but extremely useful instrumentality for getting us to twist our heads around so that we can see that something has happened. The thing may be built on faulty, or even in some cases false, principles, but there is no denying that it has worked.

The point is that it is extremely difficult to make sense out of much of the contemporary world without McLuhan's perspectives, or something like them; and if, as Jonathan Miller said on a BBC program reprinted here, "he opens doors to chaos," he also, as Miller goes on to say, opens others on productive vistas. That we are shaped by what we shape, that media are extensions of ourselves, that electricity has changed both time and human intercourse, that acquired forms of knowledge stand in the way of new knowledge, that discontinuity and simultaneity have replaced sequential movement not only in art and formal thought but also in our most basic sense of how our lives proceed—all these things are true, and yet we were unaware of them or only murkily aware of them until McLuhan.

The job now, as the most useful essays in *McLuhan: Hot and Cool* indicate, is to work with what he has given us in renewed investigations into the very problems his own writings have thrown up. McLuhan is not so much wrong as at the same time excessive and insufficient. Tom Wolfe, for example, isolates an important area in which McLuhan's inadequacies might be usefully explored: his inferior knowledge of physiology. The way the senses are organized in relation to each other, a subject about which there is little hard knowledge, has a great deal to do with some of McLuhan's more overblown assertions.

His apparent inability to distinguish between information and knowledge is another ground on which to turn McLuhan's shortcomings, as through a judo move, into a source of strength for us. Boulding touches on this in what seems to me the most significant criticism yet made: "The message is not just another medium, as McLuhan is continually saying, for the message consists of the processing of information into knowledge, and not the mere transmission of information through a medium." Boulding turns to other matters after this, leaving the point still resonant and awaiting development. In a rather different way Harold Rosenberg's remark that one of McLuhan's chief contributions has been to "help dissolve the craft-oriented concept that modern art works still belong in the realm of things contemplated instead of being [active] forces" is also only the beginning of an exploration of potentially great fruitfulness.

McLuhan's relevance to art and literature is in fact what his literary detractors have notably failed to come to grips with, so busy have they been deploring his seeming put-down of the printed word and his ostensible praise of mass media (it may come as a shock to them to hear McLuhan say, as he does here, that he thinks most of these media "pure poison" and that "it would be a good thing if TV were simply eliminated from the United States scene"). In her essay, "One Culture and the New Sensibility," Susan Sontag scarcely mentions McLuhan, but does concern herself with issues he has raised, chief among them the matter of "form" and "content," which is, I think, the crux of any future discussion.

Like McLuhan, Miss Sontag finds the distinction untenable as applied to contemporary art. And like him, she is turned off by considerations of art as moral information or spiritual catharsis. She is very good on changes that have made it less and less possible to see art in those humanistic ways. Yet she is deficient, if not so extensively as McLuhan, in not being able to see, or at least to argue as though she sees, that the distinction between form and content in art was never valid and that we have not simply come into a new use for content as form but into a condition in which seeming content, "subject matter," no longer is needed to serve as pretext and instigation for aesthetic action.

The point is central to any estimation of McLuhan. The widest hole he leaves to our understanding is the result of his confusion between "form" and "medium," his failure to see that medium is a physical designation while form is an aesthetic one. This is to say, for example, that the form of a novel is something crucially different from its physical existence within the medium of print, which is what enables us to make distinctions among novels, not on the basis of their content, a process to which McLuhan rightly objects, but on that of their formal, or aesthetic, properties. And this means that what we have to defend against McLuhan is the fact that there *are* differences that matter, not only among media but within them. But we are never going to accomplish such a defense if we spend our energy trying to blot out those other differences which in his snaggled, petulant, megalomanic way he has succeeded in putting before our consciousness.

Susan Sontag and the Question of the New

Although it knows how to simulate an independent life, criticism is obviously not an autonomous activity. Called into being by art, it has to answer to art, which means to do the tasks—of illuminating, locating and making connections—that have been set up by art's continual establishment of new forms. In one sense criticism is the annals of artistic movement, debt, change, crisis and new impulse. But criticism is also answerable to the world beyond the aesthetic, and this has meant that it has included among its functions a speculative activity designed to make art itself answerable to life.

There has always been a kind of criticism that has made sketches of the relationships between formal art and informal consciousness, sketches based not only on knowledge of aesthetic history but also on perceptions and intuitions about the general culture, the state of thinking and feeling and experience outside the technically aesthetic. At its best, which means when it takes up a celebratory function as well as an analytic one, this sort of criticism is a form of continuing, engaged, philosophically informed aesthetic thinking. Its proposals are these: to be able to dis-

cern what actually is coming to be born, to distinguish it
from the stillborn, to welcome it, extend it its validations in
public consciousness and, most basic and necessary assis-
tance, make room for it by pushing aside, metaphorically
at least, what in the form of dead bodies has been taking
up all the space.

This species of thinking and writing has been much
more prevalent and developed in France than it has ever
been here, and much more honored. American critics
have rarely possessed any substantial philosophical power
or interest (Edmund Wilson accomplished important things
without having had any such power or interest at all, but
would have been more important, I think, if he had had
some) and have shied away from metaphysics as from a
contagion.

That Susan Sontag is philosophically oriented and has
something of a metaphysical impulse to her thinking (although she would undoubtedly reject the word vehemently)
is among the reasons why I think her one of the most
interesting and valuable critics we possess, a writer from
whom it's continually possible to learn, even when you're
most dissatisfied with what she's saying, or perhaps especially at those times. For the past several years she has
been the chief voice in America of one main tradition of
French criticism, which is one of the reasons, I'm convinced,
why she is disliked, where she's disliked, with such ferocity
and xenophobic scorn.

I have been using the words "critic" and "criticism." But
if Miss Sontag has accomplished nothing else, she has made
us aware of a growing inutility and regressive principle
in our use of these sanctified words. When she said in the
preface to her first book of essays and reviews that "what I
have been writing is not criticism at all, strictly speaking,
but case studies for an aesthetic, a theory of my own sensibility," the remark was thrown out as an afterthought, a
footnote, whereas it ought to be front and center, the

motto for everything she has done. And that would include
the journal of her recent visit to North Vietnam, reprinted
in this new collection, *Styles of Radical Will*.

The point isn't that there is criticism, neat, familiar,
unquestionable as a procedure, and then there is what
Miss Sontag does, odd, peripheral although maybe useful;
but that what she has been doing, or attempting, is more
interesting and more relevant to what is going on than is
most traditional criticism. (At least, on a pragmatic test,
I don't know of any critic more interesting or more relevant.)

Her sensibility departs from that of the traditional
literary critic in that she is very little interested in, or at least
in writing about, fiction (except as it enters extreme modes,
as in pornography) and seems to care nothing at all about
poetry. (She is interested in drama but is not a very good, or
at any rate not a very sophisticated, drama critic, since she
continually announces as discoveries of her own what has
been understood in drama criticism for a long time: the
supercession of naturalism, the shift in concepts of character,
the necessity to get past psychology, etc.) But she differs,
too, from the traditional critic of general culture in that
she is deeply involved in aesthetic awareness. We
might call her a critic of ideas, except that she has always
wished to treat ideas sensuously, aesthetically; or decide
that she is a philosopher of cultural forms, except that
philosophy for her has always been a drama rather than a
method.

The truth is that Miss Sontag ought not to be examined
under the prevailing American definitions of the literary
or cultural critic, any more than the aesthetic developments
she has been talking about ought to be examined under
the rubrics of the criticisms traditional in their realms.
Ever since the New Criticism, its mission accomplished
and its effects guaranteed, receded into history, we have
been unable in America to come near agreeing on what

aesthetic intelligence is, although this kind of intelligence is surely what we should want to mean when we speak of criticism at all; and it is this kind that Miss Sontag possesses.

By aesthetic intelligence I mean a kind which is not that of the scientist or poet but partakes of both; it is that particular kind of informed but open and intuitive consciousness needed to think and talk about what *has not yet been talked about* because it has just now become present, in the form of increment and augmentation of consciousness itself. A faculty that has to come to grips not so much with experience as with what we have to call the experience of experience—since that's what works of art have to do with—it has for the most part in America been propelled and sustained by our Western impulse toward greater and more precise knowledge, and especially knowledge of an immediately useful kind. Much criticism stemming from aesthetic intelligence so motivated has had the effect of turning art back into extra-aesthetic forms of knowledge.

But the aesthetic intelligence is finding it harder to be so motivated and sustained. Like the self in so many other regions, the consciousness addressing itself to art through critical thinking has come, for better or worse, to be increasingly dissatisfied with an operation from outside, with labor across a distance separating viewer, or interrogator, and object. And it has come to be dissatisfied with knowledge as an end in itself. For better or worse: at one end the painful intrusions into thought of the troubled selves of critics like *The Village Voice*'s; but at the other, the theories of John Cage or Buckminster Fuller, the writings of Harold Rosenberg and, sometimes, of Susan Sontag.

The New Criticism, with its explorations in the interior and stress upon structure and formal reality, supported the existence of works of art as independent sources of new, aesthetic meaning; and this was immensely useful as a counterblow to the traditions of exegesis and explanation in terms of already known realities—political, moral, psychological, sociological—that dominated American criticism at the time and dominate it still in its academic and journalistic sectors. But the New Criticism, by concentrating on internal aesthetic purposes and their workings out, had the effect of turning literary and, by extension, other artistic works into models of perception and of aesthetic experience in general, at some cost to their status as unique, particular and sensuous actualities.

The alarm that many people feel at the approach of Susan Sontag, the distaste, resentment and even fury she causes, has, it seems to me, two bases, both of them related to what I have been saying about aesthetic independence or contingency. The cruder one is moral and "humanistic." She has been accused of being inhuman or antihuman for ignoring moral and spiritual elements in art, or rather for sanctioning and encouraging the immoral, pornography or camp, for example, violence or extravagance. To this the only answer is that no material or data or subject or, for that matter, mood in the aesthetic realm has anything to do with being sanctioned or deplored, needs validation or, in short, lies in the moral universe at all. When Henry James said that the only immorality he had ever seen on the stage was the production of a bad play, he told us tersely about the way morality figures in the life of forms. The moral charge against Miss Sontag, which is mainly a charge against the kinds of art she has been interested in, issues from the same morale such charges always do: apprehension in the face of new consciousness.

Beyond this Miss Sontag has marched, aggressively and with her great bristling apparatus of learning (an erudition at least as much philosophical and psychological as literary or technically aesthetic), pointing every which way but most dangerously at certain processes of literary erudition itself, into some sacred realms, to the consternation of their guardians. At the least newcomers are expected to observe the rules. And one of the chief rules is that criticism is a province of the dispassionate (and fact-finding) intellect, which it is designed to serve and, so to speak, to fill out.

But Miss Sontag, it seems, would like to fill out the body or at any rate the whole man, to return the intellectual side—especially the hermeneutic side—of aesthetic experience to a subordinate place. When she wrote, as the coda to one of her most famous essays, that "in place of hermeneutics, we need an erotics of art," she drove many persons nearly wild with misapprehension that what she meant amounted to a new barbarism, a new species of self-indulgence, a relinquishment of the hard-won rationality through which we have steadily mastered art and myth in order to put them into the service of civilized being, of "culture." What she meant, of course, was a new appreciation, a new agreement on mystery, a new delight.

She hasn't always meant it convincingly, it's true, or, to speak more plainly, she hasn't always demonstrated that mystery and delight are what she herself experiences. It is surely a notable fact about Miss Sontag's sensibility—her "subject" and the principle of her shift in critical method—that it so often strikes you as cold, even icy. This is the irony, detected by many, of her demand for an erotics of art. But to be caught in an irony of this kind has nothing to do with being inhuman; writers, more than most humans, are situated between what they are and what they hope it's possible to be. Nor is it a matter of any classical inability to "feel," and attempts to discredit her on this ground (like attempts to discredit her extremely interesting, and much misunderstood, fiction for being overburdened with thought, loaded with strategy instead of life) are obtuse and unjust.

For the problem of her sensibility is also the generating power of its interest and importance for us as she exemplifies and tests and expounds and shapes it into form in her writing. It is precisely classical ability to feel, which, as it works itself out in our shibboleths and humanistic myths, means to feel *the way others have*, to feel certain emotions (in certain ways) that have been sanctified as properly human and necessary, that has come into question. One of the chief resistances put up by new literature, or new art of any kind, is to being told how and what to feel. Academic resistance to the new, on the other hand, is a balking at the notion that we don't already know and haven't already worked out the proper forms.

Susan Sontag has been engaged in trying to plot the course of her new feelings, which is to say her responses as a representative advanced consciousness. (She *is* advanced; would we want her laggard?) In doing this she has indicated all the debilities and irresolutions and compensatory aggressions and contradictions that are inevitable in consciousness in transition. The chief content of that transition now is the challenge to Western literary culture, or rather to the supremacy of literature *as* culture; the growing breakdown of the erstwhile separation between art and audience, or more strictly between art as object for contemplation and as material for reabsorption into total experience; the claim of bodily experience to a place in aesthetics; the more insistent relationship between politics and sensibility. These are Miss Sontag's themes; and she is the victim of their assaults, in their status as realities, upon our preparation, training, inheritance and need for continuity—on *what we were like before*—as much as she is their elucidator and master in awareness.

What we were like before, which is to say what our models were like for the fullest, most exemplary, victoriously sentient civilized beings, was learned, complex, ironic, intellectually armored, central, balanced, full of explanation and the wisdom of the abstract. Miss Sontag is still many of these things, and the discrepancy between them and wanting to be something else, something spontaneous, concrete, sensual, ready for extremes and wise through physicality, is the failure and the fruitfulness of her writing.

To take an important essay from the new volume, "The Pornographic Imagination." In this long, dazzlingly learned, risky piece of advocacy and interrogation, she illustrates the perennial problem of how to argue for the rights of the body and the more dangerous passions without having to rely on the intellect, calling on it, moreover, for every subtle power and all sheer logical force, mustering ideas in order to get beyond them. The effect of this has habitually been to raise a new intellectual structure for exactly what the mind has determined it should no longer coercively house, to present a logic for illogical necessity.

One way of dealing with this problem is to write sensually, to evoke rather than rest on analysis, and this is characteristic of the French writers Miss Sontag admires for their writing on the erotic—Bataille is chief among them—although I don't mean to suggest that they are pure lyricists in whom analysis plays no part. But what they can do, as she has so far been unable to, is offer the feeling of the erotic, as actuality and consciousness, in all its ardor, despair, questionableness, contradiction and urgency, instead of merely a learned process of thinking about it.

But Miss Sontag is of course not French, and if this essay suffers from her coldness of temperament and almost complete lack of any lyric impulse, what's in its favor is the fact that lyrical writing about the erotic so rarely in this country is saved by intelligence from being sheer sentiment, romantic asseveration or rhetorical wish-fulfillment. Her piece is full of an extraordinary intelligence, which sets as its tasks first the establishment of the theoretical possibility that pornography may indeed be literature and second that there are certain pornographic works that actually are.

She is rather better on the first task than the second,

but she's continually interesting on both. To argue, cleanly and decisively as she does, that the main sophisticated counts against pornography as literature have to do with retrograde and obtuse identifications of fiction with verisimilitude, psychological realism and narrative logic is to say what needs saying—about fiction as well as pornography that uses the form. Here is Miss Sontag with her strong, complex intelligence focused on the new as it has to do with altered conceptions of fiction. She insists, with absolute rightness, that fiction is not to be defined by considerations of character-building, psychological complexity or centrality of theme, so that in its narrowness, obsession, extremity of theme and refusal of ordinary characterization, pornographic writing may still qualify as literature.

She then goes on to discuss a number of what she calls pornographic works, chiefly *The Story of O, The Image* by the pseudonymous Jan de Berg, and Bataille's *The Story of the Eye*. She is very good on them, even if she rates *The Image* much too highly, but the strength is analytic and very little is conveyed of how these erotic writings actually reach and move the imagination or why they should have a place there. And something else very curious emerges. I have been going along with her in calling a whole class of books "pornography," but a distinction should really be made, and Miss Sontag inadvertently provides one.

The books mentioned above and others she cites are distinguished from what we ordinarily call pornography precisely by their relative lack of explicit sexual scenes, certainly by their lack of sexual scenes composed as hermetic and single-minded substitutions for any other kind of experience, and by their correspondingly greater content of writing of an imaginatively freer and more complex kind. It isn't that they are less erotic; if anything, the books she admires have greater erotic power than ordinary pornography, but this is because of their greater literary power.

The result of all this is that they cannot be taken as representative of pornographic writing, which remains, as long as it *is* pornography, bad writing. What Miss Sontag fails to see is that she ends by defending not pornography but only such examples of writing with a sexual theme or even a sexual purpose (she defends, with much justice, the legitimacy of "arousing" through writing) as have shaken loose from the undifferentiated mass of such writing precisely through the greater literary strength and concern of their authors. I think it useful to retain "pornography" as a term (without moral condemnation) to denote sexual writing that fails as literature; that which succeeds doesn't need a defense, except perhaps against the kinds of minds Miss Sontag so admirably takes on in her remarks on the petrifaction of definitions of fiction.

"I have been writing . . . a theory of my own sensibility." With this avowal as justification, I would like to point out that from both the new essay on pornography and Miss Sontag's earlier famous one on Camp there rises an aura of will, or willfulness, a wish that something be true, an unavowed prescriptive desire. There is nothing wrong with this, there is even I suspect something extremely useful in it, but it hasn't been seen. For all the brilliance of these pieces and their true extensions of our awareness, they reveal, as most of her other writing does, how beneath the clean-functioning, superbly armed processes of her thought exists a confused, importunate, scarcely acknowledged desire that culture, the culture she knows so much about, be other than it is in order for her to be other than she is.

When she writes that Camp is "loving" and "tender," the wish she is trying to fulfill is for the sophistication that Camp possesses and denotes to be redeemed from its quality as modern sophistication: hard, snobbish, ugly, ungenerous, a means of establishing superiority over the past and over simplicity. When she writes about pornography without attention to its narrowing and unliberating effects, she reveals how her authentic and justifiable longing for bodily liberation, her longing to lighten her own burden of consciousness, mistakes the statement for the thing. One can say that pornography is always wish-fulfillment (nothing inherently wrong with that), but the important thing about this, in her usage, is that it is not so much a wish for erotic experience as a negative desire for eroticism—as subject and atmosphere—to overcome the imbalance of a heavy, weighted, complex, abstract history, the history of the mind as it has offered itself to us as identical with life itself.

I think Miss Sontag is representative in this, and that her own so impressive qualities of mind make her more representative rather than less. And I also think, after reading *Styles of Radical Will*, that she is moving into areas where the "problem" of her sensibility, its transitional quality and status as an arena where new movements are seen and tested at least partly from old perspectives and where culture is being redirected from contemplation to action, will have even more usefulness than it has had. Her talking less and less about literature and more and more about films (the new book contains only one "literary" piece, that on pornography, but three on film, including a masterly long study and appreciation of Godard, the best I know of) seems wholly in coherence with her strengths and interests.

It isn't a matter of any "death" of the novel or of a decline of verbal art in general; these things may be happening, but emphases on film as "truer" or more contemporary art don't prove it. The point here is that whatever is happening to fiction, the new status of film as an art means that the questions it poses are exciting, immediate and full of possible connections with the general culture. More than this, film is an art cutting more deeply into "actuality," trafficking more directly with life than fiction does and in fact taking over some of the functions fiction at one time was made to fulfill. (My own opinion is that fiction is better off stripped of its burden of "information," of portraiture and sense of actuality; denuded in this way, it can begin to be, as it is doing here and there, more purely verbal artifact and imaginative increment.)

Another point: film is a central part of our new visual and aural culture, which itself isn't necessarily proof of an over-throw of literature but may be a matter of a restoration of balance. In any case Miss Sontag's sensibility is much more attuned to the new visual and aural culture than to the older literary one; she is much better able to detect the new and write with force and originality about it in the area of films than in literature or drama. (This is a relative judgment; I haven't meant to imply that she is not contin-uously useful and illuminative in everything she turns to, but only that as a writer on films, where her general aes-thetic ideas can get stronger and deeper purchase on materials, she is at her best.)

I spoke before of the new, more intimate and pressing relationship between politics and sensibility. While Miss Sontag has never been apolitical, she has admitted that she hasn't been able to find the way for her political pas-sions and awarenesses to enter her work on culture and aesthetics. The account of her trip to North Vietnam last year, "Trip to Hanoi," the major piece in her new book, seems to me to be a sign of a new-found ability to do just that as well as being a remarkable document in its own right.

Miss Sontag went on her journey, as a guest of the North Vietnamese, convinced that "unless I could effect in my-self some change of awareness, of consciousness, it would scarcely matter that I'd actually been in Vietnam." At first she found the country and the culture alien, impenetrable, marked by what she regarded as a boring and "fairy-tale" simplicity. Her whole weight of Western complexity and psychological subtlety militated against her understanding and possible affection for the North Vietnamese. How she was able to effect the change in consciousness she knew she had to have, so that she emerged with the sense of different possibilities of life, a potential way out of self-consciousness, guilt, moral ambiguity and the ironic stance that has been the Western intellectuals' chief weapon of both aggression and defense—all this is what the essay is about. And by being about these things, it is more centrally, refulgently and authentically about mind, consciousness, sensibility—and what is new in them—than any of the technical, analytic pieces whose bravura and cold knowledgeability have gained her her reputation.

Fiction:
Donald Barthelme

"It is one of the peculiarities of the imagination"—Wallace Stevens said in *The Noble Rider and the Sound of Words*—"that it is always at the end of an era. What happens is that it is always attaching itself to a new reality and adhering to it. It is not that there is a new imagination, but that there is a new reality." Stevens had been talking about poetry, but expanded his argument here to encompass the general action of the imagination as it issues in art of any kind. Nothing could be more useful for an understanding of what "avant-garde," "cultural revolution," "new form" and the like really mean; and as an increment, nothing could be more useful for an understanding of what goes on, or should go on, in criticism, that action which takes place halfway between reality and the imagination and one of whose responsibilities is to see whether or not they are in true relation.

My occasion for quoting Stevens is the publication of *Snow White*, Donald Barthelme's first novel, a work recalcitrant to being discussed in the habitual language of journalistic criticism. One of a handful of American writers who are working to replenish and extend the art of fiction instead of trying to add to the stock of entertainments, visions and humanist documents that fiction keeps piling up, Barthelme has previously published a volume of short stories, *Come Back, Dr. Caligari*, of exceptional technical interest and uncategorizable élan. Like those stories, his novel may be read by ignoring Stevens' dictum, read, that is, as the work of a highly idiosyncratic imagination, a *new* imagination, popping up like a wild-crested tropical bird in all our parlors. But to do that would be to truckle to the imagination in its quest for novelty, eccentric fame, autocratic rule; like any other's, Barthelme's possesses that impulse. And yet its truest accomplishment is to be representative, if a good deal ahead of those of us it deputizes for, to adhere with consciousness, craft and potency to a new reality, one not unknown to the rest of us.

In the most summary way this new reality—which exists inextricably entangled with half a dozen others of varying ages—can be described as being open-ended, provisional, characterized by suspended judgments, by disbelief in hierarchies, by mistrust of solutions, denouements and completions, by horizontal impulses rather than vertical ones, by self-consciousness issuing in tremendous earnestness but also in far-ranging mockery, by emphasis on the flesh to the anachronization of the spirit, by a wealth of possibility in which all the individual possibilities tend to cancel one another out, by unfreedom felt as freedom and the reverse, by cults of youth, sex, change, noise and chemically induced "truth." It is also a reality harboring a radical mistrust of language, writing, fiction, the imagination.

For the literary imagination whose native land all this is, so that it has itself partly been shaped by it, the problem is to adhere (as Stevens also said) without being compliant, to resist at the same time as it stays in connection, and to find in that tension the foundation of its would-be art. All writing fails when it slips out of one of those two obligations; irrelevant literature is that which refuses reality, conformist that which accepts it too readily. But even that writing which appears to be taking the most daring line toward a confronted reality may actually be serving its valetudinarian interest instead of its liberation in and through the imagination.

The trouble with much so-called black humor or absurd writing or neosurrealism (under one of whose tags *Snow White* is certain to be wrongly fixed) is that in some sense it remains subservient to the actuality from which it draws its instigations and energies. The imagination's exotic bird beating at the end of a long string, it stirs up the air but leaves it afterward as it was. A gesture indicating disaffection or the reversal of commonplace values or an appetite for mockery, it accomplishes little aesthetically, even when it provides a momentary rift in the clouds of actuality. The proof of this is that it mostly stays within the formal structures of previous literature, which are inescapably the products of a previous, a superseded, reality. Superficially, we might say *thematically* rebellious, it remains artistically tory, holding on to one or another conception of beauty, to tension and development, to character, story and plot, to moral or social or psychological "significance."

There are of course great risks in trying to make fictive art without these things: you can fall into chaos or impenetrable murk, or into total sterile abstraction. Popularity isn't likely to drop into your lap. But *Snow White's* ambitions being what they are, it runs the risk most nakedly, and suffers an immediate loss. If it weren't, for instance, for its refusal to be a "novel," a story proceeding, however wildly or wondrously, like any other, it might well become the *Catcher in the Rye* of this generation. For its "content" includes the substance of our age's newest awareness and pre-awarenesses, its behavior and bemusements, its vocabularies, costumes and stances, and especially those of the uncommitted, disaffiliated young, the disabused and not-again-to-be-taken-in.

But it is a double thing, as Salinger's book couldn't quite manage to be. Its structure adheres closely to the movements and pressures of our new reality, but at the same time it shapes itself into an independent object, not to be exploited for extraliterary purposes and not to be accounted for by extra-aesthetic principles. High-handed, unaccommodating, it fashions a critique of everything it seizes, refusing to become a literary myth for these things (for disaffiliation as in Salinger, for example), putting them to uses other than explanation, morale-building or the erection of new, putatively redeeming beauty.

On its most available level *Snow White* is a parodic contemporary retelling of the fairy tale. More accurately, the tale is here refracted through the prism of a contemporary sensibility so that it emerges broken up into fragments, shards of its original identity, of its historical career in our consciousness (Disney's cartoon film is almost as much in evidence as the Grimm story) and of its recorded or potential uses for sociology and psychology—all the Freudian undertones and implications, for example. Placed like widely separated tesserae in an abstract mosaic construction, the fragments serve to give a skeletal unity to the mostly verbal events that surround them, as well as a locus for the book's main imaginative thrust.

The only thing resembling a narrative is that the book does move on to fulfill in its own very special way the basic situation of the fairy tale. But Barthelme continually breaks up the progression of events, switching horses in midstream, turning lyricism abruptly into parody, exposition into incantation, inserting pure irrelevancies, pure indigestible fragments like bits of stucco on a smooth wall, allowing nothing to *follow* or link up in any kind of logical development. Few of the "chapters" are more than one

or two pages long (some are two lines), and there are
frequent chapter-headinglike passages, set in large black
upper case, with messages of surpassing inconsequence or
misinformation:

**THE REVOLUTION OF THE PAST
GENERATION IN THE RELIGIOUS
SCIENCES HAS SCARCELY PENETRATED
POPULAR CONSCIOUSNESS AND HAS
YET TO SIGNIFICANTLY INFLUENCE
PUBLIC ATTITUDES THAT REST UPON
TOTALLY OUTMODED CONCEPTIONS.**

What emerges through the seeming chaos of styles and
procedures, the irrelevancies and non sequiturs, are a
set of determinable facts. In a house in an unnamed city
seven men—Bill, Dan, Hubert, Kevin, Henry, Edward and
Clem—live with Snow White, whom they have found in a
forest before the book begins and who is now twenty-two
and of course beautiful. Each day the seven go out to work
("Heigh-ho") "filling the vats and washing the buildings,"
while Snow White keeps house, cooks and awaits their
return, whereupon sexual activity presumably takes place,
although it is never more than ironically hinted at. At a
later point two more "characters" complete the original
dramatis personae: Jane, a young woman who is the witch
figure, and Paul, the prince whom Snow White is waiting
for.

Moving in and out of Barthelme's prose, his literary
activity, the characters present us with *its* nature as well
as their own. From the beginning we are aware that the
fairy tale is undergoing a modernization, becoming the up-
to-date expression of a change in human typology and self-
estimation. " 'I am princely,' Paul reflected in his eat-in
kitchen." But he is not princely. It is one of Barthelme's

central purposes to establish that princes no longer exist, in a crucial double sense. As a figure in reality—the strong, decisive man, the prince of good fellows—he has been driven out of existence precisely by contemporary life, with its neuroses, communal psychological tyrannies and violent self-consciousness; and as a literary figure, the hero, he can have no stature because the reality he has been abstracted from no longer sustains the values necessary to his creation.

Reality no longer sustains the values necessary to the creation of Snow White either, or the witch or the dwarfs; it lacks the floor under the imagination, the ingredients of possible aspiration, the hunger for simulated fate, to create "stories" of any kind. There is therefore no happy ending to this *Snow White,* no denouement except one that mocks the original's, no satisfaction to be obtained from a clear, completed arc of fictional experience. Fiction, Barthelme is saying, has lost its power to transform and convince and substitute, just as reality has lost, perhaps only temporarily (but that is not the concern of the imagination), its need and capacity to sustain fictions of this kind.

Everything therefore works to undermine the *données* of the fairy story, to prevent it from retracing its classic parabola, major sorties being directed against the characters in their representationality. Thus Snow White, the least self-conscious figure in literature, is here full of self-consciousness of an exact and tragicomic contemporary kind. "Who am I to love?" she asks herself about her inability to requite the seven men. "Is there a Paul," she muses, "or have I only projected him in the shape of my longing, boredom and pain . . . is my richly appointed body to go down the drain at twenty-two?" As for Paul himself, he is locked in a grotesque incapacity to fulfill his destiny, which is of course to *reach* Snow White, to rescue her by his actual prowess and fertility from her condition of potentiality. At one point he sets up an underground observation station, complete with systems of mirrors and trained dogs, so as to spy on her; at another he enters a monastery; in the end he drinks the poison intended for Snow White. He is, as Snow White finally sighs, not a prince but "pure frog"; he is incapable of being conjured into heroic form. There is an exquisite irony in the description of him as "a well-integrated personality . . . he makes contact . . . a beautiful human being."

This desperate, comic, losing struggle of the characters to fulfill their classic roles—the seven men, for instance, are continually afflicted with misgivings, jealousies and strange psychosomatic ailments—is the outcome of a mocking humanization fatal to their existence as archetypes and of a dissolution of their story's clean, utilitarian, wish-fulfilling dream logic into ambiguity, dissonance and fragmentation. In Grimm each of the major personages (the dwarfs being considered as one) is wholly and purely a representative, an incarnation: Snow White of beauty and abused innocence, the witch of envy and malice, the prince of redemptive strength and the dwarfs of selfless service. For Barthelme's imagination those exemplary careers are agencies of an acute and devastating scepticism about hypostatized ideas in reality—goodness, evil, redemption, service—the same sort of scepticism the young feel so strongly today and articulate so badly.

But at the same time they are material for a new literary action by which literature itself is made to expose the bankruptcy of its traditional normative procedures, so that new literature might be formed on the dead ground. Fiction, Barthelme assumes, can no longer be (if it ever wholly was) the expression or interpretation or simulacrum of life and its values. Nor can it be the reader of its secret thoughts, nor the vehicle of surrogate emotions or aspirations nor in fact of experience of any kind except an aesthetic one. There ought not be a logic of fictional event, fulfilling reality's reputed craving for a compensation for its own illogic; fiction cannot be the savior or map maker of reality, nor the cicerone through its confused travels. And finally fiction ought not be an employment of language for ends beyond itself, but language in its own right, mysteriously saturated with reality, perpetually establishing a new synthesis of reality and the imagination, and doing this partly by driving out all language which has accomplished an earlier synthesis.

In one of his frequent deadpan pseudoscientific passages, Barthelme has the manager of a "plastic buffalo hump" factory talk about the accumulation of trash in the world. "We're in humps right now . . . from a philosophical point of view," he says, because since trash is accumulating at a rate which will soon reach one hundred percent of everything there is, men will have to learn how to "dig" it, and "what in fact could be more useless or trashlike" than humps? From this he moves on to a reference to "those aspects of language that may be seen as a model of the trash phenomenon." In another passage Snow White complains: "Oh I wish there were some words in the world that were not the words I always hear!" And in still another reference to the pressure of language deadening, hardening, turning to trash, to discarded actuality, Paul says: "I would wish to retract everything if I could, so that the written world would be. . . ."

What it would be is, hopefully, here, in *Snow White*. A landscape filled with the dissolving remnants of earlier literary landscapes (there are parodies of Shakespeare, Rimbaud, Eliot and others), a battleground for old beauty and new form (which is always partially ugly, since it rises in the face of sanctified notions of beauty), the book makes its way by dealing steadily with the problems of language. One "retracts" what the written world has been composed of not by ignoring it, by writing new language, but by discrediting it as the answer to one's own contemporary needs. So Barthelme retracts the fairy story by discrediting its operation now, and so Picasso, to take an example from another medium, retracted representationalism by discrediting its claims to be what art has to be.

To this end, Barthelme composes his book in a variety of styles, although if there is a predominant one it is a flat, arch, professorial tone, elevated and full of pseudoprecision, exactly suited to his mock-learned treatment of the fairy story: "Bill can't bear to be touched . . . we speculate that he doesn't want to be involved in human situations any more. A withdrawal. Withdrawal is one of the four modes of dealing with anxiety." But he is also a minor Joyce, with a mastery over a great diversity of vocabularies—hip talk, academic cliché, pure or communal cliché, advertising jargon, novelistic "eloquence"—and he employs them for ironic purposes, releasing through their juxtapositions and their fish-out-of-water helplessness as literary instruments a comic sense of reality's lugubrious, perpetually renewed struggle to express itself. But at the same time he incorporates them into the substance of his new literary act.

Similarly, he incorporates into his work a great deal of data, events, names, fads and sociological fashions, using them for both satiric purposes and aesthetic manipulation. Throwing these heterogenous contemporary phenomena into the book—all these "items" about which present-day novels could be written if one saw fiction as being in life's hire or as its nemesis—he proceeds to fashion a net full of red herrings. From Teilhard de Chardin's noosphere to Red China's People's Volunteers, from hip enterprises like "freaking out" or "blowing one's mind" to psychoanalysis, hard-edged painting, motorcycle gangs and the notion of nonevents, *Snow White* is as up-to-the-minute as *Esquire* or *Ramparts*. Yet the novel isn't about these things, not about their meaning or even their phenomenological appearance. It is about their status in the imagination. Despotically contemporary, pressing forward with their claims on our attention in actuality, they are here abstracted into comic helplessness, deprived, by being turned into *mere* language, of their tyranny as fashionable facts. Thus they remain counters in an imaginative activity, not scenes of exploration or analysis, and the book swirls past them on its deceptively wayward and highly conscious course.

It remains to be asked whether *Snow White*, having largely accomplished what it set out to do, exists now as full, confident new literature. Our habits are such that faced with fiction of this kind we fall back on an inquisition designed for subjects eager enough to stand up to it. Any ordinary novel can answer without hesitation or guile the questions whether it is "satisfying"; whether it is shapely, convincing; whether it teaches us something about our lives, or is exciting, consoling or provocative. If *Snow White* is none of these things, its pleasures and conquests must be of a new, although not necessarily unprecedented, kind. I have tried to indicate what they are; what I haven't tried to do is establish a critical hegemony over the book, the kind of bored superiority so prevalent in the rarefied academicism of our fashionable journals.

Which isn't to say that I don't think *Snow White* has faults. Most blatant among them is its author's occasional inability to resist the temptation of an easy score, to keep from lapsing into a Perelmanish genre of humor in which true verbal pressure is vitiated by a penchant for cheap incongruity or the merely bizarre. Thus Barthelme can write about "pornographic pastry" and an "electric wastebasket" to destroy documents and people; speak of identifying someone by the "blueberry flan" on his lapel; have someone say, "I am not an American citizen. I am under Panamanian registry"; refer to the "rare-poison room of her mother's magnificent duplex apartment," and to a plan which is "packed away in the special planning humidor, constructed especially to keep the plan fresh and exciting."

Beyond this, and as a broader function of the same aspect of temperament, he tends to a certain form of unseriousness which is not quite the same thing as high, conscious, daring frivolity. Bent on his purposes of retraction, on redeeming language from exhausted uses and servitude to other powers and the novel from its anachronistic storytelling role, he falls under the sway of an ironical manner that sometimes ends by being its own hermetic justification. That is to say, in wishing not to do what has been done before, he is not wholly willing to risk doing what has not been done before. Thus the book draws back at times from its opportunities to create new facts of the imagination, to push reality forward into a synthesis with the imagination that would by that very action push those facts back into reality and change it.

Kierkegaard wrote that "an intelligent man has the choice (*if* he has it) to be either ironical or radical." Barthelme's irony is of course radical, within the realm of literary process. And yet if he isn't radical outside it, if his irony precludes his being radical *toward the world,* this may be a measure less of his talent and will than of the world as it now stands. We go on expecting fiction, if we expect anything from it, to provide us with large, impregnable, vivid alternatives to or confirmations of our actual experience. The latter is beneath literature, the former seems at the moment beyond it. Perhaps Barthelme has no choice—as Kierkegaard left provision for—but to make his irony constitute his radicalism. In any case, *Snow White* cannot be asked to be the kind of novel that serves as myth, alternative cosmos, the imaginary re-creation or reorganization of the world. The brief and abstract chronicle of itself, it keeps the very possibilities of fiction alive, and by doing that shows us more of the nature of our age and ourselves than all those novels which never recognize the crisis of literature and therefore do nothing but repeat its dead forms.

Fiction:
John Rechy

The temptation is almost irresistible—and I don't suppose I shall be able to withstand it entirely—to try to score off John Rechy's *City of Night,* to set up against its grotesque and graceless exhibition a scintillating road show of your own. This fictionalized account of a homosexual *Wanderjahr* is so pervasively bad, so ludicrous a performance at all but one or two points, yet so strenuously intended to be big and revelatory and dangerous, that putting it down seems like the clearest of cultural duties. Well, cultural duties have a way of turning into opportunities for a display of the self, and indeed a good deal of what I have read or heard about the book since it came out has been characterized by just this public honing of wit and invective at the expense of the issues which Rechy's painful and symptomatic creation, and the painful and symptomatic popular response to it, have raised.

As I say, I sympathize with critics like Alfred Chester. It is so satisfying to play the game and so easy: for example, the line I would love to pursue is a theory of how Grove Press, dismayed by the failure of the age to produce enough ugly, outrageous, know-nothing yet *vital* and *talented* writers on its own, has finally been compelled to fashion one in the office. And it is even easier and more pleasurable to score off Rechy psychologically, by establishing—or at any rate asserting—how much more complex and mature are your own ideas about sex and love than his. We all like to think the mantle they took off D. H. Lawrence when he died fits, don't we?

Yet I can't see what all this has to do with criticism. I don't know how it can take account of the dreadful earnestness—which could never have been faked or formulated—of *City of Night*; or of the reasons why it should be so widely regarded, by even such a substantial and putatively reliable witness as James Baldwin, as a sort of furious masterpiece of new statement; or, most central of all, of the really dramatic way it illustrates the present widespread confusion of art and life. There exists these days a naïve and cave-dwelling commitment to extreme situations and modes of behavior, a hang-up on perversity and perversion as sources of aesthetic truth, and John Rechy's lugubrious book is *its* masterpiece.

Not that there is anything at all extreme about the pressure, temperature and effect of *City of Night,* which is exactly what makes the whistles and the eyebrows that have been going up so truly disheartening. Surely the most ferocious of the many ironies that surround the book is the fact that it should promise so much shock and perturbation and turn out to be so flat, cowed and inhibited. From one end to the other Rechy's work smells of repression, both psychological and imaginative, and of narcissism of an especially depleting and devitalizing kind. Perhaps the most unpleasant aspect of the response to the book is that among many of its admirers this enervation and onanistic self-embrace is seen as strength, or, on a subtler level, as exemplary and sacrificial: *our* story, told for us by a new culture hero.

It is a case, evidently, of the wish being father to the

thought. The particular activities that are chronicled in
City of Night—male prostitution, camping, erotic degradation of various kinds—are real, sanguinary and extreme
enough in themselves, but what happens to them in Rechy's
unwizardly and weakness-diffusing hands is another matter.
Whatever this blue-jeaned *voyage à la bout de la nuit*
may have been in actuality, it has not survived its meta-
morphosis into literature, it has no status in the imagination nor any cautionary, redemptive or insurrectionary
power. And since bad writing corrupts by recoil the life
it is drawn from, the last sad effect of Rechy's book is to
lay under a heavier onus than before the events and feelings which he presumably wished with such desperation
to understand and to redeem.

I have been calling his work a "book" and the reason for
this is that I am unable to find a way to call it a novel.
This may seem to be an academic matter, but it is actually at the center of what I think is wrong with *City of
Night*. The novel is the most open of genres in our time,
but we can still give it a basic definition as a long piece
of imaginative prose in which a transformation takes
place—experience, from whatever realm, being converted
into form. This form is then the justification and truth of
the experience, instead of—as in Rechy's attempt and in
certain works of Mailer and Kerouac, most outraged poetry,
a large part of Baldwin's *Another Country* and all of James
Jones—the experience trying to justify the form or its
deficiencies. What all these works have in common, though
they are of course of greatly uneven value, is that, in
Yeats's phrase, they exibit the will doing the work of the
imagination, and that they rest to one degree or another—
Rechy's most completely—on a belief in the direct convert-
ibility of experience into art, indeed on the identity of
certain kinds of experience with art.

If what I have been saying is true, then *City of Night*
isn't a string of short stories either, as most reviewers have

described it, since none of its parts, with the dubious exception of the well-known *Miss Destiny* episode, is developed, seized from the chaos and interchangeability of raw material and given an ineluctable shape, none is released from the melancholy of potential being through the actuality of style.

The account of a homosexual *Wanderjahr*, I called it, and this seems to me accurate on several grounds. In the first place the book simply sets down, with autobiographical fidelity we may assume, the sexual things (there are no others) that happened to its author, and the thoughts—treated like things—that occurred to him in a number of cities over a period that feels like a year. (And if it should turn out that nothing of all this really happened to Rechy, that he wrote it from someone else's story, it wouldn't disturb the description or indictment, since the book would then be another person's biography, but that person still blind, rigid, untalented and hence unable to tell us anything interesting or convincing about himself.) Beyond that there is at its back the pressure of a vague search for *meaning*, a decision to go picaresquely around an established circuit of warranted possibilities and a belief that the wandering will in itself supply the reasons for having undertaken it.

The narrative proper begins in New York, where Rechy, or his fictional "I," enters upon his life as a male prostitute. First, however, there is a segment of early history, a flash back to an El Paso boyhood, in which an attempt is made to uncover the psychic and emotional origins of the malady (instructively enough, it is never referred to as one, being described instead as a "restlessness," a "hunger," an "inner anarchy" and so on). The whole section, which sets the tone for endless self-confabulation to follow, is extraordinarily embarrassing, the quintessence of derivative Freudianism and adolescent substitution of grandiose categories and hypostatized states of being for concrete acts and sensations. Any page you turn to will yield lines like these:

"I hate you—you're a failure—as a man—as a father!"

From my father's inexplicable hatred of me and my mother's blind carnivorous love, I fled to the Mirror. I would stand before it thinking: I have only Me!

It is not a digression but the essence of any consideration of *City of Night* if a few more remarks are made right here about Rechy's lamentable style. One calls it that for want of a better word, but it is in fact nothing but an infinitely derivative literary manner, its elements appropriated by Rechy from among whatever has seemed to him to have been sanctioned and frozen as "important" writing about quests and young men's fevers. He is able occasionally to capture the speech of queens and hustlers, that is to say when he is reporting and not composing, but if there is anything that undercuts the book's pretensions to rebellion and savage new light-bringing, it is the nearly unbroken conformism of its preponderant style.

From his ugly compound words ("darkcities," "angryfaces," "somefarwhere") to his sonorously clichéd renderings of encounters and self-encounters ("we cling to each other in a kind of franticness"; "the restlessness welled insatiable inside me"; "I get the feeling . . . that silence is a person listening to me, watching . . .") and dismally arty evocations of place (Chicago has "wounded streets," New York is a "heaven-piercing" city), it is possible to see influences as diverse as Thomas Wolfe, Nelson Algren, Kerouac, James T. Farrell and, as Mr. Chester pointed out, Truman Capote and Djuna Barnes, but there may be a hundred others lurking behind these.

The point is that Rechy is endlessly susceptible to influence because he can bring none of his own to bear.

Kierkegaard said that if a man has true ideas he has style immediately, and Rechy has no ideas, true or otherwise; he only possesses what *happened* to him. The result is that it has to come out sounding as though it happened to someone else, or rather—much worse—as though it never happened at all but was always marooned in "literature."

Between these two paradoxical and reciprocal fates—to be nothing but an accumulation of atrocious and unmediated facts and at the same time to be nothing but a deposit of gelid literary borrowings—*City of Night* spends almost all of its existence. When Rechy's narrator has had enough of hustling in Times Square, he moves on to the next scene, to Los Angeles, the center of the outdoor cult and legendary slave market, then to San Francisco, then Chicago, and finally New Orleans, for Mardi Gras and the ultimate Revelation. "And I think: Beyond all this—beyond that window and the churning world, out of all, all this, something to be found: some undiscovered country within the heart itself. . . ."

This is the rhythm and the vocabulary we have been dealing with all along: the portentous music, the repetitions, the windy nonsense about "something else," a Truth still to be discovered, while what does exist—the sexual transactions and sexual prowling—are entirely deprived of their weight and specificity and anguish by Rechy's refusal to really look at them, to call them by their names or to see them in any perspective except their own. When a writer continually employs indefinite nouns like "something," "somewhere," "someone," it is a sure sign that he is still mired in adolescence, in the age of Titles instead of names, Feeling instead of emotions, Desire instead of wants.

There are times when the lacerating actuality of what is happening to him and his inability to understand it or even to confront it bring Rechy to a frustration that is close to paroxysm, and bring us to a degree of pity:

. . . this was the moment when I could crush symbolically (as in a dream once in which I had stamped out all the hatred in the world) whatever of innocence still remained in me (crush that and something else—something else surely lurking—but what—what!!).

He never finds out of course; it is in the nature of such writing that one doesn't find out. But the passage I have just quoted does reveal one motive about which Rechy is perfectly straightforward, if irretrievably dishonest with himself. He wishes, he says, to stamp out innocence in himself, and the events of the book in fact derive what continuity they have from this process, which, however, like Rechy's search for an equivalent to Love, is much more a matter of gaining in brutality, ignorance and self-deception than of losing anything at all. Why he should wish to rid himself of an innocence he has never established he had, he is unable to say, but there are enough clues, and two explicit scenes, to allow us to come to our own conclusions.

In the first scene he has the chance to rob a customer but cannot bring himself to do it. "Somehow," he characteristically reflects, "I knew—in that room just now—I had failed the world I sought." A few months later, with a similar opportunity, he doesn't fail. And so it turns out that the biggest influence of all, not stylistically or imaginatively, God knows, but what with all proper sorrow for the corruption of the word we shall have to call metaphysically, is Jean Genet. Rechy has read Genet or heard about him, learned of his choice to *be* a thief and a prostitute since society had decided that he was, and has tried to put his own illness in the service of some such moral revolution as Genet's. It is very much as if some ordinary, untalented gambler and epileptic had decided to pretend he was Dostoevsky.

The urge may be perennial but we are in an especially unchastened period of such pretension. What Rechy lacks, what all our writers *manqué* lack who wish to *be* Genet or Rimbaud or Lautréamont or Lawrence, is of course everything that the latter possess: a true dream of violence as cure, profundity, lateral vision, a language, a demon. What they lack most radically of all is the knowledge that the rebellion has to be carried out within language and form themselves, that the material is a guarantee of nothing and may be a gross impediment. Even Genet could not do justice in fiction to the extreme violence and perversity of his life; when he found the proper form, it was the drama, and drama, moreover, which broke the old patterns after having passed beyond the specificities and autobiographical *culs-de-sac* of his own existence.

But if you do not know that art has its own life and laws, you will never understand why grave, passionate, anguished or terrible events in the world cannot simply be transferred or transliterated so as to make comparable events in literature. There are no good novels about earthquakes, prairie fires, strikes, tidal waves or orgies, and the reason is that these things are too much themselves; there is no getting a purchase on them or a way into human reality. By the same token the great novels about war or murder or erotic disaster are precisely triumphant because they modulate these devastations through the perspectives, or memory, of peace, reverence and love.

The Marquis de Sade, who wished to pursue perversion to its furthest limit, was a bad novelist, but he was a responsible phenomenon and a valuable witness. John Rechy is neither. More a victim perhaps than an originator, riding the latest wave of irresponsibility in the name of action and of being true to one's calamity, he would not be worth talking about if what he represented were not worth talking about. And what he represents is the distance we have come from an understanding of realms of being, of the dialectic between body and soul and between heaven and hell, and from a knowledge that art is perfect authenticity or it is nothing.

If, as it seems, we are in a period when we can scarcely even believe in love and peace, let alone exist in them, let us by all means strike out for them with all the violence we possess, but let us remember that the end is a restoration, not a perpetual rebelliousness, and let it be our own violence, not another's. If we find ourselves homosexual, or impotent, or cursed, or a hustler, or a Negro in a white world, or a white man in a Negro world, or in jail, or in *Esquire,* or on horse, or on the road—it doesn't mean that we are artists, and may mean, if we celebrate ourselves and cultivate our pain, that we can never be. We are equal to our own lives, but our imaginations have to make a leap. The deepest shame of a book like *City of Night* is that it cradles its furies and impotencies without understanding or being affected by them, and so without understanding or affecting anything else.

Fiction:
John Updike

A few weeks ago in these pages John Wain told Buddy Glass to go home. I wish I could find someone in John Updike's fiction whose mother is calling *him*, because it seems to me that Updike's art as much as Salinger's is in a situation where somebody or something has to go. But it isn't as easy as that; Updike is his own chief character, or rather his sensibility is its own chief object, spreading itself among a half-dozen voices and physiognomies no one of which can be said to be the source, or even the agent, of the malaise.

But that there is a sickness seems abundantly clear. It is one which Updike shares with Salinger, for all the older man's greater imaginative size and richer music. The two are among the most naturally gifted writers of our period, yet they are beginning to dismay us, although Updike more rapidly, by the manner in which their fiction feeds upon itself, makes pacts with itself, quiets its own misgivings and holds the world fastidiously at bay. Updike and Salinger are coming to resemble those institutionalized national comedians whose references are to their own quirks and legends, who offer us self-portraits instead of liberating counterimages, and who remain a number of years behind the truest current feeling.

I will not detain Salinger any longer, since my commission calls only for a review of Updike's latest novel, *The Centaur*. Yet I fear he is going to hover at the back of my thought in much of what I am going to say from now on, especially as it concerns the self conscious skill-in-the-void, like riding a bicycle with-no-hands-ma, that characterizes so much "sensitive" writing today. Well, let him hover then, usefully I hope, while I go on to Updike's strange problems.

To recapitulate what we already know or suspect about this author of preternaturally scintillant but thin and arrested fiction: we find an obsessive fixation upon the past, a compulsive rehearsal of the data of adolescence and young manhood, a cult of the family and of victimized sensibility, a spinning out of a legend of quest and initiation in which rococo states of consciousness and refined conditions of memory come more and more to replace imaginative event and action. And one more fatality, that which underlies all the others—an avoidance, accomplished with a scrupulous cunning and high-wire grace that resembles a brilliant neurotic maneuver, of the supreme task and burden of literature: the appropriation and transfiguration, in one way or another, of suffering, struggle, conflict, disaster and death.

Now I know I am going to be told that only a handful of writers have ever fully taken up the supreme tasks of literature and that that is no proper standard by which to judge all the others. And this of course is true; nobody judges Ronald Firbank by it, or Gertrude Stein, or Shaw or Cocteau or Nabokov. But the point about Updike, the quality of his work which makes me bring the standard into operation, is precisely the fact that he *shuns* the major sorrows and calamities while pretending to deal with them, that he glosses them, coats them with "fine" writing and disarms them by turning them into nostalgia and soft wisdom. And he does this in the face of his *prédilection d'artiste*, which keeps tugging him to the edge of the forbidden scene for a dreadful peekaboo look.

On the surface *The Centaur* would seem to be a refutation of my argument, since it is a novel which gives the appearance of engaging death, or more precisely the immanent existence of death and the consequent need to justify and fix the value of life. Yet after I had read it, I was left with the feeling of having been present at a virtuoso act of evasion, a subtle transposition of a theme into an occasion for avoiding it. It is not so much that Updike has been disingenuous; what has happened is that his instruments have carried out the work which *they* feel suited for, that because the qualities of his mind and imagination do not include the toughness, élan and valor to come to grips with such a theme, the prose has created another and infinitely less impressive monument than the one that was intended.

What was intended, we may surmise, was a complex structure to house Updike's anxious concern with his past, with his psychic and material origins as an artist, with his family and, most especially, with his father and the latter's relationship to himself. It is the father's possible death that provides the ground for the novel and such narrative force as it possesses; for Updike this segment of autobiography offers an opportunity to justify his father and attempt an understanding of the relationship of his death to the life that has gone before, and also to the life that is to come—the author's own.

"Honor thy father" might indeed have been the motto of *The Centaur*, instead of the portentous quotation from Karl Barth—"Heaven is the creation inconceivable to man, earth the creation conceivable to him. He himself is the creature on the boundary between heaven and earth"— whose effect is to prepare the reader for a complex exploration which is never forthcoming. It is this abstract impulse to write something large and significant after the exceeding smallness of his previous books, the culmination being the gilt and evanescence of the stories in *Pigeon Feathers*, that one detects from the first sentence of the new novel.

In that sentence, Caldwell, a fifty-year-old science teacher in the high school of a small Pennsylvania city, is struck by an arrow in his ankle. One of his unruly pupils has shot him and thereby converted him, for the purposes of the novel, into a present-day Chiron, the wise and humble centaur who, suffering from an incurable wound at the hands of Hercules, patiently educated the young until he gave up his immortality as a reparatory sacrifice for the transgression of Prometheus. From this point on *The Centaur* shuttles between the myth and its reconstructed scene and Caldwell's (and Updike's) Pennsylvania-Dutch town circa 1047.

Every character in the modern story, which occupies the greater part of the novel, is an avatar of a figure from the age of the myth. For example, Zimmerman, the coarse and powerful school principal, is Zeus; Pop Kramer, Caldwell's aging father-in-law, is Kronos; Peter, his son, who narrates much of the story, is Prometheus. In case we are in any doubt, there is a three-page "mythological index," which was suggested, Updike with unforgivable archness tells us, by his wife. The strategy—let us show that we recognize noble undertakings when we see them—is designed to raise the inhabitants of the modern city to the eternal status of archetypes, to postulate a continuity for all human existence in its multifarious showing forth.

But however pretentious and dismally schematic all this sounds, the mythologizing is not, I'm afraid, what brings the novel down. There are long stretches when the parallels remain implicit and unobtrusive, and others when they seem entirely to be forgotten; for the rest they are merely ineffective, a bit distracting and faintly ludicrous (except for the couple of occasions when they become resoundingly ludicrous: to make modern re-creations of mythical archetypes is one thing, but to reverse the process and speak of Artemis as "tittering around the woods with a pack of Vassar freshmen," or of Pholos as having "once been a semi-pro shortstop," is sadly another).

No, the mythological aspects of the book constitute an inept bravura enterprise, but one which is at least specific, locatable and possible to dismiss. What can't be dismissed, in order to get at something else, is the entire texture of the book, the quality of its engagements with the issues and experiences it has proposed for itself, the way in which it explores, dramatizes and finally memorializes them in a work of art. And in this central respect, despite the high sheen and delicacy of Updike's prose—or rather, as I have indicated earlier, as a result of that—all is deflected, daunted, genteel and cold, all is "writing."

Or almost all. In the boy's direct relationship to the father there is the possibility of a breakthrough into something more than a safe, enameled and narrowly literary vision. The father—an awkward, naïve, self-lacerating but somehow noble and dedicated man, weighed down by debts, social unease and the misery of having to teach mostly thick-witted or rapacious youths—believes he may be dying of cancer. His son is a germinating artist, self-conscious and convinced of his special future. Before he can possess it, however, he has to assimilate and come to terms with the fact and meaning of his father's possible death, and at the same time help the older man reach a sense of the worth of his own life as a teacher and sacrificial figure.

Updike arranges a few scenes of clear, resonant confrontation, but for the most part, here as everywhere else, there is a continual process of sidling up to an alarming or vivifying truth and then backing away into mummifying rhetoric or unearned lyricism or stippled preciosity or sententious statement:

> Alton distended. Her arms of white traffic stretched river-ward. Her shining hair fanned on the surface of the lake. My sense of myself amplified until, lover and loved, seer and seen, I compounded in several accented expansions of my ego, the city and the future, and during these seconds truly clove to the center of the sphere and outmuscled time and life. I would triumph.

> . . . he discovered that in giving life to others he entered a total freedom. . . . Only goodness lives. But it does live.

> For it is at about that age, isn't it, that it sinks in upon us that things do, if not die, certainly change, wiggle, slide, retreat, and, like the dabs of sunlight on the bricks under a grape arbor on a breezy June day, shuffle out of all identity.

> Somewhere there is a city where he will be free.

> And yet, love, do not think that our life together, for all its mutual frustration, was not good. It was good. We moved, somehow, on a firm stage, resonant with metaphor. . . . Yes. We lived in God's sight.

He has not demonstrated it. *His* stage is not firm or resonant with metaphor, but nearly always crepitant with literary genius on display. From it come repeated showers of irrelevant sparks, dazzling accuracies of perception which stand in the way of movement, intricacies of feeling which have the effect of occluding the major passions. Pascal wrote that "perpetual eloquence is wearisome," but in Updike's case it is more than that: it is destructive of true eloquence. The writing is forever moving from event to embroidery, from drama to coy detail. The boy wakes in crisis and there is an inevitable stasis while we are made to observe with him "the glass bureau knobs like faceted crystals of frozen ammonia." The house echoes with hints of death, and with no excuse of irony or chiaroscuro, we are deflected from them by being told how "the brown powder, Maxwell's Instant, made a tiny terrain on the surface of steaming water," and how "on a stiff tablecloth a loaf of sugary bread lay sequined with pointillist dabs of light."

The occasions when Updike is able to escape from his own pointillism and sequined prose are invariably those on which his memory of youth becomes unself-conscious, objective and dramatic. There is a description of a basketball game which is a set piece that works by its employment of eloquence for ends beyond itself, by the disappearance of the solipsistic and self-rehearsing author from the scene:

> Adolescent boys as hideous and various as gargoyles, the lobes of their ears purple with the cold, press, eyes popping, mouths flapping, under the glowing overhead globes. Girls, rosy-cheeked, glad, motley and mostly ill-made, like vases turned by a preoccupied potter, are embedded, plaid-swaddled, in the hot push. Menacing, odorous, blind, the throng gives off a muted shuffling thunder, a flickering articulate tinkle: the voices of the young.

This is rich provisioning, but it isn't catered, it isn't brought in from outside to impress us with professional expertise. Nor is it precious or self-indulgent or arbitrarily vivid. Once before, in *Rabbit, Run*, Updike wrote an entire book which for all its faults maintained a steady vision, subordinating its author's virtuosity to a complete imaginative purpose, using his human weaknesses—his fear of fact and necessity and pain, his dream of an impossible freedom—as a source of strength by going out to meet them and fashioning a tale and a metaphor to contain them. *The Centaur*, designed to be a complementary vision, the positive fairy tale after the flight from the ogre, rests finally as a pastiche, a sly exercise, a piece of bravado, an evasion and a dead flat ground from which, we may hope, its extraordinarily endowed author can only rise.

Fiction:
William H. Gass

In Alain Robbe-Grillet's remarkable collection of essays
on fiction, *For a New Novel*, there is a passage which most
lucidly sets forth the principle of aesthetic action itself.
"The function of art," Robbe-Grillet writes, "is never to
illustrate a truth—or even an interrogation—known in advance, but to bring into the world certain interrogations
(and also perhaps in time certain answers) not yet known
as such to themselves." A little further, he sketches the
condition of hostility and retardation—natural, inevitable
and needing only to be accepted to provide a partial liberation from itself—against which the literary artist struggles in his effort to bring to birth those forms whose
potential existence he has discovered and which now
await the actuality only he can bestow:

> The writer himself, despite his desire for independence, is
> situated within an intellectual culture and a literature which
> can only be those of the past. It is impossible for him to
> escape altogether from this tradition of which he is a prod-
> uct. Sometimes the very elements he has tried hardest to
> oppose seem, on the contrary, to flourish more vigorously

than ever in the very work by which he had hoped to destroy them; and he will be congratulated, of course, with relief for having cultivated them so zealously.

Here on my desk is William H. Gass's *Omensetter's Luck*, which I have no hesitation in calling the most important work of fiction by an American in this literary generation. Here it is lying almost midway between those ambitions and recalcitrances which Robbe-Grillet has identified as being the true artist's truest pressures. For on the one hand Gass's novel is marvelously original, a whole Olympic broad jump beyond what almost any other American has been writing, the first full replenishment of language we have had for a very long time, the first convincing fusion of speculative thought and hard, accurate sensuality that we have had, it is tempting to say, since Melville.

Yet there is also something refractory, stiff, retrograde. For *Omensetter's Luck* hangs back at times and most crucially at the time of its greatest potentiality for freedom, burrowing for comfort and safety into the familiar, not daring fully to cast off its cargo of literary inheritance, employing certain ritualistic narrative procedures which its entire pioneering thrust denies and seeks to abolish. It is as though Gass, having ventured out without looking back, has been overtaken and seduced by the past, which cannot conceive of being wholly left behind.

Yet just because of this, this freedom caught by the tail, it seems to me to make up that kind of incomplete, contingent and vulnerable miracle which can renew an art more powerfully than total revolutions, those hermetic masterpieces whose price is always a sterile autarchy.

For a novel to be problematic in this way, poised between discovery and nostalgia, having made no absolute repudiation but also no pact with the expected, is an anomaly in our culture of sluggish continuity or spastic novelty. The tendency, when confronted with it, is to subvert its impact by seizing on what is familiar in it—its "theme" or "characters"—celebrating that and then assigning to what is new and unprecedented a role as augmenter, regenerator, reinterpreter of the known. "The most penetrating (original, illuminating, powerful) image of our alienated condition (social repressions, political mythologies, sexual ambivalences)" we say of works which are actually proposing a new kind of beauty, which is to say a new form.

Omensetter's Luck is not the most original or powerful *reflection* of anything. The beauty it proposes is not an enhancement or a ramification or an analogue or a mere reversal of the old. To see what it is and why it is so significant requires us to get past the difficulty we have in understanding how a thing can be called beautiful if it does not take its sanction from what has already been determined upon as the nature of beauty in that particular realm, that is to say if it does not contribute to the aesthetic "heightening" of the familiar.

The word "beauty" is under a cloud these days and this is not the place to examine why. But it will advance my point just as well if I substitute the word "use," for that is what most talk about American writing has come to these days, a backward spin of the wheel of literary theory which, if one analyzes it, is as philistine and uncomprehending as a frozen conception of beauty. In any case *Omensetter's Luck* does not fit into the prevailing uses of the novel in America. We are so accustomed to seeing, or imagining that we see, or complaining that we do not see, the novel advancing thematically—the sensibility being extended to cover previously unreported areas of public or private behavior, wit deployed against hitherto sacrosanct targets, language in the service of ever deeper or more complex moral investigations—that we have effectively made fiction into an adjunct of all our other disciplines. We attempt to learn from the novel what has not

been given us by social scientists, gurus or eloquent gangsters.

Yet since fiction can serve only illusorily as psychology
or sociology or philosophy or political theory; since fiction
has no reason for being other than to test and exemplify
new forms of conciousness, which, moreover, have had
to be invented precisely because actuality is incapable of
generating them; since fiction has to assimilate all our
concerns while remaining resistant to their special pleas
and claims in order to be able to place before us the full,
irreducible shape of concern itself—since these things
are true and yet we want the novel to give us either confirmation or new energy, we mutter and protest that it is
not doing its duty, that it should be and in fact is being
replaced by other media.

Well, certainly, let the novel of information and booster
shots be replaced, since the only existence it has ever really
had is as a fiction devised by the utilitarians of the literary
world and as work by writers who are not artists.

Lest anyone think I am arguing for a novel stripped of
anything palpable, reduced to shadows, abstract gestures
and a game of *mere* forms, and that consequently *Omensetter's Luck* must be some sort of monster of reverbera-
tions without an initial sound to set them in motion, a
graph without data, let me say that all the comforting
materials and processes which utilitarians demand in
fiction are present: nouns, verbs, adjectives and names
which really *are* inseparable from things, actions, qualities
and characters and places; and also a tale, and also development, and also a denouement. But in Gass's book, materials from the world outside fiction are turned, or as
nearly as the resistance of tradition will allow, into what
Robbe-Grillet calls interrogations, which is to say that they
are released from their incarceration in our habits of
thought and perception, our smooth, completed, self-con-
fident and mostly *literary* way of deciding what we know

before we know what it is we have to learn. Every artist has to fight against a world unmediated by art, but also against the rigid imperium of all the other art that has preceded him, all the "literature," good or bad, which intervenes between men and what they see and feel.

The novel has a place—Gilean, a small Ohio town; a time—the 1890's; protagonists—Henry Pimber, a sensitive, defeated man, the Reverend Jethro Furber, a preacher obsessed with carnality, and Brackett Omensetter, "a wide and happy man." There is also a narrative, though we shall see that it is untrustworthy as a smooth-running railroad into the land of dreams: Omensetter's arrival in town and the disturbance it brings; the increasing tension between him and Furber; Pimber's suicide, whose instigation is his conviction that Omensetter possesses life as he cannot; Furber's hints that Omensetter has really murdered him; the running out of Omensetter's luck; Furber's own collapse; and Omensetter's final defeat.

The book begins with a prologue (beautifully written but a little diversionary since it doesn't quite establish what it proposes to) in which an aged townsman shakily remembers, like an uncertain muse of history, the events that are going to be recounted, at one point introducing a crucial note of warning to the reader: "It was Omensetter's luck. Not a story, an illness." Yet the illness which, we learn, affects everybody, for a while has the character of a story, a series of events, locatable in time and space, composing a moral and psychological crisis in which Furber and Omensetter are the chief participants.

To Furber, Omensetter, who does "everything that didn't matter and made [him] feel good," is a mysterious, inimical being, outside moral or spiritual categories, outside, it would seem, any of the familiar and reassuring modes of civilized concern: judgment, consciousness, choice, evaluation:

He stored his pay in a sock which hung from his bench, went about oblivious of either time or weather, habitually permitted things which he'd collected like a schoolboy to slip through holes in his trousers. He kept worms under saucers, stones in cans, poked the dirt all the time with twigs, and fed squirrels navy beans and sometimes noodles from his hands. Broken tools bemused him; he often ate lunch with his eyes shut; and, needless to say, he laughed a lot. He let his hair grow; he only intermittently shaved; who knew if he washed; and when he went to pee, he simply let his pants drop.

Against this "unnatural" naturalness, this refusal to take thought or make choices, this "living by not observing . . . by joining himself to what he knew," Furber opposes a fanatical principle of separation, the mind and moral imagination holding off experience through unceasing judgment, with a desperate inverted Prometheanism. Furber's childhood had been a supreme preparation for an eventual life of violent, arid internality:

> They denied him every book they had not carefully examined themselves, just as they forbade him the Hazen's fence and later the stone quarry and the bluffs beyond town, and finally all farmyards because of the geese and railroad stations because of the engines, then funerals, cemeteries, zoos and circuses, cellars, closets, attics, deep woods and vacant houses, athletic contests, fires, rallies and revival meetings— indeed any form of public excitement—and they tried to shelter him from the noise and violence of storms, too, as well as from every other remarkable exertion of nature.

The "fierce puritan intensity" came to mask an atrocious consuming rage for the forbidden. He dreams, hungers, holds his dream and hunger static, arrested, without issue:

> In the theater of his head, in the privacy of Philly Furber's Fancy Foto-Cabinet—what thrilling horrors were enacted,

what lascivious scenes encranked. Come to the skull show,
honey. Gets no babies out of it, just fun . . . fun thin as
tish-ee paper and all rumply crumply.

Thought is desire, palpable and ready to jump:

Mrs. Tightsqueeze was eyeing him. What if my thoughts
spilled out, madame, what would you do? Ah, what if yours
did? Her dress held her fiercely braced. A regular full-bodied
tumbletit, aren't you? fat of love. Oops . . . ah . . . caught. Is
that mustard on the tablecloth? No, ma'am, I spilled some
thinking.

Furber is tormented but, more subtly, really sustained by
moral imperatives and their counteragencies; to have knowledge of evil is, for him, to have life, and he dreads Omensetter because the latter's existence is pitched apart from
moral considerations, in pure physicality. The power which
Furber has over the townspeople, and which Omensetter
passively threatens, derives from his being an incarnation
of judgment, the dark warden who stands over every possibility of unconscious, unintimidated, above all unnec-
cessary, and therefore free, movement.

In his mortal struggle with Omensetter he craves for
the townspeople to "give up their hope of living like an
animal and return to an honest, conscious, human life,"
the life which Omensetter menaces with his presence.
Furber has reasons; Omensetter has being, but this can
only be from the "dark way" since its actions negate the
only basis on which being can rest for Furber. "We know
that men are evil, don't we? Don't we?" Furber pleads.
"Yet Omensetter doesn't seem to be. He does not seem.
Seem. Is this correct, this—seem?"

The enigma lies in Omensetter's refusal of words, his
refusal, really, of self-definition, which enables his presence to suggest the nonnecessity of any definition for men's
lives. And what Furber comes to see, in terror, is the

manner in which his own life has been imprisoned in definitions, in words, as surrogates for experience: "Yes, words were superior; they maintained a superior control; they touched without your touching; they were at once the bait, the hook, the line, the pole and the water in between." Words, the inhabitants of the metaphysical realm between being and nonbeing, were the instruments you could use to have both the illusion of life and none of its consequences:

> The ladies egged him on; in Eve's name, they dared him; so he made love with discreet verbs and light nouns, delicate conjunctions. They begged; they defied him to define . . . define everything. They could not be scandalized—impossible they said. Indecent proposals such as in, on, up, merely made them smile.

But while Furber is a "character" who on one level embodies this double thrust of language toward actuality and nonbeing, and Omensetter is one who incarnates being beneath language and thought, Gass's book is not *about* their relationship, except insofar—as we shall see—as it falls back into convention. On one level a newly apprehended vision of the largest perennial antinomies—being and seeming, body and spirit, the self and otherness, man and God ("For whatever Omensetter does he does without desire in the ordinary sense . . . with a kind of stony mindlessness that always makes me think of Eden . . . Omensetter seems beyond the reach of God")—the novel becomes an arena for the encounter of language and idea. The work is neither allegory nor dramatic poem nor even single metaphor, no matter how complex; it is a new structure whose elements (but not whose themes) are the relationship of language to action, thought to language, truth to its data and being to nonbeing, and whose description is therefore that of the way existence might be if we could truly grasp such relations.

The novel *is* Gass's prose, his style, which is not committed to something beyond itself, not an instrument of an idea. In language of amazing range and resiliency, full of the most exact wit, learning and contemporary emblems, yet also full of lyric urgency and sensuous body, making the most extraordinary juxtapositions, inventing, coining, relaxing at the right moments and charging again when they are over, never settling for the rounded achievement or the finished product, he fashions his tale of the mind, which is the tale of his writing a novel.

To choose what to quote is an alarming task, but here are two passages which, I think, display Gass's intentions, and the great virtuosity he brings to bear in order to realize them.

While he conducts church services, Furber's mind is invaded by the memory of Omensetter's wife, whom he had spied on as she sunned herself on a rock:

> Her navel was inside out—sweet spot where Zeus had tied her. She was so white and glistening, so . . . pale, though darker about the eyes, the nipples dark. Open us to evil. He made a slit in his lids. Burn our hearts. Shawls of sunlight spilled over the back of the pews. Nay-ked-nessss. The droplets gathered at the point of her elbow and hung there, the sac swelling until it fell and spattered on her foot. Nay . . . nay. To enclose her like the water of the creek had closed her. Nay . . . proper body for a lover. Joy to be a stone. Please, the peep-watch is over. Please hurry now. Hurry. Get out of my church.

He invokes the spirit of a predecessor, a minister martyred by Indians a hundred years before, and all spirits, gods and dominations:

> You lived with Indians—very well—but I've fallen among people. Is there no one who will pity me? Speak and say, oh great recumbency of sky, vast chest and hollow water bottle,

would you spit upon your image, eh? Ho, Barlar? Grunn?
Petvich? Hooloo? Kishish? Quarckaling? Sull Yully? Nannar-
bantandan? Tuk? Too rooky, won't reply, all tweetered up
with ravens, swifts and fowling hawks. Anyway let's have an
answer . . . some bird of omen . . . no ghost . . .
shreeeeeeee. . . .

He can also write, on scattered occasions, badly, with a
lapse into other people's acquisitions, into the appearance
of literature:

Men, in my experience, are the worst disease.

The leaves were learning of the cold.

Yet these failures are isolated and minor and in no way
shake the edifice of his achievement. What does shake it,
however, is its partial organization along narrative lines,
its compulsion to tell a "story" while its whole internal
action struggles against the reductions and untruthfulness
of storytelling, while its verbal action is struggling to *be*
the story. For narrative, which Bernard Shaw long ago
called "the curse of all serious literature" and which every
major novelist since Flaubert has either abandoned or used
ironically, is precisely that element of fiction which coerces
it and degrades it into being a mere alternative to life,
like life, only better of course, a dream (or a serviceable
nightmare), a way out, a recompense, a blueprint, a lesson.

To impel Furber and Omensetter along destinies as
"characters," to make them function within a plot, a lifelike
series of events, as Gass reluctantly and, one feels, with
only half a mind does, is to return them from their aesthetic
existence as pretexts, arenas for inquiry and containers
for verbal and imaginative action, to the status of representatives, local, circumscribed, exemplary and therefore
usable as art refuses to be. As Gass's events unfold—the
finding of Pimber's body, Furber's campaign against Omen-

setter, the latter's loss of power under Furber's charges that his "unconsciousness" is murderous and his "luck" is at the expense of others—one feels the structure of the book straining for verisimilitude, for acts that will justify the qualities of being that have been exhibited. As the narrative moves to its climax, the book partly takes on the reductive nature of a cautionary tale, an allegory of truth and error; there are moments when it feels like *The Oxbow Incident,* a story about men's prejudices and injustice; and others when it resembles a genre of philosophical fiction in which characters are embodiments of opposing faculties: Furber as sterile, destructive mind, Omensetter as fecund but naïve and therefore equally unreliable body.

Yet though the book is self-divided and suffers from a certain opacity and unclarity that are direct results of the intrusion of plot, the writing survives the tow of the past, even though it is prevented by it from reaching the fullest open water. Again and again Gass brings to birth unknown realities, truths about truth, questions out of what had been acceptances. Near the end of the novel Furber is confessing the sources of his hatred for Omensetter. "'Listen,' Furber said, 'when I was a little boy and learning letters— A . . . B . . . C . . . , love was never taught to me, I couldn't spell it, the O was always missing, or the V, so I wrote love like live, or lure, or late, or law, or liar.'"

This sentence, which both contributes to a whole and has its own irreducible and complex wholeness, traces the action of the entire book. What Gass has written is a work of the imagination and the mind whose study is the mind and imagination themselves as they grant us the instruments of knowing, which are at the same time the sources of all our inability to know.

*The ambition of a writer like
myself is to become consecutively
more disruptive, more dangerous
and more powerful.*
—ADVERTISEMENTS FOR MYSELF

*I can't stand it when
the artist exhibits himself.*
—THE JOURNAL OF EUGENE DELACROIX

Norman Mailer:
Art as Life, Life as Art

To be a writer in America; to test its possibilities and
dramatize its perversions; to test writing against the life
of action and that life against the necessities of the mind
and to be caught *visibly* in their contradictions; to try to
create oneself as a myth and to try at the same time to be
an immediate physical force; to stagger openly between
wisdom and foolishness, lucidity and dementia; to risk and
to play it safe, to fall and to be resurrected; to be a conscious, exemplary, half-clownish and half-grave and naked
public destiny; to throw the ego against the impersonal
rubrics of the age; to try to move and shake the times
while representing an unappeasable nostalgia for the artist's indifference to temporality; to be Narcissus and to be
Prometheus; to be a cloud of discontent that bumps the
stagnant heavens into motion—these have been the significances, never more potent and instructive than they are
right now, of Norman Mailer.

Mailer is a phenomenon in the face of which distinctions crumble and categories dissolve; it is perhaps the
chief way in which his ambition to be "disruptive" and
powerful has come to be fulfilled. His career has been

almost impossible to follow and judge if we think of it as
an American literary life among others. More like that
of a movie star, it can be seen moving to successive new
currents in the public air, its principle of momentum and
its spring of aspiration being compounded of both the
artist's hunger to insert his consciousness into the folds of
the world's experience and the fevered, twitchy compul-
sions of the gallery god, the externalist for whom fame is
the indispensable protection, *at every moment,* against
inner chaos and the oblivion that waits for all ego. He is
the self-made man of literature, the parvenu who having
arrived feels the Furies still at his back and knows he has
to cover up the fact that his origins are at least as much as
other men's in ordinariness and prosaic dreams.

He is the writer-out-with-the-boys, the jolly poet of
tough talk, the philosopher of the uppercut and the meta-
physician of the sixty-yard pass for a touchdown, but he
is also the dying god, the stricken prophet, the St. Sebas-
tian of modern utterance. The most savage critic of America, he is held more tightly than any of his contemporaries
in the grip of one of her chief horrors and blasphemies:
the cult of success. At one and the same time he incarnates the American careers of "winning" and "losing,"
time pinioned and time transcended, *making it* and being
left out, intimidating the world and being spread-eagled
by its indifference. In his strange arrogance and equally
strange candor, his contradictory hungers and rival ambitions, he moves, usefully for us all, at the center of a
quintessentially American confusion of all the realms of
being.

In a conversation a few years before she died, the
greatly gifted and extraordinarily modest American writer
Flannery O'Connor said this about Norman Mailer: "Why
does he have to push himself forward all the time and
make such a spectacle of himself . . . why can't he let
his work speak for itself?" Poor unfashionable Miss O'Con-

nor, so much more purely and simply a writer than Mailer, so much more committed an artist, could never have come to understand what moved him or how representative he is. For her, writing was an act by which you outwitted the world and mortality while remaining a "loser" by nearly all the world's standards; it was a continuing gesture against formlessness and chaos, and at the same time, being a power held in trust, mysteriously enough also against pride. Answering an ancient sense of vocation (which Mailer no doubt recognizes but which it is not in his interest to acknowledge), she saw the writer as a sacrificial figure whose business it is to disappear behind his work, having in any case placed his truest self there. That the writer should crave to be adored in his own flesh-and-blood actuality, that he should hunger for power other than that of the new forms and signs he has introduced into men's consciousness—where they immediately begin their new, independent, risky life—were things she could scarcely comprehend.

Flannery O'Connor represented one extreme pole of the writer's self-positioning in the world, what we might call the "classic" attitude of distance, abnegation, impersonality and submission to the sovereignty of the imagination as reinventor of men's lives and not as meddler in the world's business. It is an attitude toward the relationship between art and life that has dominated most non-bohemian aesthetic enterprises; it is the characteristic stance of the great novelists of the modern era—James, Proust, Joyce, Mann and Kafka—and it is most tersely and familiarly summed up in Yeats's implacable dictum that "the intellect of man must choose/Perfection of the life or of the work." The ego must go into making or doing, the self must sacrifice something to the universal.

Yet if this is the classic position, Mailer's has not been the traditional romantic one. A romantic of an extreme kind he assuredly is, but he has never wished or tried, as the pure romantic literary ego has almost always done, to replace life with literature; he has not defended writing as a truer existence or sought in it a redemption of the insufficiencies and betrayals of the one we are forced to endure. Nor has he ever indicated that he would be content, in that sly and perhaps ultimately most gratifying romantic way, with being one of the world's unacknowledged legislators.

He is a new kind of American romantic, his own man and yet also very much the product of our times. As the voice of the abstract and engineered and hygienic has grown louder, his own has risen; as politics has threatened us with madness, he has cut his extravagant capers, turning messy cartwheels in the middle of a deadly oratorical contest and a *tableau vivant* of lies. Yet he is not simply an opposition, a jester undermining with slapstick and violent guile the ruling self-assurances of the age; he is no antic, sage defender of what has been lost. A voracious, unclear, partly inherited and almost wholly anarchic demand that the world be reconstituted, be made *equal to him,* puts him in the company of the great dissident and utopian literary egos—Rousseau, de Sade, Tolstoy, Lawrence —with the difference, apart from questions of genius, that he is a contemporary American who knows that prophecy, like any other commodity, has to be sold and that ideas are bought today mainly in conjunction with personality.

He is no lonely prophet, prepared for false or misleading fame or for obloquy and exile, except as the latter are provisional, sources of a notoriety that guarantees that one will continually be talked about and that a great welcome for the hero-recognized-at-last is already being prepared. For though he is a citizen who mistrusts the realm of the civic, he has been passionately engaged in trying to win a muscular new citizenship—a status not wholly consistent with a prophetic role—on the strength of his victories in the marketplace. He wants *in,* and it is not at all that he is sure of himself as a potential benefactor of you and me and is therefore outraged at the obstacles in the way of fulfilling this vocation, but that he feels a terror of being left out. And this terror, shaped beyond question by many strands of private pathology and imbalance, is also and much more importantly the general cultural dread of all outsiders in America, the inward void carried around by everyone who for all the reasons of our history has not been allowed simply to fill the space allotted to him but has had continually to prove his right to it.

"The one personality" which Mailer "feels absolutely insupportable," he tells us in *The Armies of the Night*, is "the nice Jewish boy from Brooklyn." That such a being cannot possibly be a representative American figure, much less a mover and shaker, is the premise on which much of Mailer's acrobatics and histrionics take shape. One would go to the end, to the other side of personality and coherent being, to be *pertinent*, literally to figure in. And Mailer has willed and worked and buffaloed and even at last written himself into pertinence and power in one of the most fascinating and instructive episodes of our recent cultural history. More than any other of our writers he has intervened in the age, which has had to listen to him. He has come to matter, more securely as time goes on; and if it is not precisely in the way he has wanted, if it continues to be ridiculous to call him the *best* American writer, he nevertheless matters in a way that only a man with so mighty and precarious an ego as his could find disappointing.

What it has meant to be a writer in America has been a very different and lesser public thing than, say, what it meant at one time to be one in Russia or to be one at nearly all times in France. The American writer, existing much farther from the centers of power within the life of public affairs, has also lived farther from those less visible centers where the processes of general self-awareness and self-definition go on among a people. As a result we have not come to know ourselves through our writers to the degree that certain other peoples believe they have, nor, on a more programmatic and utilitarian level, have we thought to claim our writers as our national glories. (Whether or not to teach people what they are like is the true function of the writer is another question, one that Mailer's whole career has not failed to touch at many points.) Writing, Victor Hugo said, is "civilization itself," and on his death was given a sumptuous state funeral for having been in a position to say it without embarrassment. For most of us writing is at best a minor act within civilized society, one of its attributes, a divertissement, a sort of skill in putting into formal verbal modes what we already know or sense, a change of pace or an enlivenment, and no true source of prophecy, discovery or power.

We have never given our writers state funerals of the kind the French gave Hugo, or the kind—elegiac, appreciative and yet somewhat impersonal, the tribute to a human faculty more than to a man—they give even their most aloof and difficult poets such as Paul Valéry or Paul Claudel. We have almost never named them ambassadors and have never renamed streets after them. And it would be all we could do to imagine an incident taking place in this country that would be a counterpart to something that happened in France in 1934.

It was a summer day in Paris. The newly elected Popular Front government was having to deal with tremendous tensions that were gripping the whole country; a general strike was about to begin, rumors of a coup and countercoup filled the air. A journalist stopped to talk to a group of workmen who were getting ready to join a huge protest march. What we need today, one of them said to him, "is a real man to lead us, a fellow like . . . well, a fellow like Gide."

There is of course something very ironic and amusing to us in the workman's having put forward André Gide, of all French writers, as the "real man" he wanted for his leader. Yet the French are much more open and resilient about such matters than we are. For all Gide's well-known homosexuality and his lofty aesthetic of indirection and deliberate inconclusiveness—his cultivation of sensibility as what must have seemed to be very near an end in itself—he was not an incongruous choice to throw the first paving block. A short time before this he had made a journey to the Congo and had written a violent indictment of the European administrations there, a book that was to result in measurable reform. But he had had an effect precisely because he was not ordinarily a writer on such subjects, he was not an expert but a representative of literature, which kept the national conscience and had prestige that could easily be transferred to other areas. And this prestige was of just that kind which testifies to a reality of manhood and of leadership: a great writer—and one did not have to read his books to know it—was the kind of person whose qualities are summed up in the German and Yiddish word *mensch*.

To be a *mensch* is, most centrally, to be what a man should be, to have courage and so to stand up to the world; and this is what, as the French have always somehow known, writers do. Though the peasant or the laborer is not likely to have consciousness of anything beyond the fact that there is a general pride taken in this action of the writer, and though he may conceive his respect for great authors by an act, it may be, of something close to patriotism, and though he may feel contempt or envy or bewilderment, too, the respect is no less genuine for all that.

It is one of the public weathers that help support the artist, who will ordinarily be satisfied with getting his more intelligent acclaim from narrower sources. The artist knows that his heroism lies in the valor of what Ibsen called "sitting in judgment on oneself," in turn a function of another kind of valor, that of original creation, which is to say of being able to imagine newly, being able to stand up to the past, to habit, convention and the tyranny of what is expected. The specific heroism of the literary artist lies in his volunteering to handle words, those things right under our noses (we all write, if only letters; we all speak, if only to ask directions), those hot potatoes which, if we think (and that is what writers make us do), can cause the most incalculable burns, the most undiagnosable wounds.

To be a good writer, then, where these things are even unconsciously known, is to qualify as a man and, whether or not you are interested in being one, as a leader. In cultures where such credentials are more or less freely given, where the very justification for being a writer, and therefore a real man, does not have perpetually to be rewon, a man can *write*. He may have to battle for the recognition of his new forms against the delaying action of conventional aesthetic wisdom, but he does not have to fight for the independent value of what a writer does nor to be taken seriously as a contributor to and custodian of universal values. In those cultures where literature has had a tradition of being a force, a source of universal energy, such a recognition as the one which that Parisian laborer gave to Gide is far from being an eccentric act.

In America it would be unthinkable, outside, that is to say, the reveries and ambitions of Norman Mailer, who has actually run for mayor of New York and who has all his life dreamed of being president (and late, strange actuality: he has gone into the streets and become a species of leader, a role we will catch up with later in this narrative). For Gide, who was sustained by the tradition and who knew that his own work as an artist was a very different activity from his appearances in the world of affairs, writing was the ground and not the substance of his possible effectiveness there. But for Mailer a tremendous and unremitting tension has gone on manifesting itself.

Mailer has felt, with an anguish and intensity he has only recently begun to turn fully to his use, the opposing pulls of action and contemplation, of life and literature; his ego has run between vision and immediacy and has sought its prizes and sustenance in *all possible* and so inevitably contradictory roles and vocations: writer, activist, leader, insurrectionary, lover, moralist, prophet, All-American, performer, bouncer, sage. He has wanted in the worst way to *count*, to be a man the world knows about, and even more, to borrow a phrase from the adolescence he has never wholly shaken off, to be "king of the hill."

Now, the king ideally unites in his person all the strengths and faculties, all the potentialities and aspirations as well as the tragedies and defeats of his subjects. But for the writer who wishes to be king a crucial limitation is all too apparent: his castle, as Ibsen's master builder was aware, is "in the air." The writer stands up to the world, but he does not do it in the way that boxers, mountain climbers, generals, racing-car drivers and certain kinds of criminals do. For the writer courage is so much less palpable, so much more a matter of symbolic rather than real action, so uncertain and often dilatory in its effects. The point, Ortega y Gasset said, is that "real things are made of matter or energy, but artistic things . . . are made of a substance called style."

This is why literary men have often felt the need for palpable collisions, for risks that might draw blood, and why they have often sought out men of action as companions, models or vicarious selves. Thus Brecht hung out with the German middleweight champion in the twenties, and Hemingway cultivated bullfighters and an entire way of dangerous physical life. And thus Norman

Mailer, in his overwhelming, confused and voracious need to be a *mensch,* and above all to be able to see himself and be seen as one, has surrounded himself with boxers and criminal types and has frequently used his fists—at parties and on street corners—and come several times into the realm of criminality himself.

To have seen Mailer at one of the times when the need for action—for violence really, something to make the world *feel* his presence and to make himself feel that he is unmistakably in it—has mounted to an intolerable itch while there also mounted a hunger (there is no other word for it) for degradation, is to have been given knowledge to undercut legend and exorcise publicity. The night Mailer stabbed his second wife some seven or eight years ago, he was in almost the exact center of a decade during which he seemed to have abandoned fiction and when his reputation was, for the second time in his career, nearly stagnant; and these things were elements in what happened.

He had thrown an enormous party at the West Side apartment where he and his wife and children were temporarily living. At its height between two and three hundred persons filled every room of the large, nondescript place, a crowd made up of swingers, literary people, movie stars and starlets, boxers, minor politicians and fringe figures of every kind (Mailer's own father was there, a little, vigorous man with a pertinent name, Barney). All evening long little ripples of violence stirred in the rooms: fights quickly broken up in corners, sexual stalkings and contretemps, envies and jealousies staging themselves as in group therapy. Toward midnight Mailer, who had disappeared, returned with blood caking his mouth and one eye swollen nearly shut. He had been in a fight outside, whether with a guest or a stranger on Broadway nobody knew.

He went around then stirring things up, challenging

everyone to more violence, relishing his status as a source
of waves of danger, intimations of disaster. Yet he was
desperate, one could sense, for some culmination, something to relieve the craving. Pity and terror? The catharsis
he wanted, one guessed, involved going through to the
end of some atrocious, exhilarating experience that would
cruelly stretch his civilized qualities, his nature as a
reflective man (which is what the novelist, vis-à-vis the
life of action, most centrally is), overturn and break his
upright cultured self and show him finally in a vastly perilous and infinitely rebellious condition: existentially alive,
he would doubtless have called it, all contradictions resolved, every warring appetite given satisfaction, not
through fiction, which is a *theory*, a substitution through
words, but by bruises, blood and afflicted flesh.

With perhaps twenty guests remaining, he suddenly
ordered them to divide themselves into those who were
"for me or against me," then decided the matter himself,
pushing almost everyone, including his wife, into the line
for nonsupporters and commanding a few others, as
embarrassed and unhappy as the rest, to stand at his
right hand behind the family maid, who, he kept mutter-
ing, was the only person who had never once betrayed
him and who stood there now strangely silent, as if reconciled to what was going on. The guests one by one dis-
engaged themselves from the humiliation that covered
everybody, went home and learned the next day that less
than an hour after their departure Mailer had stabbed his
wife in the stomach.

He was taken in by the police of course, examined
in Bellevue and then, because the injury was not too serious
and because his wife, who had at first expressed great
fears for her safety, later refused to press charges, he was
rightly let off. Rightly, because Mailer was no ordinary
wife beater and no conventionally violent man, either.
Whatever paranoid elements entered into his action (and

he was to show signs of these internal legends of persecution on many occasions afterward), the affair's deepest significance both for Mailer and for society was spiritual rather than psychological or criminal, for it demonstrated a certain crucial relationship between realms of being and faculties of the self. Mailer was a man with an *idea* about action and violence, someone caught in a pervasive contradiction: to write is to act without acting. If he were to find the means of resolving it, it would be a general boon.

Out of this far-flung and insatiable activity of assertion and impatience, this need to have it all ways at once, this perpetual rash overstepping of limits, has emerged a strangely relevant figure, a Faustian, autonomous-seeming ego to whom many eyes have turned in an age of shackled, swamped and ill-defined selves. These have been the sources of much of Mailer's appeal: his absolutism, his independent light, the manner in which he continually appears to re-create himself, the example he sets of a man who refuses *to take orders*. And the source of his relevance beyond these psychic and personal regions (although it is a relevance never wholly separate from them) has been his occupation of a position halfway between the artist and the activist, his status as a man incarnating the breakdown of the old distinctions in these areas, his populism in intellectual matters and his philosophical drive in physical ones. It is a position that throws light as no other American writer's does on some changes that have taken place in our attitudes toward culture, toward consciousness and its relation to the objects of consciousness, and toward literature and its relation to both.

With no other American writer is it so necessary to keep shuttling between the man and the work, not in order to bring into play some scheme of biographical criticism or to get confirmation about one from the other, but because Mailer has made it impossible to separate the two. With the partial exception of one or two of his novels, and to an extent that makes Henry Miller his only, and distant, rival, Mailer has lived in public, discharging his personality (whenever he isn't physically demonstrating it) as successive waves of comment, opinion, rough poetry, visions, prophecy and exhortation. Everything he writes, moreover, is an *act*, of a kind he likes to call existential, although as we shall see he has given the word a set of idiosyncratic and wholly unhistorical meanings. It is one of the mainsprings of his effectiveness and yet at the same time one of the blurring effects he has had on intellectual discourse that he has so strenuously insisted on the existential nature of these literary actions; and it has become increasingly clear that he has done it in order to separate his writing as widely as possible from "pure" literature, from writing conceived of as an alternative to action, as contemplation, the creation of pure forms and ideas.

As Diana Trilling was the first to point out, Mailer is a writer with a deep romantic hang-up on art, but also a profound mistrust of it, of its seductions, its mysteries and necessary disciplines, of its slow, impalpable and indeterminate effects, above all of the way it recommends itself in place of history by standing outside time. To such a temperament as his, and with his special reasons for hurling himself about, art presents in its most extreme intensity a danger that many writers have felt, and most severely in our time: that it will become a surrogate for the writer's own life, inhibiting action and eventually coming to take its place. Thomas Mann struggled perpetually between the alternatives and made their relationship one of the major themes of his work; Proust yielded entirely to the aesthetic realm and raised his epic novel as the exact and legendary replacement for his life. Norman Mailer is an artist *malgré lui,* a man whose ego has needed to know *at once* of its triumphs and so of its reality, and an American who has known that here the efficacy of art has been thinner and more remote than nearly everywhere else. And so he has never allowed the fundamental recognition to take clear shape or be made into an avowal: that he is caught, in tension and revolt, between doing and making, between action and creation, finally between being an artist and being what might turn out to be more of a *real man.*

Mailer has talked on occasion about style. His basic assumption about it is a rather romantic, Hemingwayesque notion that it is the equivalent in writing of performance in sport, a sort of devil-may-care grace, and also a means of intimidation ("part of a man's style is what he thinks of people and whether he wants them to be in awe of him or to think of him as an equal," he wrote in *Advertisements for Myself*). But he has spoken very little about art. When he has talked about it, it has almost always been in one or another of two veins, the utilitarian or the nostalgic, which may appear to be contradictory but which are really the complementary poles of his continual passage between the world he wishes to affect and amend and the ideal one that seems to stand incorruptibly alongside it. "Art," he once wrote, "is a force. Maybe it's the last force to stand against urban renewal, mental hygiene, the wave of the waveless future." Such a remark indicates a rather muddled and conventional desire to hold out, to champion certain fundamental human values in a depersonalized age, but it tells us very little about art or about what Mailer thinks it can do.

Something else he has written does. In *The Deer Park* the talented, self-betrayed film director, Charles Eitel, recalls to himself "the final desire of the artist, the desire which tells us that when all else is lost, when love is lost and adventure, pride of self, and pity, there still remains that world we may create, more real to us, more real to others, than the mummery of what happens, passes and is gone." In this elegiac mood, his eye on transience, aware of the possibility of a redemption of experience through the creation of alternative worlds, Mailer came as close as he has ever done to acknowledging his unassuaged but mostly suppressed longing for aesthetic disinterestedness, the intermittent pull of his imagination in the direction of making fictions that have no stake in ordering the world around, browbeating it into changing itself, but only in offering increments to what exists.

"The sour truth is," Mailer wrote in one of the most famous passages of *Advertisements for Myself*, "that I am imprisoned with a perception that will settle for nothing less than making a revolution in the consciousness of our time." We will see what kind of revolution he has made, but it is clear that questions of consciousness—how it is affected, what forms its revolutions take, how art may transform it and so on—are central to everything Mailer has attempted in the formation of the body of his labors.

All the shifts between fiction and journalism, the new use of novelistic techniques in his reporting, the calculations of the immense confessional autobiography he has steadily been publishing, the tone and timing of his manifestoes, the abrupt metamorphoses into poet, playwright, city planner, moviemaker—these things display something rather different from the internal growth of a mind and sensibility, the gestations and epiphanies of a consciousness ruled by itself. For Mailer has been at least as much impelled by his changing ideas about how to invade the consciousness of others, how to make the revolution he so desperately covets take root; he has been our supreme exemplar of the politics of literature, the model technician of writing as power and persuasion.

In the same paragraph in which he asserts his hunger for the revolution Mailer goes on to claim it: "It is my present and future work which will have the deepest influence of any work being done by an American novelist in these years." This may turn out to be true, but if it does it is unlikely to have very much to do with Mailer's own achievements in fiction, which after five novels and a scattering of shorter pieces are of a minor and not very memorable kind. He has had far less technical influence on other writers and less imaginative influence on the American reader than Bellow, Salinger or Nabokov have had, or than John Barth, Thomas Pynchon, William Gass or Donald Barthelme are having now. And this is because for all the hoopla of his self-canonization as a novelist he is essentially a traditionalist when it comes to fiction, having neither innovated nor carried any existing mode to the end. His fiction, one is sometimes tempted to suspect, is fashioned in sincerity all right, and has its proper victories on occasion, but it is also his way of claiming legitimacy as an artist in order to then use that prestige for a hearing for his more pressing ambitions.

When *The Naked and the Dead* was published in 1948 Mailer was twenty-six. He had published a few stories, one of which had won a prize in a writing contest for college students, and he has told us how he came back to America from the Pacific determined to write the first big novel about World War II. The ambition reveals something about how closely he was tied at the beginning of his career to a shallow and essentially bourgeois, although also complicated, idea of the uses of fiction. A novel in this view is, in the first place, a way of getting at public experience, the larger the experience the more potentially significant the book; it is a way of transferring events to a different and presumably more "meaningful" plane. Beyond this a novel is an instrument for infusing emotion into fact, which theoretically lies dejected and incomplete until this happens. Finally it is also an entrant in a race;

the first big novel about a large historical phenomenon (or about anything that has aroused general interest—but a war of course is best) will get to the tape first, a tape spun out of middle-class notions of success and of the nature of artistic work as a competition like any other.

Mailer was formidably equipped for participation in such a sweepstakes: he was the possessor of considerable storytelling ability of a traditional kind, he very much wanted to do something for the facts which were waiting to be lifted into "art," and he had unrivaled energy and competitive spirit. As it turned out, the book was better than its auspices. It was "about" the war, certainly, but it was something more than a war novel if we define that the way the book-selling trade does. In one way or another its antecedents in American literature were Crane's *Red Badge of Courage*, Dos Passos' *Three Soldiers* and Hemingway's *A Farewell to Arms*. The first book set down a model for a tale of education in the nature of manliness, the latter two for an education in the nature of the world's treacherous ways of involving and assaulting the soul through its largest and most impersonal forces.

Yet Mailer stood at a point in American consciousness that was the result of events that had altered the relations between the self and society in the time between the publication of his book and those of Dos Passos and Hemingway; and he was, besides, by temperament, no lonely representative of a flight from the world's cruelty and waste. His book is much less disillusioned, less nostalgic, more political, external and socially "active" than theirs, active, that is to say, as an aggressive inquiry into society and into what we might call national psychic truth. He speaks, as Dos Passos might have done, of America's "stricken, raucous" quality, but he never proposes any kind of exile from it. We may say that he lacked the ground—if he had had the inclination—for any lofty, aristocratic self-exile from America, the interposition of a style, if not of physical space, between one's own being and what has been offered as homeland and theater, a ground such as both Dos Passos and Hemingway possessed in their inheritance of ordinary, unquestioned "citizenship." For Mailer, to write was a way in, an immigrant's papers.

A speculative matter. But what is undeniable is that the chief fascination of *The Naked and the Dead* does not lie in its battle scenes, descriptions of Army life or evocation of the general flavor of war, the elements that made it a best seller. The most memorable quality it has rests in Mailer's having been able to isolate certain strands of American actuality, the reality that lay, we might say, behind our presence in the war and made it possible to endure and even to enjoy: our hard, cold Wasp strain, our arrogance and confidence, our fear of not being arrogant and confident. Against these things he threw the questioning, "liberal" force of his own Jewish, urban and outsider's temperament.

A part of his temperament. For Mailer was clearly more ravished than a programmatically humanist writer would have been by the ostensible villains of his tale, the officers such as the general whose limbs "stirred with an odd ecstasy" before he fired a field gun, the steely, mystically brutal Sergeant Croft, who Mailer has declared is the character in his fiction with whom he feels most closely identified and whose motto was "I hate everything that is not in myself." This is the beginning both of Mailer's own Promethean and narcissistic lyric and of his awareness of an American fatality, and if anything can be said to be, it is the "subject" of the novel.

The Naked and the Dead marked a thematic shift in American fiction, something that was at the same time a renewal, at a more sophisticated level, of the political concerns of the prewar years and an opening into a new, more pertinent field of psychological inquiry. And yet to see it this way is to perpetuate that academic handling of literature by which theme and subject are made to constitute the heart of writing, and style, illegitimately separated from matter, is regarded as a kind of instrument.

The point is that Mailer's first and biggest novel made no real impact on literary sensibility and has had only a thin and local influence on the course of American writing during the generation since its appearance. When everything original about it has been seen and acknowledged, when it is granted that its vigor and relevance make it far superior to the run of popular fiction, it has to be said that *The Naked and the Dead* remains at bottom a conventional work of literary art. As it shapes itself into a tale, it proceeds along predictable lines, creates no convincingly new style and offers no new purchase on imaginative reality, nothing that can be used by other writers as a model of a *way of seeing*, or as incontrovertible vision by anyone else. Having absorbed his influences and found a way to dramatize his interior experiences—whose central element was his ambiguous position between ideality and the cutting edge of the world, between the kinds of manhood represented by generosity and by power—Mailer had produced a novel more than equal to his purposes. But these purposes, which can only be discovered within the work, did not include the extension and reinvigoration of the imagination, its *ransoming*, through the creation of new form. We are not used to asking for it, but a novel that doesn't in some manner change the way we look at the world, not just at the particular subject of the fiction, is going to die with time. Proust taught us more than about social hierarchies, Joyce more than about Ireland, Conrad more than about the sea.

The Naked and the Dead made Mailer very famous at an early if not unprecedented age. The novel had gotten to the tape first, and Mailer had now to see what might lie on the other side. He had now also, on that grosser plane along which bourgeois ambition and the fire-breathing goddess of success impel many American writers' lives simultaneously with their struggle to turn experience into literature, to try to hold and extend the reputation he had won. The law—no one knew it better—is that you aren't allowed to stand still. It was no surprise that when Mailer's second book, *Barbary Shore,* which came out three years after *The Naked and the Dead,* proved to be a public failure of rather large proportions, his morale was severely shaken. When a few years after that *The Deer Park* fell something short of recouping his literary fortunes, Mailer was forced to revise his battle plan, to enter on a new mode of literary and public life, in order to give new impetus to the flagging revolution whose instigator and custodian he so much wanted to be.

Mailer has frequently defended *Barbary Shore* and even gone so far as to call it his favorite among all his books, and there is something touching in this parental preference for a deformed or retarded child. For the novel is hopelessly bad, ponderously written, confused, uncertain of what it wants to do, unconvincing in its structure and its imaginative premises. That it has had its admirers can be explained by the fact that Mailer (and it is something important to remember about him) has always had devotees who are simply tone-deaf and wholly uninterested in literary art, who leap upon certain books with all their senses frozen except one. You see them with a feeler out waving for ideas or attitudes that are as close as possible to their own and that therefore offer confirmation or the consolation that there is someone who is *publicly* expressing what they believe.

The ideas of *Barbary Shore* had heavily, if opaquely and in unrealized fashion, to do with what Mailer called "the remnants of my socialist culture," its vision being of a world of power where such culture was no longer relevant, so that a new one had to struggle to be born. A good many persons in the same boat with him, then or now, are clearly going to be interested in such a novel, although a good many more have been unable to see in it anything but strain, fog and idiosyncratic will.

The Deer Park, coming four years after *Barbary Shore,* exhibits many signs of a recovery of powers and of their extension into new territory. In his third book Mailer's old-fashioned novelist's attributes, his inquisitiveness about how men behave in society and his instinct for the dramatization of events, reassert themselves; his imagination rids itself of the labyrinthine philosophy and the coerced fantasy of the previous novel; and he breaks into a clear ground of straightforward characterization and coherent narrative. The new novel is more "objective," more independent, and therefore less of a wrestling match in the dark with something one *thinks should be said* and more a tale to contain things whose outlines have already been perceived.

Pitched considerably beyond any kind of explicit politics, *The Deer Park* is still a political novel if we think of that as a work whose instigation and final ambition have to do with erecting a fiction out of the way men are affected by their organizations and the way the values which they are encouraged to hold or which they defy are rooted in a public soil. The American reality in this novel is that of a deer park, a preserve organized for the gratification of appetites and for the testing of styles of combat and pursuit, and its ultimate sources are in an energy that is at the same time a sickness—the American dream locked in and turned on itself.

The novel is also a vehicle for the unfolding of Mailer's never wholly unpolitical dualisms; these are psychic battles, that is to say, which can only be resolved—as all his work has gone on telling us—through some radical change in the organization of society. This is a very different matter from the "healing" through the creation of counter-organizations of the mind, the sort of thing D. H. Lawrence meant when he spoke of "shedding one's sicknesses in one's books," that most contemporary artist-novelists have sought, and it is another sign of Mailer's confusion about the uses of imaginative writing.

In the three main characters to whom Mailer has allocated segments of his divided being—the narrator Sergius, the fallen artist Eitel, the Luciferian pimp Marion Faye—the psyche and the moral self strive for reconciliation and a choice among ways of proceeding in the world. Mailer as Sergius is the "spy and the fake," the intruder into the park, the student weighing curricula; as Eitel he is the potentiality for the corruption of the ideal, the artist betraying the obligation to hold out against grosser forms of power; as Faye he is the moral insurrectionary, secretly hungering for peace and love but coldly setting about a transvaluation of values.

The psychic wars are carried on within a context of observation of American styles and ambitions that is mostly hard, detailed and full of shrewd reportorial accuracy. Mailer's gift of mimicry, a talent he was later to transfer to his journalism, is here at its most memorable within the body of his fiction, and it is a mimicry of people of the world of power, agents and products of a society that holds out and thwarts various and conflicting possibilities of fulfillment—love, idealism, sensual experience, transcendence, conquest, wealth, violence—a society organized, brilliantly and dismayingly, as a deer park.

Nothing opens out as a way. "I was still an anarchist and an anarchist I would always be," Sergius ends by knowing. The deer park is a maze in which the life of man in society loses itself. Art is brought down by cowardice and greed; love is a matter either of desolate conquest or mutual pity; Promethean immorality leads to disaster. The world is made up of rage, betrayal, self-deception and a universal cannibalism. Though a sort of disenchanted morale survives, the book's final consciousness is the prayer of Faye for a cleansing explosion, with the atomic tests in the desert as its political referent: "Let it come . . . let it come and clear the rot and the stench and the stink, let it come for all of everywhere, just so it comes and the world stands clear in the dead white dawn."

A few years later, at a time when Mailer seemed to have given up writing fiction, he said of the role of the artist that it was to be "as disturbing, as adventurous, as penetrating, as his energy and courage make possible." And yet for all the sophisticated adventuring and disturbing portraiture in this novel, for all the interest it sustains in its shabby and sinister high life, it strikes one at a distance of a dozen or so years as thin, not very penetrating, technically, and so in the end morally, safe. A persistent strain of melodrama runs through it; a sense of danger that comes more from tough poses conceived outside the novel than from any true internal peril it distilled from its neoromantic preconceptions. It remains powerless to affect the imagination in any permanent way because of its lack of inventive reach, its reliance, when all is said and done, on what lay at hand. What these things were, what Mailer reached out for, was, in the first place, a set of characters who constituted a typology, a gallery whose inhabitants seemed more reported on than given birth to, and beyond this a narrative structure whose rhythms of incident and denouement had their inevitability more in the conventions of narrative than in the exigencies and pressures of a new and startling fiction.

There is no substantial new aesthetic environment for Mailer's characters (a described place is not the same thing as an environment), and hence no inevitable new being. They act and speak within an atmosphere we have been exposed to before—the producer Teppis, acutely as he is drawn, comes from the lore of Hollywood, Eitel has been seen in the newspapers—and the passions that move them seem finally to have been transferred from the writer's experience rather than to have been fallen upon in the writer's movement through his material. One subtle difference between the novel as original creation and as a "fictionalizing" process for one's experience is that in the latter there is always an effect of scenario, arrangements for keeping things moving, a line of expectations to fill.

To take the closest look of all, Mailer's writing, so often sharp and decisive, is at least as often flabby and imprecise, bullying its way past intellectual difficulties (a characteristic that will be discernible in all his work), or thrusting sentimental evaluations in place of original feeling. The malady is not simply the excess and imprecision that can be found in the work of torrential writers like Dostoevsky or Faulkner (the kind of writer about whom Flaubert wrote that while lesser authors like himself searched for the *mot juste* to complete delicate structures, they were raising great dominating mountains). Mailer's stylistic faults have not simply been the price of eloquence but the cost of confusion about both language and life.

He writes, for example, that Faye "had killed people" and "had almost been killed himself" and that "these were emotions he considered interesting," and the misuse of the word "emotions" is revelatory of Mailer's perennial distress at certain central points where things and processes have to be distinguished. In another vein he writes an ostensibly grave self-colloquy for Eitel, who reminds himself of "how far down one could go" and expresses the hope that he and his fellow sufferer, the girl Elena, "would make something of each other," something, presumably, of renewed moral stature. After saying that Eitel was "full of tenderness for her," Mailer ends by writing, "She was adorable. Her back was exquisite," and the reduction in feeling, the anticlimax, are the results not of an ironic intention but of a deep and—as it will turn out—persistent flaw in sensibility.

In a short and little-known work, *Genius and Apostle,* Kierkegaard set forth the decisive condition for self-contained, independent artistic activity:

> The lyrical author [by which Kierkegaard meant the poet or artist in the widest sense] is only concerned with his production, enjoys the pleasure of producing, often perhaps only after pain and effort, he has nothing to do with others, he does not write *in order that:* in order to enlighten men or in order to help them along the right road, in order to bring about something; in short, he does not write *in order that.* The same is true of every genius.

Not a genius, or at any rate not one whose particular features he had shown as yet, Mailer was and would always remain in some sense what Kierkegaard meant by an apostle, a man who craves to bring something about, to have an effect. This is a clue to many things in his career and the chief way to understand why he all but gave up writing fiction after *The Deer Park* in order to practice, as he has never stopped doing, as a performer, a personality and a quotidian prophet, a commentator as close to his audience as a scoutmaster plunging up the trail with his troop at his heels. For whatever it might have been in itself, *The Deer Park* had had a public reception so disappointing and inconclusive as to strike at the center of Mailer's present-directed ego, his need for immediate effectiveness among men. A very minor success of esteem and a somewhat larger one of scandal, the novel left Mailer's reputation pretty much as it had found it, and left the revolution whose Lenin he was supposed to be bogged down in rumor, gossip and an *enfant terrible*-ism that was aging and so needed quicker, more brilliant stunts to attract a crowd.

What Mailer turned to now was in no way the result of any kind of clear purposeful decision. Do you decide how what is ravaging you should be manipulated? A complicated, protean being, elusive even to himself, Mailer seems always to have discovered himself in new roles and gestures rather than to have summoned them. This is why his famous candor and spontaneity often have the quality of appearing to be responses to interior pressures whose operation remains dim to him, as though he were living in obedience to a plan worked out in council halls to which he has only limited access.

This is the deepest meaning of what we call "representative being." Mailer's has not been the great conscious scheme for making good, the blue-printed program for seducing the bitch goddess. He would be instructive if it were that, but narrowly; as it is he has carried within himself the tides and eddies of our American age and has been as much a product as an originator. His very self-destructiveness, that impulse to step to the edge of disaster that has periodically shown itself—his brawls and arrests, the stabbing of his wife, the manic interloping jumps into activities and realms where he is made to look foolish, such as his proposal to run for mayor and his would-be intervention in the Liston-Patterson heavyweight championship fights—this impulse exhibits the marks of an ego unmoored, avid, uncalculating, an ego bent on a blind elbowing through and finding its justifications afterward. Even though Mailer never fails to take up such behavior in retrospect as existential action, and even though it has a clear utility for keeping his name and persona dangerous and giving them the febrile publicity of a legend, it retains all the quality of unconscious and unanticipated American violence, the violence of a revolt against consciousness and predictability.

But Mailer resumes consciousness after each eruption and moves zigzag through his accumulating destiny. Fame, efficacy, are the spurs. The failure of his second and third novels was surely instrumental, but even if they had been much more successful, it is doubtful that Mailer would have gone on uninterruptedly writing fiction. For the novelist in this country can of course win fame and fortune and even status as a shaper of new styles of behavior and morality (Fitzgerald and Hemingway are the obvious recent examples), but it is nearly impossible for him to win prophetic mastery, the power to impel men in the wake of his dreams. And if he is fundamentally an apostle rather than a lyrical genius, he is going to fret and chafe under the conditions of austerity and social celibacy that being an artist in fiction has generally required. Thomas Mann's *Tonio Kroeger* contains the perfect epiphany of this potentially agonizing dilemma: the young writer looking on enviously at the dance he is prevented by his nature and vocation from joining. At a turning point in his life Norman Mailer, whose own nature and vocation have never been clear to him (and who has brought this unclarity and lack of definition into a dialectic with his precise self-canonizations), made a leap and joined the dance.

He was to write in *Advertisements for Myself* that he had come to feel that it "was more important to be a man than a very good writer." Yet all the evidence is that the distinction was only tactical and provisional. Mailer has never stopped writing, never gone into the desert for stocktaking or drastic revisions, nor does he ever seem to have undergone that crisis in which a writer comes to feel that being immersed in language, that quintessential abstraction, is a sickness and an alienation. He is no Rimbaud, horrified by his own verbal moon voyages, nor, at the opposite pole, is he a Flaubert, who believed in being "as bourgeois as possible in your life in order to be that much more revolutionary in your work." He has wanted fame, power and triumphs, and so he needed to become a better, or at least a bigger, man in order to then become a better or bigger writer—the guise of manhood he had long ago settled on—although a writer of a greatly changed kind.

To be a man of action while remaining a writer, he needed to proceed now without the screens and obliquenesses of art; the indirections, time lags and impersonal commitments of the imaginative process, of *making things up*, stood in his way, as they stand in the way of anybody hungering for the dance. And so he set out to attempt his "entrance into the mysteries of murder, suicide, incest, orgy, orgasm and Time" (a characteristically mixed bag of the apocalypse) through a supremely ambitious and yet hot-handed kind of journalism, a rapidly created and idiosyncratically principled reporting on the face, the mind and the fate of the world that does not have to be imagined or invented, and on himself as its most acutely representative figure, its ubiquitous citizen and rebel.

In the columns he began to write for *The Village Voice* and the pieces for *Dissent*, both of which journals he had a hand in founding, he took up directly all those themes that had occupied him in his fiction, or, more accurately, that he had not been able to make wholly convincing as elements of a universe of fiction: the deadness and hypocrisy of American life, the imprisonment and suffocation of the ego, the exhaustion of all the old political ideas, the need for a new basis of morality that would incorporate extremity, danger and perversion; the quest for heroism and apocalypse through sex and violent physicality, the liberating role of the Negro, the hipster and what he came to call, in a hundred misleading but always resonant ways, existentialism. Later, in a more far-flung periodical journalism and in *Advertisements for Myself,* he would move on to his full role as intellectual action painter, prophet without portfolio and philosopher *maudit*.

"My passion is to destroy innocence," Norman Mailer wrote near the beginning of his second incarnation and career. His readers "must be prepared," he went on, "for a dissection of the extreme, the obscene and the unsayable . . . my nature is nothing other than to search for the Devil while I carry with me the minds of some of you."

A likely story. In this age of publicity and put-on, bulls have to be invented in order for their horns to be seized, new forms of heroism conjured up so that heroes may be acknowledged. When all distinctions have been blurred between the wars of the spirit and those of the ego, men come forward to *introduce themselves* as culture heroes, and a certain kind of traditional human modesty disappears. The arrogance that takes its place is seen as our own inimitable mark upon the face of time and fills us with enlivenment, hope and depression, outcomes of a cooperation with a violent, seductive ambition in which charlatanism and true passion are difficult to distinguish.

Mailer was one of the inaugurators of the new age of the put-on. For whose foolish hope has it ever been to *destroy* innocence? Has any serious writer—Aristophanes, Swift, Céline?—conceived of that as his project or mission? De Sade? His project in this realm was to destroy the belief that innocence still existed, to ruin the notion that it could remain intact, an answer instead of a question; and he sought, it is clear, however perversely, to create a new innocence. (Have we ever thought about artists as creators of fresh innocence, a creation out of a recognition that we are guilty of everything except portraits of our guilt?)

In the same way, what writer who has felt himself implicated with the devil has ever announced it in Mailer's way: outside the work, programmatically, like an item in a job résumé or a squib for who's who? To decide and proclaim that one is a culture hero: nothing could better indicate the point we have reached in our sense of what part the ego may play in culture and the formulation of values, our feeling for the allowable contours and limits of personal assertion in matters of spirit and imagination, than this public act of self-definition and aggrandizement, this usurpation of the prerogatives of one's fellow men.

We have always had our devil trackers and wrestlers with innocence, our literary workers at the extremities and our eloquent besiegers of the unspeakable. Hawthorne, Melville, James, Whitman, Mark Twain: nineteenth-century American writing is a set of logs of voyages of these kinds. But with the exception of Whitman, who was the first to make the full connection between the uses of personality and those of literature and from whose strategic bravado Mailer has undoubtedly picked up clues, these writers declared themselves, if they spoke of it directly at all, as victims not heroes. If there was heroism, it lay in the work, in *being able to do it* in the face of everything that spoke against doing it, and not in any gift of personality, any Promethean role in the fate of the American society or any mesmeric stance vis-à-vis others.

The ethos told such writers to move privately (literature was itself so much more a private matter then), guardedly; it frequently forced them into apologies. What one wrote was on a level of utterance that might or might not be absorbed back into the national consciousness under the aegis of literature, an uncertain sponsorship. To write was to take the risk of incurring silence, which is to say that literature offered no guarantees to its creators; as newly made, impersonal myth, it could be held outside the intimate lives and psychic reality of readers as *culture,* the disinterested sphere of educated men whose eyes were trained on artifice. The times did not provide for Mailer's kind of self-assertion; the American artist worked at best in an atmosphere of silence, that absence of outcry or fanfare that marks the probationary period of an activity the nation has not yet legitimized for itself, certainly not as power. If the boat carrying the latest installments of Dickens' novels was met at the pier by avid readers, it was in part because to Americans England was where literature—sanctified, unquestioned and mysteriously conceived—properly came from. In obedience to the impropriety of his own claims in a deeply provincial culture, and out of the insubstantiality of all his grounds, the American literary artist's sense of his vocation was still largely derived from classic models of forbearance, sacrifice and exile.

The fate and demeanor of Henry James—self-exiled, sorely gifted, as ambitious as anyone yet painstakingly defending an artistry remote from use or practical consequences for the ego—stands as a measure of the distance we have traveled in order to arrive at Norman Mailer. Yet even for writers much closer to him, for Hemingway and Scott Fitzgerald in our own generations, nothing spoke of cultural heroism or of the messianic. Their fate was to struggle or intercede or connive with innocence and finally to be brought down by its presence in their own lives, not to labor as an agent of its destruction. And their demeanor, however flamboyant or aggressive it might have been as social behavior, was not the life style of a *soi-disant* savior. Hemingway may have set Mailer a model for the reaping of publicity or for the conception of writing as the National Open, but there was nothing of the prophet or the light-bringer about him. Neither he nor Fitzgerald, more modest and more naïve than Mailer, more purely writers of fictions to set against the inadequate truths of the world, ever imagined he was leading a crusade against the shapes and weathers of the realities that already were.

With the insufficiency of his fiction as a source of prophetic power, and so with his true ambition still unsatisfied, Norman Mailer, now in his early thirties, set out to find the devil and the means of saying, by more direct methods, what had not yet been said. The process touches on much of the intellectual history of the past decade. That in these ten or twelve years Mailer has taken more and more of us with him is beyond argument, but that he has carried along our minds is something else again. If by mind we mean intellect—and in present-day America, impatient with distinctions, full of renewed contempt for the abstractions and thus the impotence of pure thought, is such a meaning still secure?—then it seems clear that our recent assent to Mailer has been something other than an unalloyed intellectual phenomenon, just as much of the earlier assent to his fiction was something other than a pure aesthetic one. The necessary distinction at this point is between intellect and consciousness; the latter is what Mailer has come to affect in us, although the event has been rather less than the revolution he has so often asserted he craved to lead.

What we have recognized is a personality who thinks, and it is a recognition that has had to crowd its way in among many physical reactions. Personality and thought: we have traditionally kept them separate, apart from the occasional exception we make for someone like Nietzsche, whose real ideas have been radically distorted precisely because they have been read through the screen of what he was *like*. What Mailer is like, though, makes all the difference, lends almost all its significance to what he thinks and gives his thought the power it has to affect us.

In Mailer's quasi-philosophical and theological journalism and in his pseudoscientific excursions we have been offered legitimate thinking, but also a game played with traditional kinds of thinking—a game in so far as it is conscious in him; in so far as it is not, the outpourings of blind and embattled ego taking on the functions of rationality. As much wayward and self-indulgent expressionism as purposeful mockery, as much solipsistic maundering as objective inquiry, Mailer's body of comment and opinion has come to recommend itself as a strange, exemplary way of dealing with experience at a time when other familiar ways seem to have been stopped in their tracks. Our period exists with an awareness that the old inherited categories of learned political and social inquiry, the old dispassionate categories of public knowledge and knowledge about what is public, are no longer unassailable, in some ways no longer even useful.

Yet Mailer has not seized hold of this truth as would a visionary writer in any familiar sense. He is no Blake or Lawrence, for whom personality was always at the service of vision and not the other way round, and in whose writings we feel at nearly every moment the pressure of impersonal, cosmic values, faculties of humanity making use of their language, borrowing its genius for the struggle. Mailer has visions, it is true, but they smack as much of eccentricity as of inevitable findings; he has ideas, but they have no clear outlines or progressions. Ideas and visions swirl and mix in his activity and break down one another's walls. What happens to the old discrete disciplines and intellectual divisions when he intrudes into architecture with his absurd cities in the sky, into sociology with his proposals for jousting tournaments in Central Park, or into political theory with his megalomanic advice to Presidents?

Mailer's influence has established itself, in its shabbier purlieus, just because he often thinks so badly while doing it so energetically and, more important, with such idiosyncratic irreverence. He cannot be argued with or *traced*, which is to say fitted into chronology where matters of intellectual obligation and connection—and thus the whole heritage of our thought—have always taken on their weight and justification, but appears always with his ideas full-blown, importunate, violently immodest. He has pitted against the ruling and arrogant specialists and professionals the zest and impertinence of his own amateur citizen's proposals. For these reasons he has been able to work a

deep populist vein. And like any other populism, his has
tasted of demagoguery. In so far as he simply asserts,
declaims, steals from others, arrogates to himself general
insights, makes light of contradiction, presses the claims
of personality and ego against a seemingly arid fitness of
thought, makes a virtue of imprecision and of half-truth,
his mind appeals to the half-formed, the impatient and
the resentful in all of us. Like Paul Goodman and Norman
O. Brown, or Herbert Marcuse at this moment, he has
told a good many persons what they have wanted to hear,
he has fulfilled wishes and raised morale, at the cost of
clarity and intellectual modesty.

And yet in the past few years we have come to see that
there is a kind of material, a subject and a ground for
which Mailer's species of unprofessional thinking and his
conception of writing as the extreme promulgation of the
ego and the reckless dissemination of personality, are oddly
and even splendidly suited. He has been discovered at
last by what lay in wait for him all the time.

A writer and his subject: we have never known or failed
to remember that the world is parceled out among all
makers of ideas and images, each poet or philosopher to
his province. Sometimes the deeds are unclear, and in any
case the condition goes against the grain of many writers
who would like to have the world to themselves. Mailer
has never shaken free of this desire; and originality, the
work he alone was supposed to do, has come to him despite
himself. This originality that has lately blossomed in him
begins with a debt to circumstances, to what it was possible for him to think and espy. For a writer like Mailer,
circumstance always disposes of a great deal, since if you
are not a pure inventor, a genius in Kierkegaard's terms,
then you are an apostle and this means that landscapes
have to be searched and clues unearthed as to what is
ready and plausible for your proselytizing.

In the middle fifties, when Mailer stepped into his role as philosopher at large and thinker *maudit*, what was present in the atmosphere for his use—what he had not drawn up out of himself as original utterance—was a triad of potential motifs: the Negro as post-Western man, the hipster as contemporary hero, and existentialism as weapon and deliverance. Three wraiths, legends or hypotheses for the mind seeking excitement, they were perfect instruments for the breaking up of the old psychic and spiritual means of apprehending the world and the old institutional ways of looking at it. And they were fine themes for romantic, superb, ready-at-hand characters, for a spent novelist, inspirations to a prophet's roving eye.

To be a Negro—of a certain knowing kind—or a hipster (or both at the same time, since they obviously could be one and the same person), and to live existentially: for Mailer, who was held outside all these conditions or roles by race, fate, cultural background, intellectual training and social situation, the possibilities were immense for extensions of his own ego through identification or sponsorship. Even more, the opportunities for cultural heroism, for light-bringing, were ravishing: these definitions of experience, these strategies for moving through life and making one's fate, seemed to ask for the zeal and eloquence of an apostle to bring them out of the darkness of cultural rumor and sociological abstraction into the light of personality, purpose and imaginative enthusiasm.

It was challenging work for a novelist who distrusted fiction, and Mailer set out to write an immense, journalistic, timely, semiautobiographical, quasi-factual epic of attitudes and ideas, using as central characters these figures that had solicited him out of the ethos, and using existentialism as the ground or plot for the unfolding of their destinies, which were at the same time his own. What he took existentialism to be is the starting point for our knowing without prejudice about his later work in all its embarrassments, aberrations and victories.

Mailer has used the word "existential" (or its noun or adverbial forms) over and over again in his essays and journalism ever since it first popped into his vocabulary. One can imagine him pouncing on it with a whoop when it first caught his eye, one of those seductive fragments of language that hint at new worlds of meaning and significance as they whirl past us on the way to the textbooks. That he ever read Sartre, to say nothing of Heidegger or Kierkegaard, is difficult to believe, but what is not hard to believe is that he knew the value of having so much work done for him. Stripped of its philosophical complexity and all its intellectual accuracies (as well as its doubtfulness), the word served him as shibboleth, talisman and motto. From the realm of philosophical discourse and speculation he brought it over for his use as the engine for the juggernaut he was about to set rolling.

When Mailer spoke of the necessity of living "with one's existential nerve exposed," he betrayed a far-reaching philosophical and historical naïveté that at the same time wonderfully revealed his instinct for intellectual demagoguery. For that expression is simply a harsher and more accurate description of the process we ordinarily call "popularizing," which is the cutting away of complexity, the spreading around and the making palatable of what is by nature circumscribed, difficult, often painful and always hard-won. To popularize: one of the chief paths to becoming popular yourself.

But the naïveté that accompanied the demagoguery was not feigned, the way naïveté so often is in this writer-personality; it was simply exploited. It sprang from the fact that Mailer has always found it intolerable that thought and action should in certain crucial ways remain separate from one another, that there should be different and sometimes opposed states of being and orders of functioning in the world. Though existentialism indeed has been and remains a way of proceeding intellectually that attempts to reduce the gap between thought and action and between intellect and feeling, it remains a process of the mind and spirit, not a property of the nerves and muscles, a light and not a power plant. Sartre, it has been remarked, does not live existentially, just as Plato would not have dreamed that it was possible to pursue a Platonic existence. There are realms of being and acting that do not spill across one another's boundaries except at the risk of losing the life that is in each of them.

The reckless use of such a word—"death is an existential continuation of life"; "that is the existential venture, the unstated religious view of boxers trying to beat each other into unconsciousness, or, ultimately, into death" —is a central revelation of how irresponsible Mailer can be, how he refuses to understand what he does not know. This word, with its cachet and currency, its portentous, *stimulating* sound and ring of humanity at the business of living dangerously, has served him in his wildest flights and led to his most dangerous and most contemptible formulations. There is no better illustration of how the word has served him as a cover for his intellectual malfeasances and a banner for his crusades than his statement that "existential politics is rooted in the concept of the hero." No, it could not be more wrong; totalitarian politics, the politics of immolation and disastrous ambition, is rooted in that concept.

Yet the sentence offers a clue to the other side of the coin, the other side of Mailer's troubled, impatient, disconsolate, crude and forceful mind. For if he is a demagogue, that is only one of his personae. And he has shown us—none of our writers more—how motives for everything are multiple, the uses of ideas various and arbitrary, the fate of what we say diverse and unaccountable. And so for all the inaccuracies and perversions of meaning, for all the shameless popularizing and the thefts from greater minds than his own, finally for all the ambition masking itself as heroism, we have known, increasingly so, of an authentic side. And that is the side from which existentialism—poor, ill-treated, overworked bit of ideation seeking an outlet and an immortality in language—has come, at bottom, in the confused intention he has had for it. For he has meant by it—often unknown to himself, quite simply, wonderfully and with the ludicrousness that is never far from any of his actions—truth, reality, more specifically the truth and reality of feelings and personal life under siege by politics and culture in these days.

"Great writers and artists ought to engage in politics only to the extent that is necessary to defend themselves against politics," Chekhov wrote, and brought together many of the questions that bristle around the phenomenon of Norman Mailer engaging in what he has wanted to. An older, different idea of art and of its relation to politics is at work here, but then perhaps a different idea of politics, too. To defend oneself against politics used to mean to remain liberated for art, in the familiar and fundamental sense of preserving room, freedom of choice, protection against the violences of power. But it also meant keeping one's freedom to refuse compromises, to refuse, in other words, the central thing that politics does and that art is the one human activity that is not compelled to do. This freedom was a function of a believed-in difference of realms, and Chekhov, with his art that had nothing to offer to life except its own perfect balance and refusal to compromise, is the great exemplar of its practice.

To defend oneself against politics is to defend against culture, too, or it is, at any rate, for those who know the difference between culture and art. As soon as it has become institutionalized (which is to say as soon as it has become itself after having been art), culture is an ally of politics: both try to hold things steady, safe, organized; both bury truth under utility. To defend against both politics and culture has been the traditional romantic literary position, but also the stance of the writer who, like Chekhov, James, Joyce or Proust, did not want to be *interfered with*. For Norman Mailer, striving to interfere, at work upon no aesthetic counterpart to consciousness within the world, protecting nothing that the world threatens and wishing mightily to discover himself as a man among men, politics and culture were not so much the enemy as a homeland temporarily in alien hands.

The real enemy was what had come over politics, its infection. To a certain kind of mind, the antithesis of Chekhov's, politics always bears the possibility of a redemption for the imagination and the private self to a point where the political comes to be identical with redemption itself. But if politics comes to stand in the way of its own promise of salvation, if it is moving directly against life and if art is no longer what you can or wish to throw up against that fatality, then literary skill, imagination, the apostle's fervor, have to step inside, work like an insurgency to change things from within. For this activist task, a word and a concept such as existentialism recommends itself as a locus of energy at the intersection of language and event.

Existentialism in this way became for Mailer a springboard to efficacy, a means of leaping into the heart of things. Once there, in the center of that political world which had spread to incorporate and corrupt so much of feeling and psychic reality, he would employ it for a general liberation. For it was something he could pass on to others, it was the name of a secret society devoted to the discovery and exaltation of *authentic* life; and he would reveal to his readers what was required to pass its tests for admission: "to be an existentialist, one must be able to feel onself—one must know one's desires, one's anguish,

one must be aware of the character of one's frustration
and know what would satisfy it."

The tiny mysterious rosette in the lapel, the secret
handshake, the password: there is something childish and
coerced in this conception of existentialism as something
to qualify for. Yet who would not want to belong to this
fraternity whose principles and aspirations have been enun-
ciated a hundred times before in Western humanism but
which rise again in each new generation like a noble,
beleaguered enclave of revelation? To feel, to know, to be
aware of oneself: nothing in these phrases is outside of
what we have always known we ought to do and be. Even
so, hearing them again under the aegis of a new word—
pragmatism, dianetics, existentialism—fills many of us with
a sense of seduction by something original and vivid. Yet
when he wrote in the introduction to *The Presidential
Papers* that "this book has an existential grasp of the
nature of reality," Mailer—in addition to being redundant
as well as chic—was saying that in it he was trying to be
himself, trying not to lie, and trying to make politics, where
so much of reality was besieged, be itself and not lie.

The main incentives to lying, both for himself and for
the political society, lay in the fact and condition of being
bourgeois. Middle-class America, or America on its way
to becoming middle-class as in the nineteenth century, has
always lied in order to protect the actual and the material.
We can go further and say that all political society lies to
itself, although bourgeois society lies in a particularly pas-
sionless way. A fearful slippage occurs, the earth trembles
under men's feet, when anything is allowed to question
(as art in some way always does) the arrangements, bal-
ances and finality of the organized material world. The
bourgeois mind, Nicholas Berdyaev has written, is the
idolatrous mind, the one that prefers the visible to the
invisible. For Norman Mailer, would-be idol smasher,
bourgeois America (its projections barbed in his own flesh)

was dying because it refused to know its anguish and the character of its frustrations under the armor it had put on against the invisible.

That he had thought of himself as a novelist is very much to the point here. The novel has lent itself to many uses (and many devaluations), but as imaginative enterprise it has always come to us as "news" of the invisible, of what exists beyond the recognitions of the naked eye, as possibility, alternative, redemption through a disbelief in what the world says about itself. The very forms of the novel have mirrored changes in what has been felt necessary to discover in prose, what has been left to do, rather than pell-mell responses to alternations in society. The passage within fiction from a Balzacian procedure to a Flaubertian to a Joycean and beyond reflects discovery accomplished and thus unnecessary to repeat, something that artist-novelists but not sociologist-critics have always understood.

Norman Mailer's lack of unassailable originality as a novelist—an absolute matter capable only of being temporarily disguised by fame, provisional fortune or his own bullying insistence on his uniqueness—has been the affair, fundamentally, of his equivocal and tortured relationship to the invisible and to the necessities of aesthetic discovery in this time. Fiction, that slowly achieved, bodiless, *ineffectual* system for changing the world, could not contain his impatience nor assuage his disconsolate wish to see himself as the recognized source of change. Turning to the world directly, or rather to those exemplary and edifying violent wraiths he had spied on the psychic and social horizons, he proceeded to employ them as new hybrids of the union of imagination and actuality, inhabitants of the visible world but with energies and purposes to discover and broadcast which would set the guardians of the visible on their ears.

Jean Malaquais once described Mailer's ideas about

hip and the hipster as "a gorgeous flower of his romantic idealism." This is true and useful but does not go far enough, since it leaves out of account the failed or stymied novelist beneath the journalist and commentator. A remark by Ned Polsky to the effect that in his famous essay "The White Negro" Mailer confuses acting with acting out brings these things to their right and suggestive complexity. For the Negro and the hipster—the white black man—have to be understood as characters in the nonfictional novel Mailer began to write, not as accurately seen and described figures in a passionate sociology. Mutants treading between the visible and the invisible, between existence and hoped-for life, they were at the same time his own desired selves. And so he set about investing them with being along the lines of his own hungers and frustrations, and having them act out careers halfway between fiction and the violently real.

The hipster and the Negro were Mailer's spacemen, sent out to the region he craved to occupy but from which he was barred by his self-consciousness, his whiteness and his burden of culture. They were the selves he would have been if he had not been his own: singular and autonomous egos sprung from mass life and bourgeois undifferentiation by ennui and oppression, the one coolly seeking "a sexual life which will suit his orgiastic needs," the other moving light-footed and exemplary in that area "where all situations are equally valid." Creatures of a dream, they bore resemblances to men we see, but having been summoned into being from half-being for the imperious purposes of the dreamer, they could not in the end lead their own lives or suffer their own debilities.

At the heart of Mailer's vision of him, the Negro danced at the end of a string whose other end had once been attached to notions of "gaiety, rhythm, and capacity for spiritual richness." That in Mailer the terms were now "extremity," "purifying violence" and "Promethean re-creation" left the Negro nearly as unseen as before. The process of corruption by deputization, the making of others into representatives of a condition we insist on having present in the world—inferiority, purity, menace, heroism—goes on all the time and is carried out by male supremacists, anti-Communists, New Leftists and every sort of government.

The black power movement is in its most central and vigorous thrust a reply to this pressure that others be something we wish them to be. What was not known about the Negro when he was converted into a deputy was his truest suffering, his anguish in trying to obtain the first creation, the recognized properties which, however betrayed, are what make the rest of us know ourselves as men. It had been our exclusion of him from our simplest condition that was destroying the Negro, but for Mailer, white, reckless and romantic, he was made to function as the agent of a complex superlife.

So, too, the hipster, the self-excluded. For Mailer, hip was "an exploration into the nature of man, and its emphasis [was] on the Self rather than society." Go past the foolish, crippling dichotomy (everywhere in Mailer we would encounter this romantic, intellectually naïve opposition of self and society) and the point to be made is that such exploration was precisely what the hipster, or the kind of man meant by the designation, was incapable of. With his very existence dependent on remaining isolated, uncommitted and closed to complexity; with his overwhelming concern being the establishment, through successive hermetic jolts to his senses, of a simulacrum of passionate life; with his fingertips filed and his antennae raised in order simply to survive—the hipster was the outlaw, the secessionist and the victim, not the adventurer. Like his counterpart at the antipodes, the academic, he was—and is in every new incarnation—the narrower of consciousness not its expander, and what he told us about existence arose unperceived by him from the sterile ironies of his fate.

In the same way that he mistook the hipster's victimized and jungle-trained consciousness for a liberation, Mailer inverted his psychopathic element and offered it as a new movement toward authentic being. He did more: he inverted the previously unquestioned bourgeois judgment and spoke of the psychopath as a force and an exemplar. And it was in fact a brilliant addition to his arsenal of intimidation, and an enhancement of his reputation as the man who turns the party dangerous, that he announced the condition as a positive form of human identity—doctor, lawyer, Indian chief, psychopath—so that a scary new career was loose in the visible world.

But the psychopath (if the word is to mean anything), far from being the intrepid Viking of the psychic seas, heroically "trying to create a new nervous system" for himself, is the arrested and agonized victim of precisely that attempt. He is pinioned and spread-eagled on the field of his own chaos by his rebellion from necessity, his inability to accept his own nervous system, his decision in the depths to turn the knife in the wounds that have been inflicted on him. It is no brief for the bourgeois spirit to say that it is right in its consideration of the psychopath as an alien and a scene of defeat; whatever victories may be in the bourgeois world, the psychopath has not achieved one in any universe.

But for Mailer, seeking triumphs over the conventional as well as the possibility of new life, the psychopath was the man who made virtues out of irredeemable losses and regrasped his ego in the same terms which had delineated its destruction. Beyond this, he was the man who employed the collapse of his communal self as the principle for a renewed and augmented solipsism, in a kind of mad homeopathy. "At bottom the drama of the psychopath," Mailer wrote, "is that he seeks love. Not love as the search for a mate, but love as the search for an orgasm more apocalyptic than the one which preceeded it."

Perhaps nowhere in all of Mailer's writing has his fundamental contradictions, his furious demand that the world reconstitute the ego out of its own substance, his confusion of realms and faculties—love as an orgasm, orgasm as therapy—been so starkly exhibited. But it was the mark of his writing everywhere during this period, the perpetually recurring point at which his energy, courage, craving for action and exasperation with impotency, real or imagined, inexorably ran up against what will not be broken through: the conditions and obligations of existence—finiteness, choice, sacrifice, hierarchy, reciprocity, debt, time. Love is mutuality or it is a destruction of itself; therapy is the release from compulsion or it is a new accession of sickness. One more incarnation in the world's long line of artistic victim-rebels, the hipster—psychopathic or not—lived by a denial of freedom, or rather by the terrible freedom to be involved in nothing beyond his own sensations. What was "coolness" for nearly all its practitioners in its heyday but—in the interests of literal self-preservation to be sure—being encased in ice?

Looking back on hipsterism, it was a case of "out of the tundra, into the refrigerator." For aberrations of this kind always spring from the effort to escape other aberrations. The tundra, the depleted bleak landscape of American life, the defoliation of its generous and sensuous growths, stretched undeniably to the horizon. Norman Mailer peopled it with his journalistic dream figures undergoing ever intensifying personal and hermetic apocalypses, his surrogate egos wresting their potential health from an unlovable world through rape, or testing themselves in psychic corridas in which they were their own bulls. Yet if in his continuing polemic against an American society so mendacious in its stated morality, so exhausted in its public psychic life and so frozen in its political behavior as to

make understandable these and many other kinds of seces-
sion, Mailer may have offered nothing but wish-fulfillment and adolescent posturings as an itinerary and a plan
for escape, he nevertheless did present something vigorous
and almost wholly accurate as a description of where we
had to start from.

It was this portrait of an America depleted and armored against self-recognition which laid the basis for the
position of mantic captain in our forces that he was later
and at long last to win. Glints of prophecy show themselves
in the political, social and personal journalism of these
years, as well as evidence of an egotism on the hunt for its
representative role. In that opaque region which he filled
with his voice, with his stream of memos to the rest of us
and with the pages of the diary he kept in public, there
are acute insights in isolation, fragmentary knowledge,
brilliant descriptions, courageous confrontations and manic,
energizing questions raised, but also misconceptions, lies,
romantic fallacies, grotesque theories and an unwearying
ascription of universal meaning to what are the most idiosyncratic of ideas.

Yet from this staked-out territory of our recent cultural life, this circus ground on which Mailer pitched his
tent, there rose something not amenable to classification
along familiar lines of logic or consistency or intellectual
coherence. The show Mailer was putting on had to do with
two things—personality and consciousness; which meant
that the writing was more and more in the world, up to
its ears in the world, and was as blind and violent or as
clear and disciplined as the leaps and turnings of his
personality, in its struggle to express itself, made necessary.

It was also portentous, grandiloquent, full of a strange
candor and, in a way that was unprecedented for serious
American writing, what we have to call chummy:

I might as well confess that I have a terrible time writing political articles.

The Republic is in real peril, and we are the cowards who must defend courage, sex, consciousness, the beauty of the body, the search for love, and the capture of what may be, after all, an heroic destiny.

Self-pity is one of my vices.

Advertisements for Myself was the anthology and summation of the first phase of Mailer's second career. A book pulled together from many sources—already published journalistic pieces and essays, unpublished fragments of diverse kinds, newly written self-revelations and manifestoes—it came on every bit as strongly as it needed to, for what was at stake was its author's viability, which meant his plausibility, if not yet his certification, as a culture hero. It was a unique book: an assertion of stature as a writer at least as vigorous as any demonstration of it; a seduction, a sharing with readers of the problems of being a writer and of those of being a man with the ambition to make others take him seriously as one; a confessional that was at the same time a dazzling strategic move. Personality and consciousness, whose interaction was becoming the ground for many new means of dealing with American life, found in this book the document that legitimized their marriage.

A personality that writes and that cannot leave off writing, even though to write never fully satisfies the craving to see the self's prowess measurable and irreversibly at work on the world's substance. Norman Mailer was never a hipster himself but the posture's chief theoretician and one of its dream merchants. He did not live coolly (there were arrests, brawls, scandals, hot flushes of sudden impetuous flights from abstraction, lunges at the bull), walking on

cat feet through the anteroom to orgasmic salvation, nor
was he seeking to remake his nervous system but to
bring it into coherence with his temperament and consciousness. And he was no outcast ("I was a psychic
outlaw," he announced in *Advertisements for Myself*) but
a man working very much from within, that is to say
someone shrewdly and avidly exhibiting, at an admission
fee and to the drums of publicity, the movements of the
bourgeoisie's nightmare figure: the renegade from prevailing values, the man who is working at his own law.

For Mailer's admiration of the hipster-Negro-psychopath
of his dreams was the mark of his exile from exile, of his
having to proceed as a personality and a voice, instead
of as a *new being*—the powerful, mysterious, autonomous
latter-day noble savage, who brings indictment and cat-
aclysm and an infinite threat to bland, organized sanity
everywhere he saunters in our society. And yet it was just
Mailer's form of articulated personality and not any kind
of new being (there are no new beings, ever; what there
are, are new dilemmas, new values and new means) that
was able to gather more and more momentum as a double
agency: a source of identification for many other egos
seeking assertion, and a radiation of consciousness about
what life in America was doing to the self.

Defiant, talented, unabashedly calculating and ambitious, spread open to all blows and all possible laurels,
grievously outweighed in its wrestling match with America,
untraditional and yet nostalgic, Mailer's personality on display was a theater where entertainment and instruction,
freed of the dogmas of professionalism and newly decom-
partmentalized, merged in the bestowing of a consciousness for the times.

Advertisements for Myself was published in 1959,
when Mailer was thirty-seven, and was followed four
years later by *The Presidential Papers*. Between the appearances of the two books significant changes have

taken place. Having won, or, more accurately, having rewon, the initiative and having daringly exposed itself to all possible critiques, the personality has become more confident, or at least less uncertain of its ground. The voice has been heard often enough and loudly enough to be able to dispense with preliminary remarks or introductions; the eccentricities, the idiosyncratic stances and even the dementias have come to be absorbed into a way of looking at the world that is more and more integral and has therefore begun to take on the attributes of an indivisible—if not yet irresistible—force.

The writing has shifted more of its attention from the self and is less embattled and tormented, its private subject having become more of a public possession, its public subject more specific and detailed. President Kennedy, with whom Mailer identifies, is both the book's chief figure and its ideal reader. For the writing has moved further and further into the heart of the political world, that world being conceived of now in its most traditional and yet also its most flexibly contemporary senses, that is, as the moral and physical organization of society through laws, arrangements and exercises of power, and as that which distills the air that citizens—who are private men in the condition of trying to endure the pressure and absorb the benefits of the organized existence of others—are allowed to breathe. Politics as substance and as spirit: we have never been able to construct the right bridge between them.

The word Mailer chiefly wielded to try to bring these two realms of politics into coherence and the beginnings of a single vision was his old implement, existentialism. But now what he considered the existential had taken on new and more impersonal uses for his consciousness and imagination, to go along with those of clearing a subjective passage through the obduracies of one's own life and of being a way of claiming authenticity for the self. It had become more of a means of investigating and judging public men and matters, society, the nation's colors and codes, our true aspirations and the fates we were likely to incur. He still made his mad pronouncements; the romanticism kept flaring up, as when he made that declaration about "existential politics" being "rooted in the concept of the hero" and was peeved that Kennedy looked as if he wasn't going to be one, or when he wrote, in his grandest philosopher-*manqué* manner, that "death is an existential continuation of life." But he had begun to understand, even if he was not yet letting on, that what lay behind the brandishing of the word was simply his own way of trying to get at the truth. The existential was that which contained the meeting of feelings and data, of appetites and facts, and it was this which provided hope for a living opinion, a wholeness of perception and idea.

What was America like in its inability to bring about this union? Against the professional rhetorics (with the visions of experience they offered or implied) of our social and political destinies—the official, the journalistic, the learned and academic—he set his own new kind of reporting. Its substance and manner were compounded of his novelist's predilection for the particular and the sensuous, his half-apocalyptic, half-domestic inquisitiveness (with the fertile tensions this division gave rise to), his increasingly nonideological formulations, his humor and gall, his recognition—however muddled—of the claims of the irrational and of how rationality itself needed a gift from below, a blessing from the body.

More than anything else, this writing introduced into talk about America the sense of a self to combat the growing feeling of powerlessness of the self, the sense of individual consciousness of what it was like to live here, not as a "sensitive" victim or a critic with an eye on the lessons of history but as a man of many parts—critic, victim, aggressor, indicter, aspirant, citizen, inheritor. If the new journalism of which Mailer was a prime instigator could be characterized by any single spiritual impulse, it was this insertion of subjectivity into our accounts of the world, of personality into the atmosphere of impersonal evaluation in which so much of our self-consideration as a people was being expressed.

The self that Mailer threw into the battle against abstraction and generality and institutional thinking in America, and for consciousness about the means there might be to restore the specificities of selfhood, was a marvelously strange mixture of candidness and stealth, nonsense and sagacity. This double enterprise—to attack on all our behalfs "the mediocre compromises of what had been once our light-filled passion to stand erect and be original," and to bring about his own ego's brilliant survival—demanded that all caution be thrown to the winds. And this meant that he was continually overshooting his marks, finding himself breathing in atmospheres not made for his body and in which his mind had then to invent survivals. He was forever trying to walk on water, going under and coming up with a new tactic already planned.

It was his style, his urgency and self-definition, but also his posture as a representative. For to push ego and personal being in America was to have to push them past the point of reason, balance and plausibility in an overcompensation whose justification lay in the tactics the situation required. You offer hyperboles, he must have reasoned—in so far as he reasoned about it at all—when precise truths, well weighted and shapely, have taken on the quality of artifacts. And you celebrate the self improbably when its probabilities are leading to despair.

The hyperboles were of behavior as well as of language, and at the center of this kind of bodily exaggeration and inflation was an awareness that his own role included the raising of morale, on many levels, from the social to the metaphysical. His role included, specifically, the breaking up, through antic or embattled example, of the old fixed notions of the apportionment of roles in society. To intrude without shame or reticence into scenes that had not been written for him was to overthrow the pigeonhole, to undermine the confidence of some, and the despair of others, that everything was in its place, and so to offer new possibilities, chimerical as they might be, of unpredictable and *whole* human careers. Mailer was rapidly becoming the rallying ground for antispecialization in America, something that was and remains one of the sources of his appeal to the young.

His intrusions were numerous and self-publicized; long before George Plimpton, a lightweight and essentially frivolous exponent of the art of having more selves than is allowed, Mailer came on in the splendors and sorrows of Proteus. The first Liston-Patterson championship fight was perhaps the classic instance of his self-metamorphoses, the one that best reveals what Mailer, as personality, mind and ego, and as deputy for all those things in the rest of us, saw himself called upon to do.

He took his place at the center of the event, not merely in its physical aspects (he elbowed in to the new champion's dressing room after the fight, cakewalked up to him, threw a playful right hook and announced that he was the only man who could make the return bout a financial success by handling its publicity) but in what he implied were its metaphysical ones as well. In his essay on the fight he asserted that Patterson's defeat was due to the failure of his adherents to give him enough psychic support, so that he was literally struck down by a "psychic bolt" and not by his opponent.

The chief delinquents had been himself and James Baldwin, with whom he had recently quarreled. But ten months later, when that literary and prophetic axis had presumably been patched up and Patterson's more humble followers had had time to recharge their batteries, Liston again knocked Patterson out in the first round. The thesis had been given a deadly blow, but by that time Mailer had moved on to new interventions elsewhere. The truth was that Liston was simply stronger, tougher and more skillful than Patterson, so that his victories were amply explainable within the natural realm. But that left Mailer confronting a realm of existence which had no need of his intervention to proceed and define itself, and therefore left it impenetrable to any attempt by the private self to have a hand in a public phenomenon. Even more, it denied the metaphysical efficacy, the power to affect things in their essence, that was Mailer's promise when he spoke for the self in America.

Still, though we might have remarked his foolishness in this particular caper, the sympathy—grudging as it might be among the "clear-headed" in our midst—survived and grew. It was present, always under siege by reason and a remaining sense of fitness, throughout his one-sided confrontation with President Kennedy. This was a remarkable combination of love affair and citizen's arrest in which Mailer undertook to lay at the Chief Executive's door all the feelings, hopes, doubts and accusations that Americans who were not President (in this sober game of ego and lifesmanship being President was all that counted) had no means to put there themselves. It was all in the interests of participation, efficacious democracy of the kind that had disappeared with the town meeting; it was also in the interests of the humanization of the nation's greatest institution and so of the national life; and Kennedy, who Mailer acknowledged had a good start (for a President) toward being human, was being asked to lead the parade arm in arm with our writer.

Mailer claimed to have played a crucial role in Kennedy's election (by virtue of his *Esquire* report on the convention; for example, in items such as "one kept advancing the argument that this campaign would be a contest of personalities, and Kennedy kept returning the discussion to politics"), and he made this the basis for establishing a little White House in Brooklyn Heights. From there he issued a stream of advice, adjuration and warning, never letting the President forget that there was *someone out there*, that this someone was America's representative man in search of a viable future and that America could not be governed without a leap of the imagination to encompass the man's passions, doubts and fears:

> . . . talk on television about the things you do not understand. Use your popularity to be difficult and intellectually dangerous. There is more to greatness than liberal legislation.

> Show us you understand our condition, put a hostage from your flesh in to our doomed city, or know that we can never trust you completely, for deep within yourself may be contained a bright and psychic voice which leaps to give the order that presses a button.

> It is possible that he does not understand or is lacking some of the necessary and vital emotions of most people.

When Kennedy was assassinated, Mailer mourned with the rest, but his ego had to add that the greatest loss was that the President would no longer be around for him to address and so improve the climate of political discourse. Mailer felt himself now, and was indeed on the way to becoming, an element of the national scene, a trait of our behavior and an aspect of our self-understanding. His voice issued from the public air not as an oration but as a conversation amplified, like that of a character listened to in a drama. And in fact he had become histrionic in the full meaning of that word: the mode of his life and expressions was dramatic, designed for a theater, language and gesture in step, both almost never less than extreme, tactless, "colorful," exemplary of an American drama of combat and arousal.

He had written no fiction for several years, all impulses toward imaginative creation seemingly swallowed up and appeased in that journalism which put images to work and made characters out of actual men. But it turned out not to be so; suddenly he began publishing serially in *Esquire* a novel he called *An American Dream*. It was an act that was at one and the same time a piece of bravado (Can one write this way, with a deadline rushing round every month? Yet what about Dostoevsky, harassed beyond endurance, overwhelmed but managing to bring it off?), a challenge to his ability to write fiction again at any pace, and a gesture to the rest of us that he knew how public he had become and that he was going to stay *up there*, as on a high wire, while he entertained our hopes or fears that he would fall.

He made it; which is to say he made the monthly deadlines and brought the novel to a conclusion. Yet beyond this limited physical act the success became equivocal. The work of fiction that emerged from the stunt exhibited enough that was weak, forced, immature and simply incompetent to give some justification to Elizabeth Hardwick's judgment that it was "an intellectual and literary disaster." An effort to see it as something more calls on us to see how catastrophe may retain its own face yet become, through the matter's particular risks and significances, a kind of strange triumph, a new, maimed heroism.

An American Dream issued from the mode of inquiry and state of morale that had marked Mailer's "Kennedy" years, during which he had been attempting to define and project both a vision of America's malaise—abstraction and institutional thinking, violence suppressed and festering, the "animal" in all of us nearly extinct, love under siege by lies—and a myth for its healing. It promised a tale of the American unconscious, offering both the form and procedure of a dream, that royal road, as Freud described it, to the self-knowledge we ordinarily suppress. Archetypes of terror, lust, hunger, moral dilemma, emotional paradox and contradiction, cowardice and courage, would take their places in a narrative that would explore regions never before articulated, territories from which our imaginations had up to now drawn back.

Such was the ambition. And the book does have certain qualities of dream and unconsciousness, the sense of having been written out of anguish and the wish to come to grips with demons. For Mailer, moving on as our spokesman, the central American dream had now to be given an alternative reading, its savage implications brought to light and its underside made explicit. He would *re*-dream, then, releasing as fiction, as painful, redemptive fable, the truths of American ambition and desire, which had until now been hidden in the protective sheathings of political rhetoric, national cant and the illusions of abstract, wishful history.

Yet one sees from the beginning that in his descent into the unconscious Mailer has lost much consciousness of a sort such explorations have always required. A writer for whom form as the central aesthetic question has represented something precious and the search for the *mot juste* something finicky, he is now more than ever operating without aesthetic wisdom. It is as though the particular reality of fictional existence and what is required to erect it have dropped from his sight and he is therefore proceeding as a blind, embattled amateur; he is going to offer us his dream, *as we all might have written it,* composed from the elements of national low art and fable, popular imagining and myth-making.

He will not write "well," will take no pains, conduct no artistic experiments. The artifice he is after has nothing to do with, flies in the face of, the fictions of art, since it is the fiction of American life itself that he wishes to set down. In this sense he wishes his book to be real, not biography but true and representative night-thoughts, hot from the dark arena; and the work's glory will be the strength and daring of having imagined it at all. And thus it will not be the conquest of actuality through a victory over the recalcitrance and exhaustion of imagination—the central literary act of our tradition—but once more personal, assertive, a hope of victory through passion if not craft.

In this noble and disastrous struggle with contradictory necessities—he will write a book about how the American imagination is working now and what we are dreaming of, but he will not attempt to create any new form for the imagination and so hope to avoid the cold isolatedness of aesthetic artifice—the main ironies of Mailer's literary career are again on display. From a language demoralized and even deracinated, a language giving continual evidence of a conflict between being fiction and being self-expression, an anguish rises more steadily and centrally than from the book's ostensible subject and themes.

Throughout, Mailer, in wishing to be himself, is forced to fall back on literature, more accurately on the literary. What is at work is the strange fatality that overtakes anyone who tries to force his experience directly into language, without undergoing the experience of language itself, its indirections, resistances and metamorphoses through context. He will fail to perceive that the literary has replaced experience, has become a sly, deadly corruption of actuality, an improbability. The writer's battle is always with the idea of literature, the idea of image, metaphor, simile as trained animals, confident of their task, so that his task is simply their manipulation *as before*. Bad writing by passionate people who feel deeply and are impatient always draws from what has become cliché as literature or else twists itself into the bizarre and grotesque in the effort to avoid cliché.

An American Dream is a disaster in this way: it accepts language as an instrument of experience without looking at it to see what it has become; and so swings between cliché and grotesque flights from cliché. There is also simple carelessness, and redundancy, and overripeness, all of whose sources are in impatience, unmediated feeling and a will that cannot openly acknowledge its dependence on an idea of the literary:

> I felt as fine and evil as a razor and just as content with myself. There was something further in her I needed, some bitter perfect salt, narrow and mean as the eye of a personnel director.
>
> I cried within like a just-cracked vase might shriek for cement. . . .
>
> I swam through some happy mood, deeper than air, more profound than water.
>
> She had taken lately to smiling at me with a droll mocking compassion and very wound-up spite which promised portfolios of detail if I were ever rich enough to turn her tongue just once.
>
> He filed the needle to a point.
>
> She did not look in the least like Marlene Dietrich, but the glamour was there, that curious hint of no-man's land where one cannot distinguish exhaustion from the shade of espionage.
>
> She looked a little like a child who has been anointed by the wing of a magic bird.
>
> The separate cheats of her body and her life collected on one scale of justice to match the weight I could put on mind—her life up to this moment was the equal of my own, good to good, bad to bad, the submerged vision of my sex moved with a freedom from vanity or the haste to give pleasure.

The novel moves with no impulse of parody or satire and with absolutely no humor, only a straightforward appropriation of stock figures and sentiments: the blond hard nightclub singer secretly looking for love and secretly doomed; the playboy who magically combines chic, money, looks and wit; the tough cops with whom one can at least *talk;* the international tycoon full of heart, terrifying wisdom about power; the mafia gangsters sending off animal odors; the Mickey Spillane housemaid ready to be tumbled by any handsome caller; and the worked-over literary rubrics of passion and desire, psychic adventures in dark *inner* places, yearning for innocence, quest for identity and confrontation with the beast and coward in oneself.

Yet something counterbalances these disasters of literary imagination, and it is precisely the sense the book gives off of having incurred the catastrophe as a price for daring to dream the way we so literarily and megalomaniacally do. In its very unsophistication as literature, its exemplary, failing struggle with expression, its unashamed appropriation of the ethos of something near soap opera, of brittle romantic narrative and egregious national mythology, it is closer to the age than a great many superior "fictions." In writing a bad novel in which his own personality sought to function as the drama and the art, Mailer once again demonstrated that his true interest and the source of his vigor are in the midground between transcendence and actuality, between art itself and the necessity to be directly a man.

Mailer then went back to journalism, criticism and speculation. The accumulation of several years of political writings, together with assorted uncollected pieces of general comment going back to 1960, was published in the volume called *Cannibals and Christians.* In this strange book, aggressively presented as a work with an "argument," he attempted to shape his growing view of America as sundered into opposing sects or tribes whose separation had to do with the ways in which the world is regarded. The cannibals—roughly America's early stock and nominal Christians—saw the world as having to be purified through the "devouring" of all unfit, alien and lesser men; they were, loosely, the natives, the right wing. On the left were the Christians, who were not believers in Christ at all but "Jews, liberals, Bolsheviks, anarchists . . . Keynesians, Democrats . . . beatniks . . . moderate Republicans . . . doctors, scientists, professors . . ." They were all those who believed in science, progress and discussion, and in the absolute necessity of preserving human life.

Yet they were also, Mailer argued, those who had started every war since World War II, those who "poisoned" the air with scientific developments and kept on reducing the quality of both moral and physical life. Through some vital deficiency—a lack of belief in the devil, an alienation from the knowledge that violence is inherent in man—they were at least as much a source of our sickness as the more straightforward and "natural" cannibals.

The book as an entirety scarcely makes the argument, except in an introductory statement and in integumentary passages. It is filled largely with Mailer's more recondite speculations, on "cancer," the mind-body relationship, American fiction seen as the Golden Gloves, the mystical effects of technology. The ideas, being the outcome of occasional writings, were all peripheral to his major theme, or in any case not organic developments of it. But the major theme was itself clearly an afterthought, something imposed, awkwardly but with characteristic bravado, to counteract the impression that the book was simply Mailer collecting himself once again. Yet if the unity it strove for did not take shape, another kind of unity was present: that of the continuing action of Mailer's personality, invading realms that had been guarded against the likes of him, cutting its (now more philosophical) capers, secreting (it is the only word for it) poems to show that even *that* isn't closed to him, speaking up, thinking, often badly and sometimes ludicrously, but thinking anyway, pushing thought like a series of lefts and rights in a never-ending boxing match, throwing out ideas and impressions at a rate that would wear every opponent down.

And then back to fiction, to something not assigned or set up as an immediate challenge. *Why Are We in Vietnam?* was announced as a novel, and nothing in that loosest of designations can be used to exclude it. It is imagined, is a rough narrative, employs characters and reaches a denouement. Yet the book is at least as much an act of Mailer the vaudevillian as the work of a novelistic imagination. In a skit that combines politics with the psychology of the tall tale and plays on its audience's expectations about the public limits of utterance, he makes himself felt again as a danger to the established turns. Nothing in Mailer's whole canon gives off such an air of the small, ambitious, outrageous boy elbowing his way into his elders' discomfitted attention. And yet the book, with its sexuality that is all verbal, a matter of epithet rather than experience, and its scatology that is designed to raise blushes and at the same time be a proof of its author's manhood, salvages something, as politics if not as fiction. It is politics assaulted and overturned, its congealed monolith splintered, its proprieties mocked, its outrages surpassed; this scatological fable confronts American political reality with the unblushing self, the impudent, testifying ego whose agent, witness and chronicler Mailer had come so significantly to be.

September, 1967. Norman Mailer is at his home in Brooklyn Heights when the phone rings. As he writes in the book that is to issue from this call, he is not one for answering the phone lightly, but he decides as a gamble to answer it

this time. The caller is Mitchell Goodman, an old acquaint-
ance, who wants Mailer to participate in an anti-Vietnam
demonstration in Washington the next month. Mailer hes-
itates; the event smells of inevitable failure, and "there
had been all too many years when he had had the reputation of a loser; it had cost him much." Besides, "the damn-
able habit of consorting with losers was that they passed
their subtle problems on."

But he accepts, is given an assignment to write about
the affair for *Harper's Magazine,* goes to Washington,
takes part in what happens there, returns to New York
and at a furious pace turns out an account that was originally intended to be twenty thousand words but finally
runs to more than a hundred thousand. It is a book, not a
report, and it is the best book he has ever written, the
culmination of his multiple careers, the thing he was
slated to do. With it he has entered American consciousness
in a central way, all doubts ended about his qualifications
for being central, most of his claims honored.

In *The Armies of the Night* the rough force of Mailer's
imagination, his brilliant wayward gifts of observation,
his ravishing if often calculated honesty, his daring and his
chutzpa all flourish on the steady ground of a newly coherent subject and theme. His subject, as it has always been,
is himself, but this time a self balanced between objective
events and private consciousness in a more original and
more resonant way than it has ever been before. And his
theme is just that relationship between the self and history,
the ego and actuality, which he had been seeking to fulfill in all his writing and with which he had wanted to
make the inimitable mark of his presence felt.

In writing about his participation in the occurrences
in Washington, most particularly the march on the Pentagon, Mailer had finally succeeded in laying hands on
the novelistic character he had never been master of before.
The character was of course himself, but a self freed now

from the dilemmas and contradictions that had trapped it earlier and from which it had only sporadically broken loose through explosive, imbalanced and often wholly eccentric gestures. The antinomies were resolved; the artist who has to invent and the observer who has to prey on facts merged into the same person; the transcendencies of art and the immanences of action moved to a juncture; and the excesses of personality found a new and strangely valuable use in the face of the opaque excesses (and history has come to be almost nothing but excesses) of our public days and years.

This is the central, rather wonderful achievement of the book: that in it history and personality confront one another with a new sense of liberation. By introducing his ego more directly into history than he had ever done before, by taking events that were fast disappearing under the perversions and omissions of ordinary journalism as well as through the inertia we all feel in the face of what is *over with*, by taking these events and revivifying them, reinstating them within a present tense of action and contemplation, Mailer has added a dimension to verbal imagination and thereby become at last the revolutionary he had never really been. The revolutionary, after all, is the man who turns things around.

Anyone who was more purely an artist than Mailer would not have been able to bring it off; but neither would any kind of traditional journalist, no matter how inventive. The feat arose from the conjunction of Mailer's special nature—part artist, part activist, part inventor, part borrower—with what the times required: an end, for certain purposes, of literary aloofness on the one hand and of the myth of "objective" reporting on the other. History is both fact and invention, annals and tale. It is indeed what we make it, but this is something we are never able to see while we are doing it. In his own person, as the representative who takes on the burden of consciousness in the midst of action, Mailer shows us in this book how we construct history, and how we do this not to have, before anything else, a particular kind of history but simply and primarily to have one. His account is neither imaginative literature nor journalism nor theory of history, but a new procedure: consciousness and events seen in reciprocity.

The early pages of *The Armies of the Night* display the notorious literary personality in all its disarming shifts between megalomania and self-deprecation. He speaks (in the third person, as he does throughout the book) of the "living tomb of his legend"; writes grandly of how the "architecture of his personality bore resemblance to some provincial cathedral which warring orders of the church might have designed separately over several centuries"; reveals that "a party lacked flavor for him unless someone very rich or social was present"; and tells us about his "illusion of genius," "the wild man in himself," the "absolute egomaniac" and the "snob of the worst sort."

All this has two functions: to "humanize" the character who is going to participate in history, and to push his sense of self to its limits, so that history will have the most formidable opponent and secret impregnator. As Mailer moves on to the actual events of the four days in Washington, his cocky stance—the self as the equal of all large intimidating public adversaries, yet also the self aware of its small size and internal divisions—becomes a representative posture for all of us. More than ever, Mailer's embattled ego is seen to be the troubled, sacrificial, rash and unconquerable champion for all of our own selves.

The ego fluctuates wildly. He arrives in Washington in a sober mood: "Like most New Yorkers he usually felt small in Washington. The capital invariably seemed to take the measure of men like him." But the "wild man" he harbors pushes forward and takes over. At a party given by a liberal academic couple in whose home he smells the "scent of the void which comes off a Xerox copy," he insults the hostess. Later at a theater rally he outrages nearly everybody by what is reported in the press as his drunken behavior. He is indeed drunk, but his actions still have wit and point, and his account of the evening is a sustained triumph of autobiographical writing.

But it is autobiography of an intense and unconventional kind. Into this report of a public meeting, in which his part had months before been corrupted into "history" by the press, Mailer introduces the most personal matters: his having missed the urinal in a dark men's room; his resentment at having been replaced as M.C.; his strongly ambivalent attitude toward the audience. And into this confession he sweeps the other participants—Paul Goodman, Dwight MacDonald, Robert Lowell—writing about them in a form of high and liberating gossip, infusing particularity and personality and queer informing detail into their remote public biographies, their status as names.

MacDonald, "the operative definition of the gregarious," "gesticulated awkwardly, squinted at his text, laughed at his own jokes, looked like a giant stork, whinnied, shrilled and was often inaudible." Lowell, toward whom Mailer positions himself throughout much of the book in a remarkably frank species of testing, a weighing of their very different personalities and backgrounds, stands "with a glint of the oldest Yankee light winging off like a mad laser from his eye," gives off "at times the unwilling haunted saintliness of a man who was repaying the moral debts of ten generations of ancestors," and moves with a slouch whose "languid grandeurs" testify to generations of primacy at Harvard and in Boston.

In seeking a shape for the relationship of the self to the historical events of that weekend and to the historical realities that had led to it, Mailer has understood how his own self has to be employed as both battleground and partial perspective, how other selves such as Lowell's, products of an almost wholly different background, an America of complex traditions, austere moralities, rooted political conscience, elegance, personal diffidence combined with patrician standards of public behavior—the older textbook American style—have to be taken into the picture so that it might be seen what a confluence of varied egos and personalities occurred at that point in Washington, within history, facing it and making it. Lowell (the New England style), Paul Goodman (the wholly liberated urban Jewish style) and the multifarious styles of the older liberals and young dissidents and radicals: something congruent and crucial to our American understanding arose from their incongruity and widely separated motives, their having come from so many starting points to that time and place.

As the demonstrators gather for the march on the Pentagon, Mailer moves brilliantly between analyses of his own feelings, descriptions of the crowd and a grand, lyrical sociology. As the tension rises, he finds himself going beyond the playacting which has subtly characterized his participation up to now, "as if some final cherished rare innocence of childhood still preserved in him was brought finally to the surface and there expired, so he lost at that instant the last secret delight in life as a game where finally you never got hurt if you played the game well enough."

He looks at the young rebels, who have started from points well beyond his own romantic and fundamentally "cultured" view:

A generation of the American young had come along different from five previous generations of the middle class. The new generation believed in technology, more than any before it, but the generation also believed in LSD, in witches, in tribal knowledge, in orgy and revolution. It had no respect whatsoever for the unassailable knowledge of the next step; belief was reserved for the revelatory mystery of the happening where you did not know what was going to happen next; that was what was good about it. Their radicalism was in their hate for the authority—the authority was the manifest of evil to this generation. It was the authority who had covered the land with those suburbs where they stifled as children while watching the adventures of the West in the movies, while looking at the guardians of dull genial celebrity on television; they had had their minds jabbed, poked and twitched and probed and finally galvanized into surrealistic modes of response by commercials cutting into dramatic narratives, and parents flipping from network to network— they were forced willy-nilly to build their idea of the space-time continuum (and therefore their nervous system) on the jumps and cracks and leaps and breaks which every phenomenon from the medium seemed to contain within it.

The balance he maintains, the breadth of his vision here, his capacity to see history whole while being immersed in its unfolding and while in the act of rewriting it, are the result of his novelist's patience and sophistication holding his ideological horses in check. The young are "villains," too:

Mailer was haunted by the nightmare that the evils of the present not only exploited the present, but consumed the past, and gave every promise of demolishing whole territories of the future. The same villains who, promiscuously, wantonly, heedlessly, had gorged on LSD and consumed God knows what essential marrows of history, wearing indeed the history of all eras on their back as trophies of this gluttony, were now going forth (conscience-struck?) to make war on those other villains, corporation-land villains, who were destroying the promise of the present in their self-righteousness and greed and secret lust (often unknown in themselves) for some sexotechnological variety of neo-fascism. Mailer's final allegiance, however, was to the villains who were hippies.

The march proceeds. In a superb passage, one in which all the strands of personality and public stance, self and community, politics and feeling, are brought reinforcingly together, Mailer moves to appropriate and give utterance to a passionate, coherent moment within the chaos and cross-purposes of life in this country in our time:

> . . . the sense of America divided on this day now liberated some undiscovered patriotism in Mailer so that he felt a sharp searing love for his country in this moment and on this day, crossing some divide in his own mind wider than the Potomac, a love so lacerated he felt as if a marriage were being torn and children lost—never does one love so much as then, obviously, then—and an odor of wood smoke, from where you knew not, was also in the air, a smoke of dignity and some calm heroism . . . Mailer knew for the first time why men in the front line of a battle are almost always ready to die: there is a promise of some swift transit—one's soul feels clean . . . walking with Lowell and MacDonald, he felt as if he stepped through some crossing in the reaches of space between this moment, the French Revolution, and the Civil War, as if the ghosts of the Union Dead accompanied them now to the Bastille . . .

And now, as culmination:

> . . . he was arrested, he had succeeded in that, and without a club on his head, the mountain air in his lungs as thin and fierce as smoke, yes, the livid air of tension on this livid side promised a few events of more interest than the routine wait to be free, yes he was more than a visitor, he was in the land of the enemy now, he would get to see their face.

From this point the intensity slackens somewhat, the writing growing more abstract, the thought more general.

"Prisoner of his own egotism, some large part of the March had ended for him with his own arrest." Yet the book remains steadily interesting. Into the account of his two days in jail Mailer inserts passages of political and intellectual autobiography, opinions on social matters, a theory and position paper on the Vietnam war (its boldest, most original idea being the argument that this most "obscene" of conflicts has paradoxically provided him and countless other Americans with "new energy"), obiter dicta on the American soul—all of it sustained and given resonance by the atmosphere of extraordinary pertinence and intimate, incorruptible dialogue that has been established.

In the last quarter of the book Mailer turns from "History as a Novel" to "The Novel as History," tracing the background of the Washington events as he was able to reconstruct it afterward. What he means by these phrases is never clear, nor in any case would they be convincing if it were. For he has not done what he thinks he has; the theory, swelling out of his head as one more avid claim on everything, no bit of glory left to chance, goes up in smoke while the true accomplishment, as with all *works*, keeps its solidity and contours.

He has divided the book into an initial long section composing what he says is a history in the form of fiction, that is to say as a true "tale" with characters, a plot, a narrative, etc., and into a smaller section making up a novel in the form of history, i.e., actual events treated as though they exemplify fictional structures and procedures, as though they possess, as he says, an "aesthetic." But what is in question here is just that word and what it has meant to Mailer, as well as what the words "fiction," "novelist," "imagination" and the like have meant.

Anything may be said to have an aesthetic, as when we speak of the art of politics or of sex or, for that matter, of life itself. But when we do this, we are simply transferring our notions of how art is constructed and, in a sense, our esteem for the fact that it *is* made, that there is something which offers an absolute truth in itself. We borrow the prestige of art when we speak of the aesthetic as a realm within life, and we do this in order to point out that we think we have found the way in which that realm works best, is most surely itself. But life is not art, and the aesthetic, properly speaking, is what has to do with art, with the way of treating materials from life so they are no longer prisoners of the actual, of history and therefore of what had to be because it was. Art is what *did not* and does not have to be, what does not have to happen.

For Mailer the problem has always lain in his notions about the novel and the novelist. Beginning with a fundamentally bourgeois idea of fiction, or of the novel in its bourgeois uses (which is not the same as its own reality), he has struggled always to make it serve the purposes of action, or, failing that, to write as a novelist *who is not writing fiction.* His idea has always been of the novelist as someone whose gifts of intuition and prophecy enable him to see more deeply than other men into society and human organizations. From this follows the notion that novels are superior reports on social or psychic or moral phenomena and that fiction is therefore a superior way of agitating for change and helping to bring it about. This is an outdated conception of fiction, and Mailer's possession of it, along with his Hemingwayesque policy of style as performance, has kept him on some wrong, if for him inevitable, tracks.

Novels, the best ones, the ones we mean when we speak of fictional art, have very little to do with such uses (what novels once had to do with them was, for that matter, largely in the realm of pretext); novelists who are artists expect nothing to change, do not imagine that their work can safeguard or resurrect men, and have no interest in being *acknowledged* legislators. The novel remains, through all its present travail, a medium for the creation of new kinds of truth and pleasure.

What Mailer did in *The Armies of the Night* was not to write a novel in the form of history or history in the form of a novel, not to produce any startlingly new forms; history remains itself and no new fiction has been shaped. What he did was to rescue history from abstraction and aridity by approaching it with certain "novelistic" instruments at the ready and in a certain large, general, novelistic spirit. They are old-fashioned things, constituents of an older idea of fiction, the kind of qualities we associate with Balzac and Zola and Maugham and textbook ideas of the novel. A more advanced novelist than Mailer, one less interested in getting at social or political reality, would not have been able to bring it off; that Mailer is only imperfectly a novelist, that his passion for moving and shaking the actual has prevented him from fully inhabiting imaginary kingdoms, is the underlying, paradoxical strength of this book.

The important thing is that Mailer refused to leave history, actuality, to historians and journalists. His aim was to do for our present situation, and by implication for all our communal pasts and futures, what our traditional instrumentalities of knowledge and transcription have not been able to do: place our public acts and lives in a human context. Writing *as he can,* as part inventor, part observer, part intervener, writing with gusto and vigor and an almost unprecedented kind of honesty, writing very badly at times (among dozens of instances are these: "they sensed quickly that they now shared one enclave to the hilt"; "On the *a fortiori* evidence, then, they were young men with souls of interesting dimension"; "psychedelic newspapers consider themselves removed from any fetish with factology") but writing always with this steady aim, Mailer has put us all in his debt. In the light of that, whether or not he is the best writer in America, the best novelist or the best journalist, would seem to be considerations out of a different sort of game.

The Armies of the Night, then a few months later *Miami and the Siege of Chicago,* Mailer's account of the 1968 Republican and Democratic conventions and, in the latter case, of the events in the streets that were so much more significant. The new book was written in much the same spirit as its predecessor, but had a rather different model: Mailer's own earlier convention reports. And while, like them, it had its fascinations in so far as it was journalism of a very high order, it fell far short of the incontrovertibility, the originality and relevance of the book on Washington.

Mailer has moved, the portrait is blurred. And the portrait is nearly everything, everything that gives to the political and social comment its acuity and vitality and, above all, its usefulness as something more than opinion. He is not present in the same way; the pundit intervenes too often, the eccentric doesn't bring his foibles and the passion of his foibles into a moral alignment with events, there is a sense of strain, as though the recognition of what *The Armies of the Night* meant to him and to his readers has put him under an obligation to be wiser and more cunning, and more of a polymath still. The personality is close to becoming an institution.

But of course he is full of surprises. No island is an island to him, no territories are uncolonizable. Within the past few years he has offered us his dramatization of *The Deer Park,* a play so old-fashioned as to seem a put-on, and two movies (with a third on the way), the second much better than the first but neither escaping a heavily amateur, self-indulgent manner, an air of having been made because everyone is making movies these days. He has shown us his architecture and will no doubt show us his paintings and sculpture in a while.

It will not matter that they will almost certainly be bad, and not matter much more if they turn out to be good. He has earned the right to do these things, and to run for mayor and ask to go to the moon, which is to say to be himself. And that is what his work has been, the being of himself, which for us has been the demonstration of how we might begin to know our own selves. He talks, gestures, fights (half bites off the ear of an actor on his film set), has become a man, will have to hold on to it. He goes on intervening, in all our issues and phenomena, wrong as often as right, foolish as often as wise. His writing slips between marvelous accuracy and weary literary postures, he is no man for self-criticism in that region. He will go on thinking of himself as a novelist and will undoubtedly write more "novels," but the heart of the country of imaginative fiction will not likely ever be his home.

Some months ago he appeared on a panel discussing the place of the irrational. Perhaps, he said at the end in his characteristic mood of sly pessimism, "the world will end with Joe Namath facing Earl Morrall across the line." The remark beautifully sums up his dogmas and his style. The world seen as combat, violence that has to be controlled, as a game and a place for the ego with a name. And the world also seen wrongly in part: pro quarterbacks face not each other, but the other team's defensive players. He can get by with it; we know what he means.

Part Two

Art and History

Among other uses every art appears to lend itself to history by possessing a history of its own. How much more does art, the totality of aesthetic works as well as the abstraction by which we hold in consciousness the faculty that produces them, seem to possess the historical as one of its attributes and identifications? We speak of the "development" of the novel, the "course" of music, the "fate" of poetry. We talk about movements, revolutions and returns (neo-this and neo-that), about avant-gardes (spearheads, colonizers of the future) and academicisms (wrong-headed repetitions performed in despite of time and change). One of our thoroughly contemporary notions about art is that of "crisis," which means that we have come to see it as periodically trapped between a closed-off past and a not-yet-open future, which, however, must sooner or later come to open, as all future does.

All this habit of mind—art seen as history, as chronological extension and time filling up with truth or beauty—is on the analogy of general human history, which, dominating the way we see time, dominates whatever is produced within its walls. And in the same way that thinking of life as history is, beneath its purely technical uses, in the interest of reassurance, so thinking of art as history serves as reassurance, too. For whatever the local, provisional quality of events and enterprises, however painful, worn, inadequate or perverse existence may seem at any time, the fact that it is going to go on—that there will always be more of this self-secreting substance, the historical—means that there are going to be new chances, possibilities, accessions and revivals, for art as well as life. Every new generation makes this more or less explicit, ours more than most; we are always in the way of having everything made good.

What may seem to be a hatred of history or a repudiation, such as characterizes our own time and in one way or another the entire American experience and its historical bases, is more often than not a willed freedom from particular histories rather than a relinquishing of the habit of casting experience into historical molds. When such a relinquishing does occur, it is almost always in association with the aesthetic as the principle of deliverance. But this is most frequently a matter not of art as aesthetic creation but as dream, myth, a potential way of nonhistorical life, such as is appropriated by bohemians at all times. But the true relation of art to the historical is usually no better understood by bohemians than by anybody else.

Art is the only unbetrayable revolution, the only one that does not restore history in a new guise. And one must argue that behind all particular revolutions in the arts is a culminating sense of history as an occlusion, a maker of impasses, a narrowing light. For the artist, history, the history of his own art, is reassuring only at the beginning, when it grants him a provisional identity as a worker in its line, an apprentice, and provides him with indications of what is to be done. But the artist finds (and it can be at once, like Rimbaud at fifteen, or quite late, like Yeats at forty-five) that he has to resist the temptation and pressure to draw from a bag of tricks which have all been used before—history is what has been used before—and that to be an artist means nothing less than to invent, to "come upon" what has not yet existed.

"Everything the artist invents is true," Flaubert said, a more profound remark than it might appear. For it is extraordinarily difficult really to invent against the multiplicity of patents taken out by previous artists. But that is what has to be done, menacing as it will always seem to all strategies of continuity, and indistinguishable as it will often appear from a quest for mere novelty. Art has even had to invent its apparent disgust and even its seeming death in order to make of its gestures new parabolas, new connections between the imagination and the materials life presents to it for reconstitution. To revolt is to invent at full speed, to seek new and unprecedented assurance in an act of creation whose one gift is its own appearance, its demonstration that it continues to be possible for men to shape realities outside history.

The contemporary crisis as it concerns art lies just there: we do not fully believe that such a thing is possible, which means that we have lost the sense (never widely or wholeheartedly supported) of art as wrestler with history rather than as an aspect of its expression. A tenacious resistance of academic thinking (historical thinking in its quintessential form), and of a humanism trying to add to its justifications, goes on obscuring the truth that physical events, or "real" events, including the lives of artists, have one history, and aesthetic events, without following an arbitrary course and without lacking in their own kind of reality, have another. Thinking of the arts as the embodiment or reflection, most subtly as the formalization—the "aestheticization"—of social or moral or psychological history continues to dominate the academic's teaching and most critical practice. Against how many pieties does one bump if one sets out to demonstrate that the chief impulse of the truest art has always been to serve, in no merely figurative sense, as compensations and atonements for such histories, for history as the annals of our deficiency.

If it is at all historical (if it has a relation, that is to say, to chronologies outside itself), art is a counterhistory; the surprises, blessings, threats and transformations it offers are distinguished by the remarkable fact that they might not have been, that they have made their appearance as the result of a kind of smuggling operation, that they stand outside history as a species of alternative to it. So positioned, they are not subject to any law of historical development (except to a principle of change kept in being by the new shapes history continually throws up) nor to inevitability of any kind. Only when, as periodically happens, an art succumbs to human history, stopping dead in its tracks under the weight of demand that it fulfill one or another social or moral or psychological function and above all that it fulfill it as before, the way previous art has been considered to do, does it surrender its freedom. New artists, new art, then come forward to reclaim it, although there is nothing inevitable even about that.

Of all the arts the theater, perennially broken down, forever lacking fuel, is perhaps the one most given to predicting its own future, or rather asserting, with dogged, blind, quasi-mystical assurance, that it is going to have one. The theater has always survived, so the almost prayerful argument runs, its history being one of perpetual recovery from dry spells, wrong turnings and persecution. A great and central human activity, it is the most communal of all the arts, the most inclusive and ubiquitous. Its history is very nearly coeval with mankind's, since even before its reputed origin in ritual there was the beginning of theater the first time a gesture was made which announced that a gesture was being made, the first time somebody "acted," performing symbolically instead of with a straightforward, useful, physical end in view.

From this origin the theater, formalized, diversified and multiplied into a wide-ranging institution full of both steadily accumulating myth and continually renewed technical consciousness, has become one of our chief public ways of knowing ourselves and even more of getting around our finiteness. This is to say that for a certain space of time it allows us to be not ourselves but our reflections, impersonations, doubles and dream children, our possibilities and theoretical incarnations. How can the impulse to bring these things into being, buckled securely on to a history as it is, ever come to an end?

Yet it may very well be coming to an end in the form in which we have known it. That latter form may go on making public representations of itself, alive in the history outside art, as portrait painters still go on exhibiting their outmoded visions, but the center of the art of drama will be elsewhere, if any art of drama finds it possible to survive. For the theater has discovered—or rather uncovered to our sight—that in the past fifteen years or so its perennial crisis, that joke, lugubrious weather or occupational disease, has taken on a deadly edge. The crisis is now one neither of style nor subject nor economic feasibility nor relevance, but of existence itself. And what lies behind the widespread failure to become aware of it, to do more than lament the current doldrums while preserving the core of faith unshaken, is the tyranny of the idea of historical inevitability and the gross, fanatic pressure of habit.

To its first Parisian audiences in the early 1950's the new drama whose principal executors were Samuel Beckett and Eugène Ionesco came variously as an enigma, a revelation, a curiosity or a good or bad joke. Without being wholly unprecedented (there are always precedents for the movements of the imagination; the avant-garde, Ionesco was later to write, "always constitutes a restoration, a return"), these new plays were publicly unprepared for.

Having leaped over the immediate theatrical past, they might have seemed to exhibit connections with an older experimental mode, but to have identified that, to have said, "Ah, yes, surrealism," would have been entirely mistaken. For *The Bald Soprano, The Lesson* and *Waiting for Godot* were not surrealist in any meaning which the word had previously possessed. Their movement was precisely toward the infrareal: nothing "above" or "beyond," no cozying up to the presumed divinity in the automatic operation of the mind, no raid upon dreams or other sources of transconsciousness. "The surreal is here," Ionesco was to say, "within the grasp of our hands, in our everyday conversation."

He might still use the word—any word which pointed to a renewed freedom for consciousness or an attempt to transform its bases would do; later "absurd" would be fastened on himself, Beckett and others—but what was at issue was that the "real," as it became the material for the dramatic imagination, brought with it a power of cliché and conventional iconography to which the imagination had increasingly succumbed. Art had been added to reality; and reality had revenged itself, as it always does, by sending back to the aesthetic field of operation its own face distorted by artifice. Reality in drama was reality as previous drama had imagined and shaped it. To break this deadlock meant for playwrights like Beckett and Ionesco to deal cannily in their different ways with just what surrealism had so strenuously repudiated: matter-of-fact vocabularies, ordinary *mises en scène,* antidreams.

A grossly upholstered English sitting room, a language professor's seedy studio, a scrubby piece of anonymous ground, were the new arenas in which was taking place the latest attempt to deliver the stage from everything predictable and reassuring, everything heretofore aesthetically legitimized, whether it was the consolation of a

mirror image or that of an exotic dream, that the theater
had been offering for so long. A couple who establish that
they are married to one another by tracing their steps
back to having awakened that morning in the same house,
in the same room and finally the same bed, and who find
this an "extraordinary, bizarre coincidence"; two tramps
whose major "actions" consist in eating radishes and car-
rots and in taking off and putting back on their shoes, and
who perform a play which seems throughout to be waiting
for known dramatic principles to start operating—such
were the new characters and plots which by their implicit
mockery of "real" characters and plots gave a new blow
to the latter's self-sufficiency and imperium in drama.

Uneasily kicked against, sporadically violated but
never wholly thrown off, a fixed conception of what characters were supposed to be and of what plots were supposed to make them do had lain at the heart of the practice
of drama ever since it had passed its so-called heroic
crest several centuries before. Such a conception was in
fact the enervated and abstracted essence of the soul of
that earlier drama, the outcome of its passage from actuality—from being plays created and performed at a time
and in a place—to a condition of ideality, its alteration
from process into proposition.

Twenty years before *Waiting for Godot,* to which
Beckett had come after a series of brilliant coups against
the remaining entrenchments of fiction, he had written
these words about James Joyce: "he is not writing about
something; he is writing something." What had become at
least theoretically unassailable as the main tenet of serious
fiction—that literature is its own reality, that fictive language is a new, concrete, independent fact—had in
drama, the slowest of the arts to register or contribute
to an era's broad aesthetic and philosophical changes, been
a troubled aspiration, a scent of freedom, a series of in-

conclusive forays into forms that were perpetually made
to smack of eccentricity and arbitrary capers. Such is the
theater's conservatism and committeelike soul.

In the middle of the nineteenth century, at just the
point when drama seemed to have settled into mere absolute reproduction of itself, the German playwright and
critic Friedrich Hebbel had set down in his journals truths
which we are still trying to overtake and turn into exem-
plifications:

> All dramatic art has to do with impropriety and incompre-
> hension.
>
> To present the necessary in the form of the accidental—that
> is the whole principle of dramatic style.
>
> Drama shouldn't present new stories but new relationships.

The latter remark might have been as much elegiac as
hortatory, since Hebbel had risen out of an era which had
contained the remarkable but hermetic achievements of
Friedrich Buechner, Heinrich von Kleist and Christian
Dietrich Grabbe. These three German geniuses had all
died young and unexalted after having written dramas
which must have seemed like monstrous sick dreams in an
age of classical repression. Stemming from rules discovered in the self, wayward, nervous, "neurotic" and blackly
visionary, their plays were to prove crucial to a future
drama. But what was most significant about them was not
their independent morale, their more accurate psychology
or their discovery of demons in an era of Goethean rationality. Technically, dramaturgically, they cleared the ground
for new uses of the scenic art.

Their plays differed widely from one another but were
united by the way they swerved violently away from
storytelling and character-building to dispose themselves
as original universes in which conflict was between ele-

ments and faculties far more than between personages or personalities, and in which language pressed forward to become a kind of plot in itself, a drama. When they were rediscovered generations later, when, that is to say, what they had accomplished was felt once again, after the renewed occlusions of history, to be *necessary*, it was with a sense of enormous wonder, a dizzying contemplation of their green islands as seen from an exhausted mainland. And this mainland might have been described as a large body of theory and practice that had itself been cut off from any new and fertile propositions.

A digression may be permitted here for a word about "mainlands" in drama, or in any other art for that matter. This persistent notion, this geography whose nomenclature is built around the continental designations "realism," "symbolism," "romanticism" and so on, remains the bulwark of academic defense against art and the chief instrument of its submission to human polity. Art hasn't for a long time been susceptible to being codified in any such way, if it ever was at all. The terminology, and its being wielded in the interests of rational control over culture, is the product of a pedagogical sortie against everything that had threatened society's accumulating knowledge; to force art into being knowledge has been the master stroke that cut off its roots in ritual and play and mysterious otherness of presence.

In the same way, the idea of succession in the arts, that chronological dragon which swallows up almost all true response in the urgency to construct assimilable sequences—social novel, psychological novel, poetic novel and so forth—and so turn art into history, is what keeps us from seeing what the artist is and why he has continually to repudiate what he has been thought to be. It keeps us from seeing that at any one time the subject of an art and its manner are almost wholly provisional and interrogatory, not answers but questions and at the same time screens

behind which the next subject and the next manner are
being prepared. The subject and manner—content and
form—are of course indissoluble, but more than that they
are revolutionary precisely in their meeting, in their not
having found any other way to exist except through each
other. And the revolution is always against the previous
rebellion, that which had thought to fix the continuing
questions into replies, so that in the heyday of the so-called
social novel, the "psychological" novel was already advancing a more radical art (as Balzac recognized about
Stendhal); during, not after, the reign of impressionism,
"post-impressionism" was sketching a new visual kingdom.

This is why the seemingly miraculous flowering of
drama in the first decades of the nineteenth century in
Germany is not to be considered an aberration, something
isolated, premature and off-center. To abstract it into
the linear perspective of time, to deplete it by making it
a historical conundrum, something which throws chronological understanding out of whack, is to end up by
being literally unable to account for it. If it arose outside
the charted course of time, in other words, we bring it
back in the form of the exceptional. And such are our
habits that not being able to account for it—the exceptional
is that which can't be accounted for—we preserve it in
eccentric and isolated existence and look elsewhere for
what we consider the true historical course of drama.

That course leads us to the theater, which we go on
identifying with drama as though there were not a deep
tension between them, one which has grown more exacerbated in our time but which has actually been exhibiting
itself continuously since a breakdown occurred in their
relationship sometime in the seventeenth century. In this
tension between drama as an act of the individual mind
and theater as an act of what we may call the social body
lies the roots of the crisis which, as I have said, we persist

in seeing as merely local and as being resolvable by will, wit or magic.

Popular expectation and hardened definitions afflict all the arts: the novel was and still is expected to be a narrative, music was supposed to be tonal and harmonic, painting to represent and so forth. But the drama faces something more than this; the public nature of the theater and what can only be called the too-human content of its operations work inevitably to keep the drama isolated from aesthetic changes and help account for its conservatism and lag, its periodic irrelevance. The drama finds itself pressed to the past by a cultural expectation reinforced by the practicalities of theater, by physical and social exigencies: a necessary physical plant, seats to be filled, a community of skills to be organized and held together, technical apparatus to be on hand, a score of other functional considerations—props, lighting, tickets and ticket takers, fire extinguishers, charwomen, ushers, press agents, programs and much more.

All this investment, these stakes, this as it were municipal and clerical disposition of things, are what help to bind the theater to the historical, to what has already been done and what has already been known. And one result of this is that avant-garde and traditional are more widely separated in the theater than in the literary and graphic arts, although not in music or the dance, which are locked into the material world in the same way as drama. From this rises the fact that a body of repetitive, banal and compromised work perpetually occupies most of the space in the theater while everything original is crowded into corners.

The struggle simply to find a space on stage, to rescue itself from the fate of being nothing but dramatic literature, has marked the course of contemporary drama ever since artist-playwrights who had emerged—miraculously it sometimes seems—from an age of mere artisans began to write it. That drama could be an art, issuing from the same order of aspiration, consciousness and morale as poetry, music, painting or the novel, had virtually to be newly established after the nineteenth-century theater's long sterility. And in order to establish this, to extricate itself from the theater as an institution while retaining it as the necessary physical ground, the "place for seeing" (the original meaning of the word), dramatists had to be guileful, to use the theater against itself, by practicing a form of judo. Artist-playwrights had to present most of their visions under the guise of something else in order to satisfy audience expectation on one level while working out insurrectionary programs on another. They had to accept, and still have to accept, that they are allowed to be artists only as the outcome of a struggle with their technic more exhausting and consuming than we know of anywhere else in the life of culture.

A pious myth retains its force: that the communal nature of the theater is its major strength, heart of its energizing mysteries and source of its values. Yet the truth is that as the theater sank more and more into *divertissement* its communal nature bound it more and more closely to the perversion of its possibilities, to banality, repetition and sentimental acts. The audience for the theater has for a long time now been much more of a quasi-sophisticated mob than a conscious collectivity; it is a horde seeking banality or else, in another mood, sensation. To such an audience, as Henry James once pointed out, sensations are what pass for augmentations of consciousness, and it has been the sensational aspects of modern drama that have gained it its public recognition. A phenomenon not wholly different from the fate of the other arts, it nevertheless has been more maiming here, less easy to surmount. For paintings and novels and poems may surmount their scandalous successes by introducing themselves into the private consciousness where response and judgment have at least the possibility of being freer.

The sensations of new drama are clearly so much more public and immediate than those of the literary or graphic arts. *Right out there in the middle of society* its altered sounds and shapes are experienced in one mood as heightened *divertissement,* in another as affront and a kind of treason. What will not be experienced, except by isolated individuals who in this very process distinguish themselves from the horde of which they are physically a part, is the drama as a work of art, as unreal, that is to say as the product of an escape from time and from that life in which sensations function as surrogates for consciousness. The sensations of new drama, like those of any new art, are instead its means of access into consciousness.

They are also the signs of its struggle with itself, or rather with its own history. Like a war waged with an external enemy while a civil conflict goes on simultaneously, contemporary drama has fought a double battle: against the theater and its audiences drugged with tradition and received notions of the dramatic, and against its own assumptions, its accumulated existence, the dead hand of its accomplished artifacts and the coating of reality—its source and nutriment—with its own images and metaphors, the "dramatization" of actual life through the example of created dramas.

The true history of contemporary drama as an art is the gradual erosion of the sanctified image of man on the stage, man as character, destiny as plot, and at the same time the increasingly radical questioning by playwrights and other theater artists of drama's own bases and *raison d'être.* And much of this history has taken place on the sly, behind a barrage of aggressive gestures, a great many of which have been feints. From Ibsen's embattled dealings with the well-made play and his final partial movement beyond it, through Strindberg's replacement of rational character by dream and psychic adventure and Pirandello's ironic dramatization of rationality as itself the source of delusion, down to Brecht's objectifications of the traditionally subjective and Beckett's motionless plays of language, the common thread has been a heroic effort to make the drama do something new while battling for its sheer existence as a form and a public act.

For the majority of audiences as well as for all but a handful of critics (compared with modern literary criticism, that of drama has been notoriously thin, wary, lashed to tradition and inherited definitions, the best of it often produced by men who are not ostensibly drama critics at all) the major new dramatic propositions of the past eighty or ninety years have been either thematic, statements about the psyche, society or human destiny; or purely technical, tinkerings with a stalled machine or else, in the eyes of technological optimists, an intransigent progression on the model of technique's life in science or mechanics.

The real revolution, a change in conception of what is actually dramatic, a birth of consciousness about the possibility that all known forms of the dramatic may be exhausted, remains largely unseen outside those widely spaced small matrices where original work is still going on and morale remains besieged but not yet overthrown. A number of recent phenomena testify to the newest confrontation with history, its own and that of the world it inhabits, which drama is engaged in at this moment. Happenings and environments represent the most extreme form of a repudiation of the artificial procedures of traditional drama, an attempt to topple the text as sovereign power and to reconstitute acting as the gestures of nonprofessionals, a set of motions like any others and one carried out in what is meant to be society's quotidian midst instead of being placed before it as if on a platter. Theaters of cruelty and of polemical immediacy issue from a despair of drama's effectiveness under its old aesthetic patents as much as from a disgust with the theater of public consolation and confirmation, what Brecht meant by the "culinary" stage.

It may be that nothing will come forward as new, unassailable creation. It is surely true that any art comes to find that its own historical momentum becomes the enemy of its renewable prowess. About ten years ago Eric Bentley wrote an essay entitled "Is Drama an Extinct Species?" to which question he found himself able to give a negative answer. But the question remains open. And meanwhile the history which gave rise to it is there to be examined.

Ibsen and Strindberg

The history of the modern theater is almost universally considered to have begun with Henrik Ibsen's change in midcareer. Much before this the drama had had a brief, astonishing life as prediction, something in advance of itself, in the work of the early nineteenth-century German playwrights Heinrich von Kleist, Friedrich Buechner and Christian Dietrich Grabbe. But there had been no continuity; the Germans had been forgotten and to this day they remain imprisoned in the status of precocious, eerie forerunners, victims of a criticism by chronology.

When Ibsen, believing, correctly as it was to turn out, that the era's stages were closed to any further movement in the line of his own earlier dramaturgically open and poetic plays, *Brand* and *Peer Gynt*, turned from epic historical dramas to begin his cycle of so-called social plays, his shift in strategy was extreme. But it was not likely in the nature of things to have been quickly detected for what it was. Along with Zola, although with far less "scientific" fervor and methodology, Ibsen appeared to be engaged in moving drama into participation in the naturalistic movement that had overtaken large sectors of fiction and compelled its attention to society's immediate dilemmas, maladies, disjunctions and distempers. Diagnostic, prophetic and hopefully purifying, the new drama banked on a recovered honesty of imagination and sight after the reign in the theater of evasion and more or less elegant artifice.

Issuing from a greatly reduced surface, one of bare planes and unresonant corners, commonplace, quotidian and "lifelike" in their materials, Ibsen's plays of the 1870's and 1880's caught the half-horrified attention of audiences by their aggressive thrusts into public domains and their disturbing analyses of contemporary behavior. They carried with them and seemed to rise out of a heavily breathed air of topicality. And yet everything that seemed new and sensational, all the muckraking, the advanced ideas and calls to order, the assaults on public hypocrisy and private deceit, were fundamentally pretexts and sheathings for something else.

It was Eric Bentley who first undertook, in America at least, to rescue Ibsen from the soapbox or dais on which his statue—his decided-upon position in the life of culture—had so long rested. *A Doll's House*, Bentley demonstrated in *The Playwright as Thinker*, is not really about women's rights, the theme that had so exercised the Victorian audience and that continues to reign in the textbooks, but about human appetites for power and exploitation. If Nora had been the husband and Thorwald the wife, Bentley argued, the theme and music of the play would have been the same. Beneath the appearances—a husband who patronizes, a wife who rebels—patronization and rebellion themselves are on exhibit; something more permanent and mysterious than sociological data is being fed into a dramatic machine.

The insight Bentley provided can be used for all the social plays. The real subject of *Ghosts*, for example, is surely not "the rigidity of middle-class Norwegian morality," as a recent critic (Lionel Abel), thinking no doubt to get past the flagrant insufficiency of venereal disease as the theme, has found it possible to argue. Who could possibly be interested in that now, or, outside Norway, have been interested in it then? *Ghosts* is "about" something far less fettered to an era or a locality; it is about the rigidities, the fatal blind movements of ideals and abstractions in a universe of fact.

Francis Fergusson's study of *Ghosts*, which was nearly contemporaneous with Bentley's writing on Ibsen, was one of the key acts of modern drama criticism. Reinterpreting Aristotle on drama so as to separate the notion of plot from that of mere physical narrative, Fergusson at the same time helped free Ibsen from the conventions of a criticism that had persisted in seeing him on his most literal plane of expression, in tying him to the superficies and instrumentalities of one segment of his vision and practice. In offering a reading of Mrs. Alving's actions as a form of "tragic seeking" not distinct in impulse and trajectory from that of the Greek protagonists, Fergusson broke through the myth of Ibsen's bourgeois and polemical spirit, which was at the same time a legend of the necessarily prosaic and tendentious nature of all naturalistic-seeming drama. What Fergusson called Ibsen's "poetry" was, as he said, his most real dramatic enterprise. It was to emerge more openly, although not with greater critical or popular understanding, when the structures of his social method could no longer contain, not even as compromise and ruse, the pressures of his sensibility's ambitions and the crisis of his awareness of the embattled situation of sensibility itself.

The kind of criticism that Bentley and Fergusson practiced on Ibsen drew upon all the complex armaments of modern literary thinking, not the least among them that gun which goes off to announce that like any works of literature plays are more than their paraphrasable themes.

They are, first of all, forms. And forms are imaginative dispositions of existential materials seeking deliverance from actuality itself, from their status before imagination is added to them, and plays are therefore also "about" the action of this deliverance and its difficulties. Our habit of not looking at Ibsen as an artist but as a sort of grim or splendid fulminator, an ideologue, or else as a kind of superior carpenter, has done more than obscure the aesthetic reality of his plays; it has prevented us from seeing him as a crucial figure in the dialectic between art and life, artist and man, which has more than ever become the subject of art itself and the ground on which it takes shape.

All this is essential to an understanding of what has happened to the drama since Friedrich Hebbel set down in his journal at a time when Ibsen was beginning his career those ideas which could lead to a bonfire for all the textbooks. Ibsen is a magnificently fertile locus of nearly everything that is misconceived and misunderstood about the drama of the last hundred years. From Walter Kerr's parroting of the traditional uncomprehending criticism that Ibsen's "was the drama of ideas" and that this is a "drama in which people are digits, adding up to the correct ideological sum," to Mary McCarthy's sumptuous insensitivity to the great playwright's entire career, culminating in her drama-instructor's dictum that the last plays "grow more grandiose as the symbolic content inflates them," the Norwegian master, whom we have still not assimilated, continues to expose the poverty of our thinking about the drama, a poverty unequaled in our contemplation of any other art.

"I have been more the poet and less the social philosopher than people generally seem inclined to believe," Ibsen wrote with characteristic understatement as the misunderstanding prepared to extend itself beyond his own lifetime and into ours. ("A great poet, to whom we shall

go by path after path now that we know one," Rilke wrote
to a friend after his ecstatic discovery of Ibsen.) The surfaces of his ostensibly naturalistic plays, their domestic and
civic details and their apparent concern with conscious
issues, had of course made it possible for people to go to
them in the wrong way. To that hectic presumptuousness
which is the most subtle form of revenge upon art of audiences and critics alike ("We know what to do with
this!") these plays presented themselves as unquestionable social documents. And this meant that they could
be confined, for purposes of tendentious praise, execration
or polemical utility, within what was already known, what
could have been said in other ways. They could be
turned, that is to say, into artifacts of public self-consciousness, elements of a civic debate, and whether they were to
be regarded as dangerous or inspiriting was not as significant as the fact that by being absorbed into society's
problems and gross tensions they could be robbed of
their dignity and distinctness as artistic works.

It was highly possible then and remains possible now,
for example, to think of Hedda Gabler as a decadent aris-
tocrat chafing under the encroaching pettiness of her
bourgeois surroundings, or as a neurotic woman moving
forward with sexual aggressiveness in order to mask a
radical frigidity. When Bernard Shaw wrote that the
trouble with such women is that they *don't* kill themselves,
he was of course partly subscribing to these views of the
play as character study. Yet it is much more mysterious
than that. Beneath the surface of the play, under the mer-
ciless portraits and the exact iconography of domestic
crisis, Ibsen was trying to fashion something else: a new
kind of tragicomedy, more metaphysical than is comfort-
able for us to think, whose elements were energy turned
in on itself and being struggling against its tendency to
nonbeing, to dissolution.

From one point of view Hedda is indeed neurotic and

the play does suggest a cold view of bourgeois propriety. But Hedda's revenge upon Lovborg, her destruction of his manuscript and then of herself, are actions in a dimension beyond pathology, whether social or psychological. Hedda cannot *live*: she is caught at the deepest level not so much in a particular set of circumstances as in human circumstance itself; she is a victim of the way things are. She is a fish in Ibsen's great, polluted, boiling sea, where creatures, ill-adapted at best, struggle to know what to do. Ibsen wrote (and very few have listened) that all his work concerned an unappeasable conflict "Between one's aims and one's abilities, between what man proposes and what is actually possible," a conflict "constituting at once both the tragedy and comedy of mankind, and of the individual."

To achieve this drama which was more than a conflict on a representational plane but which first had to represent in order to be anything at all, Ibsen rooted his methods in a poetry which was informal, hidden and besieged by the guardians of the surface, who drove it down into the depths beyond the audience's immediate eye. It was a poetry lying beyond the grasp of paraphrase and exploitable "meaning"; the conscious, public, assimilable events of the play would have to serve for that.

It was Henry James, much more than William Archer or Bernard Shaw, Ibsen's great and tireless public defenders and explicators in England, who saw his real accomplishment by seeing through him, that is to say, through the ruse and the strategy. For Shaw, Ibsen was an invaluable ally and source of morale; it was very much to Shaw's interest to stress the social content and forensic energy of the plays, to place them in the context of contemporary insurrection against deceit and evasion on the stage as in life, and this is what makes *The Quintessence of Ibsenism* much more of a guide to Shaw's own values and developing practice than to Ibsen's. But for James, situated by taste, temperament and artistic procedure as far from Ibsen as one writer can be from another, the latter's art was preserved in its integrity precisely by the fact that he himself could not make use of it, could not employ it either to justify or buttress his own.

When James wrote of Ibsen's "smoky rooms" with their "odor of spiritual paraffin" and spoke of his being "massively common and middle-class," he was indicating his distance from Ibsen's appearances, the very constituents of what was being taken for his substance. James could see beneath these appearances, however, to Ibsen's "independence, his perversity, his intensity, his vividness, the hard compulsion of his strangely inscrutable art." That the art should be "strangely" inscrutable was due to just that discrepancy between what Ibsen proposed as dramatic values and what he choose for these propositions' public life which James noted everywhere in his work. The art should have been entirely available; if it was all politics and all moral study, if its energies were essentially forensic, why should it resist analysis and clarifying study? The truth, it has turned out, is that with the possible exception of Chekhov, no modern playwright is more deceptive than Ibsen, more resistant to the easy triumphs of historical method and of a criticism which regards art as itself an aspect of history. Not even the best efforts of sensitive critics like Bentley and Fergusson have fully established Ibsen in our minds as the artist who said of himself that his "task was the description of humanity," and who, as an artist, stood apart from history in order to overcome it.

His subject, James went on to say, "is always, like the subjects of all first-rate men, primarily an idea." James was the first to see this. Later Bentley was to write about Ibsen's "thought" in order to distinguish it from the localized "ideas" for which the playwright had been held responsible, as though they were negations of feeling or emo-

tion in his plays; and Robert Brustein has pointed out that
Ibsen was far less interested in specific notions than in a
"generalized thought," something we might resurrect from
misusage as "thoughtfulness." Bentley put it most succinctly
when he wrote that Ibsen "is far less interested in 'modern
ideas' than in certain ideas that go behind them. In Ibsen
one must always look for the idea behind the idea."

Ibsen's chief idea, James said, was "the individual
caught in the fact," and Ibsen himself announced his preoccupation with this "subject," which is not so much a
theme as a recognition, a principle of aesthetic action and
an overarching attitude toward experience, when he wrote
that his work had always dealt with the "contradiction
between word and deed, between will and duty, between
life and theory in general." None of this can be paraphrased
into social information or reduced, for the purposes of an
intelligible and orderly history of drama, to conventional
notions of character and plot, even though Ibsen had for
a certain period to make use of the most conventional-
seeming procedures in playmaking in order that his dramas might take on viable shapes and weights.

Such specific shapes and weights—Ibsen's "stories"—
concealed more than they immediately revealed and were
not synonymous with the dramas themselves. Ibsen was of
course concerned with the accuracy of his characterizations,
never permitting himself to be satisfied with approxima-
tions—Nora must know the latest exotic dance for her first
gesture toward freedom, Tesman must have the exact
lugubrious gravity and the precise vocabulary of a bourgeois husband—but characterization was not what he was
most centrally engaged in. You are accurate, Ibsen knew,
as an original premise of your art; and your characters,
when "seen" truly (the poet is the man who "sees," Ibsen
wrote), will behave for you then with grace and the
utmost revelatory force. But what they are to reveal is not
identical with their reality in any environment outside that

of the stage; imagination is their new environment, with purposes beyond the reportorial, and the preliminary act of reporting done, their unassailable rightness of detail and portraiture gains you room and opportunity to pursue your deeper objectives. It is a way to bait your traps.

Hedda Gabler was the last of the social plays, the last "trap" of its kind. From then on, during the last nine years of his productive life (he died after seven more years during which a stroke imposed silence), the old and now unaccommodating Ibsen wrote four more plays. These are the so-called symbolic dramas which Mary McCarthy found inflated and which have figured in most histories of contemporary drama as aberrations. Although some critics have found them strangely beautiful, to the majority they were out of the main line of Ibsen's career and therefore cut off from the body of values and intentions by which he is most comfortably defined and located. Even Bentley and Fergusson have stopped short of these plays in their inquiries into Ibsen's hidden truths.

With the exception of *Little Eyolf*, which seems to lie outside the main movements of Ibsen's imagination not so much because of its nonsocial and nonpsychological subject matter as through its narrowly mystical disposition of domestic event, the last plays strip themselves more and more of that skin of verisimilitude, that elephant trap, which had been stretched over the preceding ones. In so doing they seem to have provided for symbolmongers (or decriers) a series of *mises en scène*—the high tower of *The Master Builder*, the mysterious upper room of *John Gabriel Borkman*, the wind-swept mountaintop of *When We Dead Awaken*—which contain nearly all the material needed for their misapprehension. The rest is provided by quests outside the familiar social or moral categories and by vocabularies less and less fixed to the necessities of dramaturgical intrigue and narrative velocity. Not taking place in a drawing room, a kitchen or a town hall, not issuing in revelations of corruption or self-deception or political chicanery, there is evidently no other word for it but symbolic.

The vicissitudes of the idea of symbolism as a literary mode or operation are brought to mind at this point. It may perhaps have been found wanting as a full, lasting poetic procedure—the name of Mallarmé continues to be associated with a thin, cold air—but nearly everyone grants to that species of symbolism a purifying, jettisoning intention, quite the opposite of inflationary tactics. At the same time, important novels considered to function symbolically have been taught as being more complex, richer, less exhaustible than classically straightforward ones. Yet plays thought to be symbolic have suffered from a twofold degradation of response.

So strong and persistent is our belief in the "reality" of the drama, its necessary anchoring in verisimilitude and one or another kind of portraiture, or so sophomoric and romantic is our impatience with these evident limitations, that we reject as arty and pretentious many nonsymbolic dramas which are not familiarly representational, or we enshrine as high dramatic art a crude and windy but "real-looking" symbolism. Archibald MacLeish's *J. B.*, for example, is a false and pretentious play which hides behind a flashy modern setting functioning precisely as a cluster of symbols. Ibsen's last plays are not symbolic, nothing in them stands for anything else, and they are marvelously true and convincing dramas. What we take for symbolism in them is their having moved away from one kind of representation, from recognizable, predictable social and psychological life and behavior, from traditional *historical* human action.

The confusion runs through all our critical thinking, but especially through our thinking about the drama. Of course, in a certain sense (and at the risk of extreme oversimplification) we can say that all language is sym-

bolic and that all gesture on the stage partakes of the
nature of symbolic action. A symbol, after all, is that which
contains in compressed form something other and larger
than itself, and it is the very process of art to force elements
from life—words, shapes, colors, sounds, movements—to
yield up implications and sensual actualities different from
the ones they ordinarily contain and express. Yet "symbolic" is not being used in this sense when we speak
of Ibsen's last plays as being inflated or soft or imprecise.
Here the symbolic is being confused with the allegorical
and is thought to exist as a discoverable "story" in itself,
for which the physical work serves as a kind of decodable
message, so that the symbolic meaning of the piece is
encountered *afterward*.

The questions posed by Ibsen's last plays, as well as
by most significant drama since he wrote, transcend
ordinary critical categories to become elements of a confrontation with the bases of drama itself. What kind of
reality do we accept in the theater? Have we ever been
prepared to accept aesthetic reality in drama, that is to
say a reality constructed not as a replica or a spiritualiza-
tion of actuality but as an alternative and a sensuous
question addressed to it? When symbolism is enthroned
by "drama lovers," when a putatively inspiriting but coerced poetry takes the place of true dramatic language
and when plays are fashioned from lax humanistic dreams
or reveries of art, we are in the presence of a desire
for reality to be presented to us in false colors, as somehow "higher," more "meaningful," more acceptable than
we can otherwise know it. At the same time, when great
plays are stigmatized by "realists" as being ruinously symbolic and thereby reduced—as Ibsen's last plays and a
great many other dramas since then have been—to interpretive schemes, to allegories of actions that antedate
them and that can be uncovered outside art, instead of
being seen as new, self-contained, unallegorical dramatic

universes, then life is similarly being asked to direct art and keep it manageable, rational, helpful and domestic.

"Yes, to be sure, the critics," Ibsen once wrote, "they are often far from adequate. They like to symbolize, because they have no respect for reality. And if one really gives them a symbol, then they reduce it to a triviality or they revile the author."

From *The Master Builder* through *John Gabriel Borkman* to *When We Dead Awaken,* Ibsen moved step by step across a perilous region of the dramatic imagination where the task imposed was to create new myths—myths of art—for the most central and unlocalized human conditions. The kind of play he had been writing was far too limited for these new purposes and ambitions. His subject, as James had said, was an idea, and now this idea threw off most of its particularities, or rather those particularities of social setting, psychological causation, the knowable relationships of lovers, citizens or family members, which had seemed to be the very arena of Ibsen's activity and had thus lent themselves to the misreading of him as a social philosopher rather than a poet.

In their different ways the three great last plays are myths of the individual caught in the fact, but now the fact has expanded toward a metaphysical dimension; it is mortality, finiteness, the ineluctability of death and the irretrievability of the past that press down on those points of consciousness, those arenas for struggle, which his characters have now more than ever become. It is greatly significant that all the protagonists are old or aging, for this is one of the means of their extrication from the limiting social milieus of the earlier plays; like their creator, they have been carried by time past the stage where social reality and social behavior are more or less decisive for moral and psychological leverage and revelation. They have in this way been liberated into more purely aesthetic functions. In the same way that Henry James freed his characters from financial worries, that is to say, from economic reality, Ibsen freed the figures of his last plays from the thick texture of societal entanglement so that they might inhabit a realm pitched beyond society's determinations and categories; and this was in order to encounter them more stringently as projections of his own self.

"In every new play I have aimed at my own spiritual emancipation and purification," Ibsen once wrote, although, as a function of our refusal to see him as an artist, we have generally refused to take him at his word. Having in a sense dispersed himself among and embodied himself in his characters all along—in Brand, Peer Gynt, Mrs. Alving, Gregor Werles, Rosmer and Rebekka West, Hedda—he now entered the final and most rigorous process of purification through his own created surrogates. Through Solness, Rosmer and Rubek he broke into an expanded tragic awareness, one that in testing the limits of human existence also tested the limits and justifications of art and at the same time threw into final question the kind of play he had written before and that was to continue its domination of the stage long after his death, retaining to this moment its power as norm and model.

With his habitual understatement, Ibsen remarked in a speech a few years after *The Master Builder* appeared that its central figure was "a man who is somewhat related to me." (All three of the protagonists of the last plays are artists or artist types.) He had on an earlier occasion asserted that none of his plays dealt with anything that he had not himself lived through. Yet there is nothing here to encourage biographical criticism, for Ibsen's work, that long lifetime of plays which he had more than once insisted had to be seen as a whole, was not his biography placed serially on stage but a series of constructions out of his being, at once tutorial and sacrificial, for which a lifelong struggle to find adequate aesthetic means had been waged. What appeared to be an aloof technology, a cold, impersonal architecture, broken into at times by an argumentative author's voice (most notably in *An Enemy of the People*) but always reinstating its control and sober purposefulness, was for the period of the social plays the necessary mask and means, his way of being able to shape plays for the actual stage.

It was also his way of being an artist involved with the world. More than most innovators Ibsen felt a need to *count*, to be immediately effective, so that his struggle with his art was seldom clearly separated from his battle to find a place, a large high position within the main enterprises of European civilization in his time. From this need takes shape the unflattering portrait we possess of him, one that obscures the purity and nobility of his self-imposed task in art; he was a dickerer for honors, a jealous colleague, stiff, hieratic and self-institutionalizing. But there was a point at which his egoism, if we want to call it that, and his aesthetic choices converged, and this was the condition of his own art, of drama in this time. Here it was only possible to count, to be seen, he thought, through the principal agency of a naturalism that had itself arisen as a reaction to the artificiality and lifelessness of previous drama but that had brought with it severe inherent limitations.

What Ibsen could never have revealed to his public was the difficulty of writing plays at all. For him—the first dramatist to come fully to grips with it, a culture hero—the difficulty lay precisely in the fact of the gradual conversion of drama's traditional strength into its weakness, of its operational premises into an embarrassment and a noose. The projection of the self in drama had always been affected and shaped by the obligation to create "others," *characters* who would function in new and artificial realms as explorer-delegates of one's own being and at the same time as creatures of the general imagination, of society's other life. With the decline of drama into

naturalistic and bourgeois forms, dramatic characters fell
under the necessity of being recognizable, familiar, involved with immediacy (social issues, moral dilemmas,
the debate over values), or else figures of inflated physical
and deprived moral stature, the stock personages of farce
and melodrama. One reaction to all this was to try to
conjure up pure dream, a stasis of lyrical and abstract
being, as in the plays of Maeterlinck.

As characters became bourgeois in the dominant sectors of the theater, plot can also be said to have become
bourgeois, middle-class stories in an exact sense, since they
made up gross, consolatory myth and fable on the one side
or reportage, sheer exacerbated journalism, on the other.
Plot had always propelled characters in a movement that
ideally was in coherence with the movements of the playwright's own imagination, but in practice, for the artist-
playwright, this had become less and less true. In practice
meant the kind of play we call well-made, which Ibsen
had adopted to far more serious purpose than did his
French predecessors in the mode, but which confined him
to a narrow space where he chafed more and more.

The state and atmosphere of the theater which Ibsen
did so much to change is faultlessly conveyed in a letter
of the French playwright Eugène Brieux, written a generation or so afterward.

> The theater . . . was confined rigidly within certain time-
> honored conventions, and lay like a lazybones in a warm and
> comfortable bed. The theaters of Paris all had their accepted
> and privileged purveyors of amusements, and their intel-
> lectual sloth was in turn communicated to the public—each
> supporting the other.

Ibsen had introduced into the dramatic form he had
taken over a moral and intellectual complexity and weight
such as it had not come close to possessing. By compelling

the past to reveal its hold on the present, and abstractions their tyranny over the palpable, he had infused the well-made structure with a depth of conflict that radically exposed the superficiality of the kinds of conflict—immediate, circumscribed, assimilable—it ordinarily dealt in. "The Ego against the Ego . . . the Soul against the Soul," James had said of Ibsen's plays and had gone on to call these clashes "thinkable things." The very notions of ego and soul were what was missing from the French plays among whose clevernesses and predictabilities Ibsen had set his harsh, steely, uncompromising constructions.

But the necessities of prevailing dramatic method, what was viable and coherent with the spirit of the age, had, since *Brand* and *Peer Gynt,* forced Ibsen to rein in and partially disguise the inevitabilities of his imagination. Plot had been a story adopted from life, from the latter's presumed operations (which presumption had itself largely been derived from previous dramatic art), and Ibsen's greatest effect on his audiences had been to have shocked them into an awareness of what such plots, such contrived destinies and biographies, can conceal, what moral and existential truths lay waiting to be exposed under their orderly surfaces. But he had not undermined their confidence in the operation of plot itself, or their admiration of plot's consistency, its logic and its mirroring of the narrative ways in which their own lives were assumed to run. If anything, he had reinforced the well-made play by having made it work so well in the yielding up of social and moral truth.

But such truths were plainly less than he had striven as an artist to bestow, something to which his lifelong battle against misunderstanding so clearly testifies. Had he been a novelist, he would have been able to make use of those integumentary and aesthetically environing elements, that atmosphere made up of reflection, opinion, point of view and so on, which the novelist brings into being (in a way that not even the most stringently operating naturalism can wholly suppress) in order to give his characters richer and more complex destinies than their literal actions can amass. We have seen something of how under the surface of Ibsen's social plays elements of a far-reaching tragic vision endeavor to shape themselves. Yet all the machinery of plot in the plays of his middle period works to the accompaniment of a hum of imaginative activity separate from the straightforward sounds of its wheels and gears: moral quests spread past the incidents arranged for their unfolding; metaphysical and spiritual actions take place in imperfect collaboration, sometimes in acute disharmony with the physical details of their stage life and the obligation to fashion recognizable portraits.

Fergusson put his finger on the matter when he said that "the most general way to understand the unsatisfactory end of *Ghosts* is to say that Ibsen could not find a way to represent the action of his protagonist, with all its moral and intellectual depth, within the terms of modern realism." Yet Fergusson, in this essay and elsewhere, left the problem as he found it, and nobody since then has fully taken it up.

Most egregiously in plays like *Pillars of the Community*, *A Doll's House* and *Ghosts*, but also in more complex works like *Rosmersholm* and *Hedda Gabler*, the machinery of plot works logically to establish necessary physical connections, narrow sequences of cause and effect which propel the action forward and against which poetic event has to compete for a place, literally for "a piece of the action." Almost all these chains of physical event originate in the prehistory of the plays; fatality emerges like the visible segment of an iceberg or like a fist thrust through a wall by a hidden arm. Or rather these similes describe what Ibsen would have wanted the process of fate to have been like in his social plays.

In actuality their denouements have issued from mechanical rather than organically imaginative progressions, from an inevitability of physical causation resembling the causation we illusorily feel in real life, in life outside art. The famous letter in *A Doll's House*, Osvald's inherited illness in *Ghosts*, Lovborg's manuscript in *Hedda Gabler*—quintessential objects and data of the well-made plot—have the effect of imposing on the plays a stringency, an inevitability of a smaller and much more limited kind than the action of the imagination, and this is due to their need to reproduce ordinary causation, their obligation to resemble the inevitabilities of physical and social existence.

There has been little room for choice, the kind of choice by which a character is shown to "elect" his own fate, as Oedipus or Macbeth does, as a consequence of his own nature and existential situation and as an image of these things, instead of having his fate thrust on him by more or less arbitrary circumstances, by a logic of happenstance. However much those happenings strive to attain the condition of fatality itself, they remain incommensurate with the characters, too local, specific and literal to contain all their meanings and implications or to support fully their stature as freely imagined beings in an aesthetic environment and dimension. Thus once the letter is in the box, Nora is compelled, by the logic of the plot-as-fate, to act on the coercive knowledge of what its discovery by her husband will bring about; once Rosmer has learned of Rebekka West's machinations, he is propelled by this knowledge (as by literal machinery) to a death intended partly to atone for them and on that account smaller in implication and in metaphoric density than Ibsen was striving to create for him.

In the same way, once Hedda has destroyed Lovborg's manuscript, which has itself come down to her through a chain of plotted, charted circumstances, she is led to destroy herself, having literally burned her bridges behind her. Or rather it is truer to say that the plot has burned them for her, and thus we feel a discrepancy, an uneasy space, between its inexorable physical action and the realities, tacit or expressed, of her own nature and being. The violent circumstances may be physical or "objective" correlatives of her moral and psychic being, their dramatic instancing, but they are by no means equivalent to it, so that what she incarnates is reflected in the events of the play like a face overflowing a small mirror held too close. The miracle is that Ibsen has been able to make her fate, with its profound implications of a disorder at the heart of existence itself and not merely in a particular social or psychological modality, as convincing and resonant as he has.

With *The Master Builder*, Ibsen moves to create a dramatic metaphor which will not have to take shape entirely underground, beneath the explicit incidents of a well-made plot, will not have to contend with, try to overcome actually, their literalizing and specifying tendencies. At first glance the new play's structure seems to stand as before and its procedures appear to make no radical departure from the past. Individualized contemporary characters act in a sequential way, events concatenate and issue in a violent denouement, something has "happened" that appears to lend itself as in the preceding plays to extrapolation as the dramatic "point." An aging architect encounters a young, poetic girl who goads and inspires him into attempting a "dizzying" feat which brings about his death. In the course of this tale themes make their appearance to announce the play's preoccupation with the pressure of youth upon age, of new force upon established energy, and with the profound hostility between the life of art and that of domestic and social responsibility.

The individual caught in the fact, to return to it once again, has always been Ibsen's subject, his basis for aesthetic appraisal of his task. But in this play both individual and fact undergo a change toward a suggestive indefiniteness, a mysterious transcendence of milieu and era. In a way that looks back to *Brand* and *Peer Gynt, The Master Builder* rises to a more complete and self-contained metaphorical status than had been possible for Ibsen to achieve as long as he was under the full exigencies of his entente with the naturalistic theater and its methods. His meanings and implications, the images and vocabularies from which they radiate, the objectifications of his intuitions, all exist now within an aesthetic environment that is more completely outside history; their disposition is more directly toward the service of his double task: to effect his own spiritual emancipation and purification, and to erect a sensual, histrionic equivalent and housing for that existential action. His imagination functions more freely as a bestower of metaphor; he enters more fully into his creation, whose laws are now more consistent with his own nature and needs; and plot, the soul of the tragedy, makes fewer concessions to the fixed mechanical movements of a well-made body.

As in the social plays that preceded it, the parabola of action has its starting point in a long history anterior to the drama's specific events, the past functioning like a body in darkness which thrusts its head into the light. Solness, the master builder, has already almost wholly become what he is going to be in the play, which is to say what he is going to do; and these actions will in turn further define him and, most important for the realization of the work as art, fix what he is in a mythic status. Events are the consequence of what he and of course, to a lesser extent, the other characters are, and the play is concerned with the exhibition—the histrionic unfolding—of such being in the form of actions which shall seem to flow necessarily and inevitably from it.

But this being is neither uniquely individual nor broadly typological. Solness, the protagonist, is a field of action within a field of action; he is the incarnation and arena of qualities and conditions in conflict, elements which we tend to isolate as "themes" but which are really ideas and intuitions brought together in an active, a dramatic, *instance*. For Ibsen the problem was how to make these ideas and intuitions, these experiences halfway between actuality and their potential new guise as art, issue in a work that would transcend personal, limited fate, that would be exemplary for a condition of existence and not a mere career; it was the problem of how to make fate universal and perennial in a bourgeois age in which the only accepted fatalities were social and what we might call *technical*.

In the way in which what is necessary and inevitable is made to work itself out lies the change from the previous plays. Nothing better illustrates this than the minor matter of the crack in the chimney. When he tells Hilde, the young girl, about the fire which destroyed his house and indirectly led to the death of his children, Solness prepares the audience for causation within the canons of melodrama and the well-made play. Yet he soon reveals that the crack he had failed to repair had had nothing at all to do with the fire; it has continued to operate precisely as an element in his awareness of mysterious spiritual connections among phenomena, and his revelation of the part it did not play in the fire is a subtle declaration by Ibsen that there are going to be no more causal sequences of the earlier mechanical kind.

The Master Builder thus expands the space available to its protagonist for the discovery and assumption of his destiny by converting much of the machinery of plot from the order of physical contingency and necessity to that of ontological urgency and spiritual choice. Solness is not free of course to evade his fate—that he has one means that the play exists—but he is free, within the dramatic narrative, to choose the events that will reveal and constitute it, in a way that has not been possible for any other Ibsen character since Brand and Peer. For the tyranny of the past, to have dealt with which was Ibsen's chief means of extending the well-made play into metaphysical areas, is no longer absolute; no longer does it act as a remorseless sequence of cause and effect. Nothing Solness does issues from his past like time bombs going off or chickens coming home to roost, figures which do describe the line of action of most of the preceding plays. Nothing has to happen simply because something else has happened; the "evidence" of the play, its imaginative data, is no longer heavily circumstantial.

The "cause" of the culminating action of *The Master Builder* is an effect of choice, not the result of coercion by a logic of physical event. When Solness climbs up the tower for the traditional wreathing ceremony, he has been led to it by an act of will which he is free to repudiate at any time. That we feel his decision to be inevitable is not the result of his having been caught by circumstances, hooked in the mouth by plot, but because of Ibsen's successful creation of a world of inevitability built up from psychological and ontological materials under enormous pressure to find just such an aesthetic resolution. Solness, as a character, that is to say as a person brought into being for just this drama, this specific aesthetic use, has gathered in himself Ibsen's consciousness and intuitions of the grandeur and futility of art, of the terrible burdens it lays on the artist's ordinary life and of the doubts it perpetually raises about its agency in the world.

And along with this awareness of art as the necessary but disastrous "dream of the impossible" is consciousness of another and related realm of besieged being: human existence in time, the tyranny of aging and the loss of the self through the erosions of time. These two recognitions of finiteness which the play simultaneously makes known as its aesthetic enterprise work inexorably, as poetic potencies and dramatic energies, toward the tragic attempt at reversal, the leap to overcome necessity, by which Solness is made into legend and the play is crystallized in an inimitable and irreducible image.

Unlike any of Ibsen's other social protagonists, Solness has gone to the end of his possibilities with internal assent if not with full consciousness, and above all with freedom from mechanical plotted pressure. His decision to climb the tower has arisen from his original promise to Hilde of a "kingdom" for her, a promise which, since he had made it as nothing more than a flirtatious utterance to an enchanting child, puts him outside any rigorous moral or social necessity to fulfill. Yet he will give her her kingdom, since that is the only way he can assume his destiny.

Again, not since *Brand* and *Peer Gynt* has Ibsen made such complex and resourceful use of a controlling image. Beginning with its narrower function as a figure for romantic aspiration in general and for sexual promise, the notion of kindgom is steadily developed into a resonant metaphor for the life of art and, beyond that, for the ways in which existence presses toward its limits and discovers them in a dialectic of necessity and disaster. In the end the idea of kingdom has been modulated, after an intricate exchange in which Solness and Hilde swiftly uncover all the meanings and implications of their spiritual relationship, into that of a "castle in the air," one built, as Solness says, "on a true foundation." No more suggestive metaphor for the nature and location of art in relation to life has ever been devised.

When Hilde, in "quiet, crazed triumph," cries out at the moment of Solness' death that she has heard "harps in the air" and apostrophizes him as "*my—my* master builder!" she gives a home in consciousness to his lucid, insane act, one that contains all the brilliance and dementedness of men's efforts at transcendence. Solness has gone too far, which means that he has reached the tragic condition, something that Ibsen has not for a dozen plays been able to achieve for his protagonists. But he has been able to achieve it for this one only as the outcome of a major shift in dramaturgical procedure and not, as is so often taught, as the simple result of a change of values or of cultural ambition. He has added his second transcendence to the structures of the well-made play; having first made it work for the revelation of moral truth by introducing into it the irrevocable and corrosive action of time, he has now moved it further from its bases and cleared the ground for a new possibility of dramatic freedom by bringing the objective necessities of plot under the sway of the internal necessities of character.

And yet character and plot remained in question as the chief instrumentalities of dramatic vision. For Ibsen the process of purification within and through his art continued to the end. Even the most sympathetic recent criticism has tended, however, to concentrate on his spiritual and moral intentions in the writing of *John Gabriel Borkman*, and *When We Dead Awaken*, viewing them, like *The Master Builder*, as problematic documents of embattled old age and tormented consciousness of the risks of art. Yet what matters much more than these thematic and interpretive considerations is the question of how these plays work aesthetically and what this meant for the subsequent art of the drama.

Ibsen's two last plays are filled with an even greater anguish than *The Master Builder*, yet they are even sterner, more sparing of means, less dependent on an intricate narrative structure and on sequential action. For these final testaments he reached a condition of lyric expressiveness that sharply reduced the plays' reliance on linear movement, on progression of causally related events. This is what has so disturbed critics such as Mary McCarthy and brought down on Ibsen the charge of pretension and self-indulgence. And the charge gains a degree of plausibility from the fact that Ibsen was indeed unable fully to solve the nearly unprecedented problem he faced; how to write directly about himself, about his moral being and existential anguish as a permanent condition, a poetic fact, within the stringencies and expectations of a dramatic method that contained little provision and no principle of morale for writing of this kind to be undertaken. Still, the plays are neither pretentious nor self-indulgent; incompletions, failures at the extreme edge of ambition, are often the signs in art of the most unaccommodating and indestructible integrity.

The last plays are not so much descriptions of Ibsen's state of being at the time he wrote them as new constructions which rescue the materials of that state from formlessness, abstraction and the destructions of time by placing them in the imagination. They are essentially static creations, informed by pure radical moral and ontological perceptions and intuitions, and what is needed for their dramatic viability is a form extensively different from anything Ibsen had thus far been able to control. He would not of course have called it "spatial form," that modern intellectual construct, but something of what the term suggests was surely the thing he was seeking. For the fact that almost all the crucial "action" the plays contain has been completed before the stage life has been set in motion, the two protagonists moving toward their deaths not as the result of a traditional dramaturgical development but out of recognitions that have been almost wholly present throughout, means that development will have to take place in some other fashion. Something other than a chain of causally linked occurrences will have to generate the necessary interest, that suspensefulness without which no drama can be said to exist.

The suspensefulness is in fact mostly created by the poetry, that web and mesh of implication, cross reference, image and suggestion which had been the subtext

of all the social plays but which here, to an even greater
degree than in *The Master Builder*, moves forward to
become very nearly the whole drama itself. It is a poetry
of discovery and lamentation, of cold recognition that the
cost of everything is everything, and of dark, strangely
exultant, lyric crystallizations of the sense and emotion of
finality, of the irretrievability of the self's beautiful and
catastrophic ambitions. The two protagonists, Borkman and
Rubek, have "sold" love and human connection for power
over the earth and over experience, the latter through
art and the former through an aesthetically informed dream
of being a great, Alexander-like tycoon. Their deaths, even
more than that of Solness, are demonstrations of their
having crossed a boundary line; they are punishments in
the moral order, but more than that they are newly
shaped aesthetic creations, legends of mortality as the
process of discovering the ruin our ambitions will always
incur.

Yet the poetry had still to have a base. For the plays
as histrionic occasions of the intuitions I have described,
for dramaturgical coherence and dramatic momentum, the
problem for Ibsen was to make things "happen" within
a structure of plausibility such as the well-made play and
his own temperament and training as a playwright required
but that could scarcely be sustained now by the kind of
linked events, replicas of "stories" from the self-drama-
tizing world outside art, such as he had been forced to
devise for the past twenty-five years. His main instrument,
the past, is no longer the principle of active dramatic
pressure, one that brings about the revelations and denouements of the plays as physical consequences or even,
as in *The Master Builder*, as spiritual ones in a sequential
line. For both Rubek and Borkman have already reached
their recognitions, and the plays, instead of being the unfolding process of these recognitions, are their swift flower-
ings. In a brilliant stroke Ibsen anticipated and partly

inspired an entire milieu of plays to come by placing his
protagonists as already "dead," as they are told by others,
that is to say already in the condition to which ordinary
drama must lead with all its parade of events. As far as
he was able, he took drama in these plays out of what
Ionesco was fifty years later to call the line of the "detec-
tive story," drama as the statement, the development and
the solution of one or another kind of paraphrasable questions.

But he was unable to go the whole way. What marks
John Gabriel Borkman and even more *When We Dead
Awaken* as transitional plays (although nonetheless masterpieces for that; in Joyce's ecstatic opinion *When We Dead
Awaken* was Ibsen's greatest work) and brings down on
them the accusation of being "symbolic" is their settings,
the wrapping of images—mysterious rooms, snow, storms,
mountains, avalanches—within which the true poetic
body of the plays forms itself. We may say that the real
work of both these plays is complete without those external elements, just as the real poetry lies in a passage like
this:

IRENE: We only find what we have lost when—
RUBEK: When?
IRENE: When we dead awaken.
RUBEK: What do we find then?
IRENE: We find that we have never lived.

Ibsen nevertheless brought into both plays this apparatus
of external scene and suggestive setting, partly in order
to accomplish physically the deaths of his protagonists,
but more subtly because he could not yet imagine how a
play whose ambition was nothing less than to exist immediately, all at once, causing itself and not being instigated
by anything outside itself, and therefore existing as a poem
does, whose passage through time is a concession to physical laws but whose end is really in its beginning—how

such a play could be written and staged. Nevertheless, great mind and tireless spirit that he was, he remarked after writing *When We Dead Awaken,* when he was well past seventy and had not yet had his stroke, that he was ready now to strike out into wholly new regions. Meanwhile a younger and equally great playwright, August Strindberg, had already moved into those territories with remarkable, beleaguered élan and great daring.

In November of 1887, when Henrik Ibsen was at the height of his fame, he received a copy of August Strindberg's new play, *The Father.* A few days later he wrote to the Swedish bookseller who had sent it to him that although the younger dramatist's "experiences and observations in the area of life" with which the play was concerned were not the same as his own, he found it impossible to deny or to resist the author's "violent force" in his new work. Eight years later Ibsen, then sixty-seven, wrote to his wife, Susannah, that he had purchased a portrait of Strindberg which the painter called "The Revolution" but which he had decided to call instead "The Outbreak of Madness."

Ibsen is known to have hung the portrait on the wall opposite his desk, where he could see it while he wrote, and he seems to have employed it both as a grim reminder of the competition from younger writers he had always feared (Strindberg was more than twenty years his junior) and, we know from certain remarks of his, as a sort of negative icon whose maleficent power he could draw on for his own "saner" purposes. In much the same way he used to keep a scorpion in a jar on his desk, provoking it from time to time to sting a bit of apple and thereby allow him to feel his own "venom" oozing vicariously and liberatingly out.

Ibsen's rechristening of the portrait of Strindberg has an interest much beyond that of gossip about the great or even that of the psychological history of artists. A private act with idiosyncratic sources, it had a public bearing as well, a significance beyond that of personality or temperament, since it tells us something about the way the art of drama, changing so rapidly at this period, was regarded by one of its greatest practitioners.

That Ibsen was well aware of the Swedish playwright's originality and power is clear, but it is also evident that he found their uses disturbing. An episode not unknown in the relations between two artists of equal genius, in this case it was a good deal more revelatory of larger cultural matters than is usual. Ibsen was himself one of the foremost revolutionaries in the history of the theater, and at the time he hung the portrait he was on the verge of his final and most far-reaching technical advances. That he should have chosen to emphasize the evidence of Strindberg's personal life (the painting had been done in the middle of his so-called inferno period, a time of agonizing visions, paranoia and headlong flights) at the expense of the very different testimony of his work was for Ibsen very much a matter of artistic considerations. For there lay at the center of his retitling of the Strindberg portrait Ibsen's own embattled confrontation with the problems of dramatic art, with the questions of how it ought to be made and what its future might be.

Besides being by temperament a more hidden and cautious artist, Ibsen had deeper roots in the technical and professional tradition both men had had to work with and through; he had a greater commitment to what we might call a theater of public acceptance and had a more conservative (one might argue, more subtle) arsenal of dramaturgical weapons. Most centrally, his sense of the function of dramatic art was considerably more "civilized," more a matter of great lofty debates within the imagination than, as he thought it to be for Strindberg, of its violent irruptions. Consequently he had a profound mistrust of the younger writer's credentials as an insurrectionary, strengthened, we may assume, by his own partial aversion to being considered one. That they were both rebels engaged in storming the same palace was something he would never have admitted, not even after it had become clear that his own last works had joined Strindberg's in effecting a procreative turbulence in the art.

Four years after he had acquired the portrait, Ibsen stopped writing, the victim of a stroke at seventy-one. In his last plays he had carried his long struggle with inherited dramatic forms and methodologies to the furthest point in his power; something in them remained held in the stage's heavy conservative tow, and something else stood outside, as an absence, a silence, a refusal to offer *what the theater expected*. In *John Gabriel Borkman* and *When We Dead Awaken* he had written plays whose plots were fundamentally static, given so to speak all at once, whose characters underwent almost no "development" and whose thought, generalized perceptions of a moral and poetic kind, resisted more strongly than had any of his work since *Peer Gynt* a process of extrapolation and codification into "ideas."

But long before that he had been moving against the entrenchments of traditional dramatic method, more specifically the traditions that had become solidified during the century and a half or so before he began his career: the belief in stage characters as participating coherently in a recognizable typology drawn from "life," the belief in plot as a series of causally connected, physically logical incidents. Ibsen had shaken the foundations of reigning dramatic art as far back as *A Doll's House* when in a stroke that was more significant as a subterranean technical upheaval than as an open moral one he had kept Nora from coming back on stage after she had slammed the

door on her husband. The play's first audiences had continued to sit and wait for it really, *properly*, to end until
it was finally understood that this was in fact the ending
the author had intended.

The unease and unhappiness of these audiences make
up an instructive episode in the historic relations between
form and content as these are experienced in the sensuous
actuality of the presence of a work of art rather than as
pedagogical terms indicating an unreal division. The prevailing academic view of *A Doll's House* is that Nora's
act of rebellion against her husband's authority was what
so disturbed Victorian moral sensibility and what therefore constituted Ibsen's revolutionary gesture. And in fact
for most minds such explicit events will always be the real
"meaning" of works of art, since works of art have always
to do with actions and qualities that are significant in
life and from which therefore art borrows its own significance.

And so it needs to be said again that the truest, most
enduring and unopposable significance, the only revolution,
has to do with the way gestures, moral or any other, are
made within the work; it has, in other words, to do with
form. And new forms, which come into being as a simultaneous rediscovering, re-expressing and relocating of prevailing existence, or content, become new experience, new
content, as the work completes and realizes itself as art.

The world is changed by such an operation. Things
are seen to have shifted in relation to one another and to
have meanings that were not imaginable before; new
forms are new significances. What most profoundly disturbed the first audiences of *A Doll's House*, however unconscious they may have been of it, was not so much Nora's
"immorality" as the fact of her absence, the fact that she
had stepped outside the framework in which characters
were supposed to be contained on the stage. The upheaval
that had occurred is that which takes place whenever an

art breaks with its immediate past, having been brought to it by the art's having stiffened into repetition and cliché, which means that it has become a confirmation of illusion rather than an accession to experience.

The prevailing illusion of the period was that life worked toward neat conclusions, and art, from which this sentiment had ironically enough been derived, was supposed to go on reflecting this. And so the audiences were unhappy, as other audiences were to be unhappy generations later when Godot failed to come, because they were not allowed to find out—fatal condition for the old easygoing entente between playwright and spectator—what had happened to Nora, what she was *now*; the play hadn't fulfilled drama's traditional task, which was to take characters along a fixed journey, to bring them from *one known place to another*. It was not suprising that the hole at the end of the play was filled in by a number of hack playwrights, who wrote new scenes in which Nora did come back, having been summoned by theater managements unable to swallow the news.

From this point on, while Ibsen was introducing all those themes that are the elements of his mistaken reputation as a social critic, he continued to take more radical sorties against the limitations of the *pièce bien faite*, against the anticipations of an age of mechanical procedures and conventional illusion in drama. His aims were almost wholly different from those of what we might call the School of Paris, for which dramatic events on the level of mere cleverly arranged events and recognizable psychology made up most of the art of the stage. (Eugene Scribe is said to have remarked that once he had his plot well in hand, the play itself could be written by his janitor.) But while he was fighting to make room within the well-made structures for his moral and poetic schemes, Ibsen, master builder, was at the same time extending the life and deceptive prowess of the genre by adding to its

technical means. This is one source of his being confined,
in our general consideration now, to a dated and narrow
achievement.

Ibsen is linked forever to something that wasn't synonymous with the well-made play but that had assimilated
its technical means. Naturalism is one of the terms we
use to see to it that art remains within the realm of "culture," that is to say within the domain of pedagogy. For
Ibsen's contemporaries—Zola, for example, or, provisionally
as we shall see, Strindberg—the word naturalism meant a
number of things, but a shared meaning was that it marked
out the field of an exploration that was at the same time a
repudiation of unseriousness and artificiality in literature
and drama, an assault on them for having taken their
eyes off what existence was really like. It was a word to
describe a procedure and a morale that were felt to be
necessary in art at the time, and *as a word*, it is useful in
the history of changing attitudes and ambiences in art.
But it was never a thing, a substance, or even a specific
style, in the same way that "absurd" art or expressionism
are not actualities but signs, climates, and terms we use
for the sake of historical order and the exigencies of textbooks. The kind of serious, socially oriented well-made
play that Ibsen seemed to be writing, and Zola actually
was, might calmly bear the label "naturalism" as long as
the aesthetic activity it denoted was going on, but in
our hands now it clouds and perverts the truth of what
the imagination was engaging in then.

This is essential to remember in the case of August
Strindberg. For Strindberg, almost a generation younger
than Ibsen, naturalism as I have been describing it was
already the prevailing serious attitude toward literary
art when he came to artistic maturity, and his first important
plays were written in its atmosphere and with its élan. Yet
Strindberg's dramatic imagination, like that of Ibsen, was

too far-reaching and original to have been content with the operation of a literary mode that understood itself largely as a principle of earnestness, a repudiation of spectacle and arid fantasy and a means of making the theater work for conscious, socially revelatory ends. Such things could not be much more than starting points, and in fact Strindberg early referred to himself as a *Nyanaturalist*, a "new" naturalist.

With less of a stake than Ibsen in maintaining a *plausible* theater, one in which a playwright worked to change things by indirection, withholdings and subtle departures, Strindberg was able to move more aggressively and quickly out of the well-madeness of naturalism as well as out of its area of social concerns, or at least socially oriented subject matter. For him, though he acknowledged Ibsen's contributions to the possibilities of a more open theater, the older writer remained essentially inside. Sharing in part what was then, as now, the reductive view of Ibsen, Strindberg saw his great fellow Scandinavian largely as an ideologue (on the wrong side of most issues; he thought *A Doll's House*, for example, was part of a feminist plot), a forensic dramatist and a man with whose spirit he felt no compelling impulse to link his own.

For all that his work plunged more deeply into psychic jungles than Ibsen's, was more "unconscious" and more taken up with extreme emotional states, Strindberg was a much more ready and voluble expositor of his own aesthetic ideas and attitudes. Ibsen's extreme reticence means that his imaginative starting points as well as his thinking about aesthetic problems have to be almost wholly inferred from the internal evidence of the plays, although there is some important help available from those scattered, lofty, understated pronouncements on process and those oblique essays in self-definition that we generally persist in ignoring: "I have been more the poet and less the social philosopher than people have generally been inclined to believe."

Strindberg has been more easily recognized as a poet, one reason being the closer coherence with our own concerns of his inquest into aberration and of his ambiguous lyricism. He was extraordinarily conscious and clear-sighted about his art, knowing at all times that he was making something new and that these new compositions whose music was one of implication, internal logic, protean change, intuition and epiphany were not going to be easily understood by the public and not easily shrugged off by other playwrights. Out of his letters, his obiter dicta and, most important of all, his prefaces to his own plays there takes shape a history of a revolution in imagination, one that amounted to nothing less than the overthrow of a sanctified way of organizing experience into the formal patterns of drama, at the same time as it was an opening out to new kinds of experience. (And it is this simultaneity, the response to the claims of new and not-yet-identified experience and the necessity to find means for its disposition as art, that we so often lose sight of because of our habit of thinking of art as the *record* of experience and not as its transformation.)

The history begins with Strindberg's first plays in the mood or genre of what we call naturalism. To this moment he is nearly everywhere taught as having composed two distinct and even inimical kinds of plays, two major kinds, that is, in addition to the historical pieces with which he filled out his dramatic *oeuvre*. "Naturalistic" and "symbolic": the two species go on bearing their names in the textbooks like identification plates outside the cages in a zoo, with nothing to connect them as the work of a single imagination except a theory of psychological change or else one of cultural inevitability.

Strindberg, according to the first of these notions,

went from the naturalistic to the symbolic in his writing when his psyche had passed through some similar process, something that is usually described (although never explained) as his deepening emotional instability and near madness. What this ignores is that during the last years of his life Strindberg wrote a kind of play that cannot be labeled either naturalistic or symbolic, that even at his maddest he was never less than lucid about his aesthetic procedures, and that in any case the word "symbolic" tells us almost nothing about the nature of his art at any time. The bias here in favor of the "real" over the "symbolic" is, however, striking; even when the later, so-called symbolic plays are preferred to the earlier ones, as by some commentators they are, the choice is usually made on the grounds of a governing notion of art as a form of pathology—interesting, important, but aberrant for all that—and a particular feeling for Strindberg as both a conscious and unconscious explicator of pathology's ways.

A related approach is through history: Strindberg's symbolic plays are seen as reflections of the general cultural breakup and ferment, as icons of the new "dissociated" sensibility and the onrushing movement of all art into abstraction. What both these theories do of course is throw on to psychology or intellectual history the burden of finding out why his art was as it was and why it showed itself as it had to.

Beyond this, these theories, these ways of looking at art as history and at artists as its more "imaginative" scribes, leave out all awareness of the artist as the man who is intent on solving the problems of the imagination. These problems may be seen as the questions that are presented to the mind and sensibility by history as itself problematic—not in its internal political, moral or social dilemmas, but in its capacity of being *all there is,* its deficiencies of being, its holes, its muddled ontology, the possibility that it might be something else. History is what has been and is; art, the imagination in its form-giving mode, is the series of acts by which it is demonstrated that actuality can be other than it has been. The problems of the imagination have then to do with the means of accomplishing this demonstration, and if you believe this about art, the resolution of these problems is the only "solution" to history that we possess.

When in his late thirties Strindberg wrote his first plays in the atmosphere of what we call naturalism—*The Father* and *Miss Julie*—he had behind him a body of traditional and *acceptable* work, plays on historical themes such as the established Swedish theater was easily able to assimilate. But during the years immediately preceding the writing of *The Father* in 1887, he had done scarcely any writing for the theater at all. The stage, he wrote, was "mere pose, superficiality and calculation," something "reprehensible" when compared to poetry or fiction, for example, fixed in conventions, impermeable to new consciousness, lacking almost all means for the expression of thought. During this period he wrote mostly autobiographical books and engaged heavily in psychological and sociological research, some of it eccentric but most of it of an uncommonly advanced and radical kind. It was a period, too, of marital discord and sexual turmoil of the kind he was to experience even more violently later on.

When he went back again to writing plays, it was evidently with a new morale and ambition. Having engaged in an exploration of his own being during the creation of the autobiographies, he was prepared now for an expansion of the self into drama, an investiture of its events and scenes with the actualities of his own experience and nature. It was something that among his contemporaries Ibsen alone, in his oblique and scarcely visible way (scarcely visible, at any rate, since *Brand*), had done. But to accomplish this, to put dramatic form to the uses of the self, meant having to apply pressure to the reigning notions of characters in drama. Inhabitants of a world outside the specificities and exigencies of personal being, archetypes and stock figures of a protected universe of publicly maintained artifice, bound to the expected gesture and the categorical utterance, dramatic characters stood against personality, against private vision and all visions of private actuality.

In the *Biographia Literaria* Coleridge had written: "There have been men in all ages who have been impelled as by an instinct to propose their own nature as a problem, and who devote their attempts to its solution." Strindberg was such a man, and we mostly see his works as those kinds of attempts; what we don't so easily see is how the solution to himself lay in his being able to solve the problems of his art, to be able to create it.

In the preface to *Miss Julie* Strindberg composed a brilliant, elaborate justification for the dramatic practices of the play, for its aesthetic choices, and a manifesto for much future change on the stage. At the heart of his argument was the recognition of what "character" had come to mean on the stage and of how his own aesthetic urgencies could no longer be contained within that circumscribed meaning and use:

The word "character" has, over the years, frequently changed its meaning. Originally it meant the dominant feature in a person's psyche, and was synonymous with temperament. Then it became the middle-class euphemism for an automaton; so that an individual who had stopped developing . . . in other words, stopped growing—came to be called a "character," whereas the man who goes on developing, the skillful navigator of life's river, who does not sail with a fixed sheet but rides before the wind to luff again, was stigmatized as "characterless" (in, of course, a derogatory sense) because he was so difficult to catch, classify and keep tabs on. This bourgeois conception of the immutability of the soul became transferred to the stage, which had always been bourgeois-dominated. A character, there, became a man fixed in a mold, who always appeared drunk, or comic, or pathetic, and to establish whom it was only necessary to equip with some physical defect . . . or else some oft-repeated phrase . . . This oversimplified view of people we find even in the great Molière. Harpagon is a miser and nothing else . . . So I do not believe in "theatrical characters." And these summary judgments that authors pronounce upon people—"He is stupid, he is brutal, he is jealous, he is mean," etc.—ought to be challenged by naturalists, who know how richly complex a human soul is . . .

The bourgeois conception of the immutability of the soul which Strindberg speaks of was a central incitement to that widespread action by which abysses were opened up before traditional art in the late nineteenth century. Dostoevsky's underground man was of course the model of the slap in the face administered to such complacency. For the theater, the bourgeois art par excellence, to which as Strindberg says the notion was transferred, naturalism was one principle of dissent. Bourgeois life being itself a life of more or less strict appearances, the life of the stage, whose art is wholly a matter of appearances, had been asked to provide the kind of reassurance that goes much beyond specific moral or social questions; reassurance lay in the manner in which things were done in the theater, in the perpetuation of dramatic forms that bodied forth changelessness, logic, completion, an exhibition and parade of the soul's categorical and perennial identity. And the naturalistic ethic was inspired, in its most interesting manifestations, by an awareness of change.

Since they are modern characters [Strindberg went on in the preface] living in an age of transition more urgently hysterical at any rate than the age which preceded it, I have drawn my people as split and vacillating, a mixture of the old and new . . . My souls (or characters) are agglomerations of past and present cultures, scraps from books and newspapers, fragments of humanity, torn shreds of once-fine clothing that has become rags, in just the way that a human soul is patched together.

The note that is struck in this paragraph is of course the modern psychological one, that accent of inquest and pathology and that awareness of the dissolution and dismemberment of the long-established unitary sense of self which the conscious elements of society had known, or at any rate proclaimed. It had been heard considerably before this in poetry, with Baudelaire as its progenitor, and in fiction, with Dostoevsky, and was now (1888) the increasingly dominant chord. But even though the theater in the early nineteenth century had for one of the few times in its postclassical history anticipated a general shift in sensibility through the plays of the German dramatists Buechner, von Kleist and Grabbe, their work had been lonely, aberrant and premature, which is to say it had not given rise to a new tradition or atmosphere, so that it was left for Strindberg, at this period of the dramatic imagination, to begin one. The thing to see now is how the increased psychological knowledge and intuition was absorbed into the making of a work of art, to issue there as something more than a report from a brilliant, wayward academy.

When we look at *Miss Julie* under the sign and governance of naturalism, it seems to be, like *The Father* before it, a work whose energies and apparatuses derive from life rather than from the stage, from an observed and inhabited world of social and psychic pathology into which acute insights have been made and a series of passionate incidents, a "plot," devised for their incarnation on the stage. A hard, violent, tightly constructed *equivalent* has been found for nature, in this case human nature in its extreme aspects of aggression, envy, fear, hatred, lust and so on. The naturalism of the play thus consists in its fidelity to these emotions as they show themselves in the world and not as abstract counters in a theatrical game, and the drama's revolutionary importance consists in its having gone beyond artifice and stock theatrical representation, in its having *told the truth*.

These are the assumptions on which the play is usually taught, and they are sophisticated assumptions for the most part. To hold them means, to begin with, to be open to the presence in art of emotion of a disturbing kind, not such an easy thing to be, and beyond that to be able to trace a kind of process, the aesthetic action itself, by which such emotion can make itself felt as significant. And yet the notion of equivalence—the idea that art making is the creation of counterparts to what exists already in other shapes—turns this way of contemplating plays and other works into a belief in art as surrogate history, as moral or social or psychological truth in a special form.

It leads finally, however much the pull of a sensuous appreciation holds out against it, to *Miss Julie*'s being seen as a psychological or sociological document, or rather as both at once, its subject being changing class relations, the decadence of the Swedish aristocracy and the simultaneous rise of an aggressive, insensitive proletariat, along with the psychosexual manifestations and analogues of such a process. In the same way Chekhov's plays, so mysteriously and deceptively clear, full of arguments that make no points and of a reality that cannot have existed anywhere else, are nevertheless interpreted as "dramatized" accounts of the descent, through ennui, failure of nerve and irresistible social disqualification, of the Russian upper classes in the face of an ascending bourgeoisie.

The trouble with such interpretations (if it weren't trouble enough that for even their historical and sociological value to remain intact the most pointed and coerced analogies to our own experience have continually to be set out) is of course that they leave almost no space for the plays as art, which is to say for their existence as new, independent truths, new actualities. *Miss Julie* is indeed taken from "life," from experiences that have been gone through and not simply appropriated from the literary, the *invented*, past, and in its action a paradigm may indeed be traced for the new psychosocial actualities that have been the arena of those experiences. That, at the deepest level, was what naturalism was all about: a wheeling movement back to the sources in history of imagination, which had been feeding off itself, with more and more jejune results, for generations.

And yet that highest value of naturalism, that *truthfulness* (which art has again and again to recover), was something that had to be won aesthetically, achieved within the work and not simply applied there, as though through a transfer from one realm to another. Being so created, such truthfulness is no longer the equivalent or the recasting of data that has been obtained somewhere else, and it is no longer describable as a truth about "nature." Naturalism, like all such denotive terms, ceases to mean anything as soon as it is asked to account not for the starting point or the morale of a work of art but for the art itself.

Miss Julie is a social or psychological document only in so far as experiences have entered into it which it is possible to paraphrase into sociological or psychological information, such periphrasis being the responsibility of its perpetrator and not a true potentiality of the work. It is naturalistic only in so far as it begins with a repudiation of stage typologies and received artistic ideas, and as it wishes to be true, or rather—and most importantly— to *not be untrue* to what has been felt and observed. The poet is the man who sees, Ibsen had said, and Strindberg always had his eyes open. But what he saw was something more complex, fatal and unlocalized, above all more personal and unsystematic, than the changing class structure in Sweden or the armaments of a sexual combat, both of which served his purposes for the play as a kind of pretext, a necessary physical and histrionic ground. His preface tells us in part what he had *noticed*: how men and women have become "split" and "vacillating, a mixture of the old and new," how human souls are "fragments," "torn shreds . . . patched together."

To write a play is a problem in imagination, and just as Ibsen had had to struggle with the technical means available to him, to find means that would still be dramatic in a theater confined to only certain kinds of imaginative arrangements, so Strindberg had to devise a new kind of play, and not merely, as he remarked, "to create a new drama by pouring new ideas into the old forms." The play he needed to create was one that against all recent precedent would not simply incorporate what he had discovered, or *seen*, but would exist as the discovery itself.

The form he was seeking, in other words, was one in which fragmentation, gaps in connections, discontinuity, self-division and vacillation would be the content itself, the true subject of the play. This was to constitute the real revolution, the alteration in experience that now had its aesthetic form, which in turn provided a new experience. Men lived, Strindberg had seen, in a new atmosphere, a changed medium, and against this interrupted and discontinuous air they went on trying to bring about continuity and wholeness by fiat, by *previous* forms of the imagination, in so far as they tried to do the thing through art. Plays had been images of wholeness, whether they were farces, melodramas or "naturalistic" and sober dramas; their very forms were in opposition to the way life was being most crucially known and felt.

At the center of Strindberg's changed dramaturgy for

Miss Julie is the remarkable compression he achieves in making the events of a single night issue in a tragic denouement. In this era of the theater such compression would have been employed only for the purposes of a swift unfolding of melodramatic or farcical events, as in the rapid, circumstantially linked, "outer-directed" plays of Scribe or Sardou. In *Miss Julie* it is the effect of a substantial cutting away of integumentary material, of all that explanation and exposition that had burdened the "serious" theater and made bourgeois tragedy, where it existed, into something very like a sermon on the logic and coherence of human life, no matter how disastrous the action being portrayed might be. The connections in this play are inward for the most part, unstated, carried by implication in the gestures and utterances of the two main characters, whose conversation is mainly a series of instigations to internal activity rather than an exchange of information, a species of repartee or a means of advancing the "action" of the drama.

(In the preface Strindberg comments on his use of the dialogue: "Here I have somewhat broken with tradition by not making my characters catechists who sit asking stupid questions in order to evoke some witty retort. I have avoided the symmetrical, mathematically constructed dialogue of the type favored in France, and have allowed their minds to work irregularly, as people's do in real life when, in conversation, no subject is fully exhausted, but one mind discovers in another a cog which it has a chance to engage. Consequently, the dialogue, too, wanders, providing itself in the opening scenes with matter which is later taken up, worked upon, repeated, expanded and added to, like the theme in a musical composition.")

The play's action advances, as it were, by fits and starts, by reversals, leaps and regroupings, although the dominant motif and impetus remains the movement toward Miss Julie's final loss of self-esteem and subsequent (implied) suicide. Yet there is no single motive for her action: "Another thing that will offend simple souls is that the motivation of my play is not simple and that life is seen from more than one viewpoint . . . This multiplicity of motive is, I like to think, typical of our times. And if others have done this before me, then I congratulate myself in not being alone in my belief in these 'paradoxes' (the word always used to describe new discoveries)."

Yet Strindberg was almost wholly alone in this "paradox" when it came to the stage. The crucial thing to notice about Julie's suicide is that it is not brought about by anything inexorable in the working of the plot; it is not even, properly speaking, a denouement at all, not an inevitable outcome of a logic of cause and effect. Jean has seduced her, as the drama's central event, but even the fact that the news will become known to everyone is clearly no sufficient reason for killing herself, and Strindberg makes no pretense (a conventional playwright would have made a mainstay out of it) of its being so. Nor is her shame a sufficient reason either, even if such a thing could have been, as it is not, "dramatized," made into an active force, a motive.

Julie has killed herself, in rather the same way that Ibsen's Hedda Gabler did, because she cannot live (we do not die from our deaths, Charles Peguy wrote, but from our whole lives), and she has discovered this truth—or rather the play is the process of such discovery—through what she has been made to feel and think and say. She doesn't hang together, she lacks a principle of coherence, which is what self-esteem ultimately depends on; she is "split" and "vacillating." The "plot" is the story of her self-division, the image of it, not a vehicle in which she travels to her destruction. And the play in its entirety is the very form of such being, the new aesthetic environment for what has up to now been only intuition and feeling.

Julie of course is only half the play, one of its duelists,

and in being absorbed in her fate we tend to lose sight of that of her adversary, the servant Jean. Nothing demonstrates better that Strindberg was not engaged in writing history than that the latter character also "loses," is made aware of his own unfreedom, his riven and incoherent self. He prods Julie to suicide but he cannot really live either, being on one level still bound to his subservience, fear and unaccountable guilt—his psychology—and, more deeply, to his invented and therefore sterile persona. They have fought each other to a standstill: "You take all my strength from me, you make me a coward," he tells her at the end.

In the most subtle fashion Strindberg has arranged one of his "dances of death," in which elements and faculties of the soul (for that is what these characters are beneath their provisional and tactical incarnations) move to administer death blows that have been conceived in a fatality known and lived through before this—the death of the consistency and harmony of the self—and that are now fictions, strokes of the imagination which has erected their new environment, so that they may be delivered from chaos, dispersion and the fate of being mere nameless impressions or, worse, data.

This new environment, a realm of existence for characters who had been dislodged from their habitual function in drama as *summary judgments* or as metonymic actions, had been built up by Strindberg at certain public costs and with some incompletions. As he had anticipated, people were disturbed and distracted by the absence of a single point of view, for this, like Ibsen's spiriting away of Nora at the end of *A Doll's House*, was more truly revolutionary than the violent moral vision that the play was in one of its appearances offering. They were disturbed, too, by the drama's elisions and ellipses, the way it moved to invisible promptings and arrived suddenly at its climaxes with only the faintest sound of theatrical machinery being heard.

Yet for the most part, again like Ibsen, Strindberg had remained within the largest conventions of the stage. His characters, although complex, unprogrammatic and unco-erced—souls now and not automata—were still recogniz-able, unified in their essential presence within the drama, possible to "identify" with, no matter how difficult that might be. His plot, though subterranean and unmechan-ical, still moved in a linear fashion, and his narrative could be repeated, which is to say paraphrased. Ten years later, after a series of further new-naturalist plays and an in-terval of silence during which for six years he lived in his "inferno," Strindberg wrote a play, *To Damascus*, that broke wholly through the bounds of drama as they had existed until then.

The True and Only Crisis of the Theater

**NOTES FOR A SCENARIO ON
DRAMA, MOVIES, ACTING,
ILLUSION AND REALITY**

1. An Admission

For the past year I have been teaching a seminar in playwriting at the Yale School of Drama. It's a famous course, Playwriting 47, which has been given continuously for over forty years, or ever since it was started at the school by George Pierce Baker, who was as famous as a professor of playwriting can be. Eugene O'Neill was one of his students and Thomas Wolfe another (both at Harvard, where the course started; on the wings of it Baker was wafted to Yale, where he was given a whole new department as well as a large Schubert-type theater to play with), along with a good many other lesser dramatists and writers. So it's a pretty formidable tradition I inherited, and I felt my responsibility. I think I have discharged it, too, the only thing that might bother an inspection board being the fact that during thirty weeks of interesting, often useful discussions with nine or ten young playwrights we talked at least as much about movies as about drama.

2. The Shortest Possible History of Modern Drama

When Nora kept on going after she'd slammed the door
on her husband, she did something more than disconcert
and bewilder audiences, who sat waiting for *A Doll's House*
really, *properly*, to end, and discomfit critics, who wrote
that Ibsen had surely turned freedom into libertinism.
She set the idea of dramatic "characters" back on its heels,
not by being an unpleasant kind of heroine, one who
acted against accepted moral and social values (this was
what we might call the manifest content of the dream),
but by stepping outside the accepted framework in
which all stage characters were supposed to be contained.
That is to say her chief dramatic reality, her final presence
in the imagination, was established at one stroke by absence, by her decision to take off, to refuse physically to
support the dramatic situation (a very different matter
from not supporting the moral one) or bring it to a
resolution. Onlookers were not to find out—fatal condition
for the old easygoing entente between playwright and
spectator—what happened to her, what she was *now*, what
she'd been brought to; the play hadn't fulfilled drama's
traditional task: to bring characters from one known place
to another. The demand was heavy for some time that
Ibsen bring her back in a new play that would fill up the
hole at the end of the first one. (It was plugged at a number of performances by new endings written by local theatrical types.)

But the holes kept opening up. August Strindberg was
responsible for some very large ones. "Time and space do
not exist," he wrote in the preface to *A Dream Play*.
"On a slight groundwork of reality, imagination spins
and weaves new patterns made up of memories, experiences, unfettered fantasies, absurdities, and improvisations."
(Isn't that a concise vocabulary for almost everything we
think of as modern in drama?) "The characters split,

double, and multiply," he went on, "they evaporate, crys-
tallize, and converge." And they also fly out of reach of
logic, conventional psychology, history, the reigning spirit
of entertainment and all structures of morality.

Almost all the interesting drama of our century has
taken shape under Strindberg's auspices, or those of Alfred
Jarry, his contemporary, or at least in the atmosphere they
made inescapable. Strindberg, the larger figure, was, like
Mallarmé for poetry, a writer in whose wake drama had
to change; a source of freedom, a new direction, or a bulky
impediment, his work meant that a principle of *doing things
differently* had sovereignty now. What chiefly had been
overthrown, what couldn't be restored to the hegemony
it had had in nineteenth-century drama, was the idea of
stage characters as coherent, consistent, orderly; as sim-
ulacra of our own presumedly coherent existences; as substitute, enacted biographies. The dismantling of plot accompanied this destruction of character, an event in
dramatic history parallel to activities in fiction, music and
painting designed to bring about the end of heroes, mel-
odies and subjects. We were no longer to be taken from
one place to another in the course of the evening, made
to feel that we'd been on a journey from darkness to light,
problem to solution, unmeaning to meaning. From Chekhov
down to Beckett, characters go nowhere, or struggle
against being propelled (the secret of Chekhov's purported
"static" quality), just as they struggle with their remaining
life as stage personages against easy recognition, against
being "identified" with. Who of us has met in the street
Gogo, Azdak, Ubu, Enrico IV, or the police chief in *The
Balcony*?

Strindberg again, in the preface to *Miss Julie:*

The word "character" has, over the years, frequently
changed its meaning. Originally it meant the dominant fea-

ture in a person's psyche, and was synonymous with temperament. Then it became the middle-class euphemism for an automaton; so that an individual who had stopped developing, or who had molded himself to a fixed role in life . . . came to be called a "character," whereas the man who goes on developing, the skillful navigator of life's river, who does not sail with a fixed sheet but rides before the wind to luff again, was stigmatized as "characterless" (in, of course, a derogatory sense) because he was so difficult to catch, classify and keep tabs on. This bourgeois conception of the immutability of the soul became transferred to the stage, which had always been bourgeois-dominated. A character, there, became a man fixed in a mold, who always appeared to be drunk, or comic, or pathetic, and to establish whom it was only necessary to equip with some physical defect, such as a clubfoot, a wooden leg or a red nose, or else some oft-repeated phrase . . . I do not believe in "theatrical characters." And these summary judgments that authors pronounce upon people—"He is stupid, he is brutal, he is jealous, he is mean," etc.—ought to be challenged . . . My souls (or characters) are agglomerations of past and present cultures, scraps from books and newspapers, fragments of humanity, torn shreds of once-fine clothing that has become rags, in just the way that a human soul is patched together.

There are other parts of the story: Pirandello gave his stage characters connections with life outside the theater, and called attention to the artificiality of dramas; Brecht told his audiences they weren't watching characters but actors impersonating characters; the surrealists cut all strings to recognizable behavior; at the Bauhaus they tried to make dramas out of abstractions, inhuman figments. Beckett came along to present the histories of historyless men, and Ionesco to detach language from personage and make speech the dramatis personae. To bring things down to the very moment: large dolls with actors *inside* them are the best things about *America Hurrah*; and mixed-media events, which use only the barest of scripts and in which nobody "acts," are where the action is.

3. Footnote and Correction to the Shortest Possible History

Certain playwrights persisted in behaving as though characters were still alive and plausible, and audiences persisted gamely with them. Certain critics went on writing essays about how character and plot are instrumentalities of exhibiting man's fate in action. Naturalism didn't die away as a category or a practice, though under dogged attack by other critics and by lyric types, experimentalists and madmen like Antonin Artaud. Arthur Miller wrote *Death of a Salesman* and many persons were brought to tears by a process we have to call identification. Forms in art are never wholly superseded. Painters have gone on painting portraits decades after Picasso blew up the genre with those three noses; novelists continue to write books about men in society as Balzac taught them to do, never dreaming that a Proust or a Joyce has supervened; there are still imagist poems coming out of Iowa. And people still go to the theater to identify with characters, not having been apprised of their death.

4. Some Clichés about the Theater

> The theater is eternal.
> Conflict is of the essence of drama. So is character. So is plot.
> Dramatic illusion is what makes the theater work; suspension of disbelief is the key to its operation.
> The theater, being "live," is a deeper, more basic, more important and more "human" art than the film.

Being a directly communal activity, the theater has the
power to bind us together the way no other art can.

We like theater because we feel our own lives to be
dramas, or would like to feel that they were.

The "crisis" of the theater is almost wholly a physical
and economic matter.

5. A Question

Why are most intelligent people, most people who are
interested in art in general, most bright young people,
most young people with ambitions to create works in the
area of performance, most good literary critics, most good
teachers, and most philosophers much more drawn to the
films today than to the theater?

6. On Boredom

That we are bored by most plays today is unquestionable.
Is this a matter of there being so many bad plays around,
or so little good acting in the good ones? But we're bored
by Shakespeare, too, and Molière and Greek tragedy (young
people have never before been so bored by classics),
by Shaw and Pirandello and Brecht. Even by Ionesco and
Genet. Tinkering with the classics, throwing out all the old
pieties of production, are measures of our boredom. When
we say that we want to make a Shakespeare play "work
for our time," we don't mean that we want to make it
relevant so much as that we want to make it stop boring
us. The Royal Shakespeare Company's *King Lear* and
Joseph Papp's *Hamlet*—the former a brilliant, steady feat
of skill, the other a clumsy, ragged affair—are united by
a common, admirable decision not to add to the stock of
boring objects. And both have been decried by people

who expostulate: "Where's the old passion, the old dignity, where's Shakespeare?" By which is meant, where's the lack of surprise, the predictability, the train that's been down the same track a hundred thousand times?

We're bored by actors, too, perhaps most by the best ones. By Sir Laurence Olivier, for example, who is a truly great actor, which is what enabled Joan Littlewood, a theater person as bored by "normal" theater as anyone could be, to say of him: "'Look at me! Look at me!' That's what this bloody chap and all the rest of these bloody nineteenth-century bastards keep saying up on that bloody stage!" This egotism, even when it's not exploited directly or even when it's entirely jettisoned, is what makes us bored—because it's of the nature of the stage—with Sir Laurence and Sir John Gielgud, Sir Alec Guinness and Sir Michael Redgrave, heirs of the nineteenth century.

Ionesco wrote, to explain his own boredom with the stage in the years before he decided to try to relieve it with a few plays of his own: "It was as though there were present two levels of reality, the concrete reality, impoverished, empty, limited, of these banal living men, moving and speaking upon the stage, and the reality of the imagination." He wasn't talking only about naturalism or drawing-room comedy; from a certain perspective, one that has freedom from convention, anyone on a stage in any traditional kind of performance appears impoverished and empty, a no longer useful lie. We find it hard to believe in "characters" any more: banal impersonations, jerry-built replicas of ourselves, surrogates who ask our indulgence and solicit our credence—to what end?

It's a commonplace now that boredom of a certain kind operates as an intention in much recent aesthetic practice. But what kind? I've always taken this boredom to mean that in certain new paintings, the films of Antonioni or Andy Warhol, the novels of Robbe-Grillet or

Claude Simon, to take only some examples, we are deliberately prevented from having what we might call enthu-
siasms, from having emotions and undergoing excitements,
whose corrupted origins lie in the aesthetic *habit of mind*
and which therefore prevent us from seeing the strangeness
and actuality of the work in front of us. It's rather like that
earlier revolution in which "beauty" was dethroned as the
aim of art, or in which at least the definition of the
beautiful was enormously expanded. The truth is that art
has continually to overthrow expectations about itself, to
move over and over again out of reach of the *aesthetic*.
In this new boredom (which is never wholly that; intimations of new kinds of pleasure stir around its edges) we
are deprived of what the artist considers false pleasures.
And a habit of liking art for its confirmation of previous
satisfactions, its repetitions, is one of the conditions in
reaction to which new art is made in every age.

Elements of a boredom which prevents us from jumping to conclusive delight, which keeps us from repetition
and complacency, are present in some of the most irrefut-
able plays of recent years: Gelber's *The Connection,* Pinter's
The Homecoming, Lowell's *Benito Cereno,* above all
Beckett's static dramas. But these works have managed
to overcome the other kind of tedium, that which we feel
in the face of the blandishments of drama generally. For
our boredom with the theater has to do with its very procedures, its declared and sanctified intentions, not with its
failures, however numerous these may be. What we have
found increasingly uninteresting as forms, the kinds of
creations drama traditionally makes, are its hitherto unquestioned means of conducting its business: illusion, impersonation, pretense, the stage as justified ruse.

We don't trust "live" replicas of ourselves; we don't
wish for surrogates to exhibit, through a series of inexorably
limited gestures, our "meanings"; we're turned off by people who *right in front of our noses* pretend to be *someone*

else. And we find it harder than ever to think of the expression or representation of emotion as having very much to do with any art at all; banality lies not in the quality or kind of emotion but in the superannuated impulse to bestow it on others. As though we couldn't have obtained it by ourselves.

7. *On Dramatic Illusion*

The idea of the stage as a magic place, a scene of prestidigitation, was never seriously challenged until this century. Through all the theater's vicissitudes of style, manner and subject, throughout all historical changes in dramaturgy, there persisted a belief in the efficacy of and necessity for dramatic illusion. By a mysterious process of sympathy and analogy, faith is engendered in the reality of what is taking place; false identities are accepted as true ones, invented acts as natural, arbitrary sequences and connections as inevitable. Acting is impersonation, imposture, the creation of beings—characters—whose "lives" (for this brief space of time) are accepted, deferred to, followed with passion or at least interest, or else rejected as not being of a worthy kind. Quarrels about acting, the classic one having to do with whether it's better for the actor actually to feel the emotions he's representing or be detached from them as pure instrument, never question the necessity of illusion but only the means of establishing it.

But then self-consciousness sets in. This sublime trick, dramatic illusion, is seen to have been flourishing in the void, for what is being conjured into existence is what has already existed: the illusions of the stage are the commonplaces of everyday life. It is felt, as Strindberg says, that bourgeois life, a life of strict *appearances,* is nearly conterminous with the uses of the theater. This is what lies behind the ensuing assault on naturalism and the recourse to dream, fantasy, the surreal and the unlifelike, as well as to poetry (unavailing as it's proved), as means of reinvigorating the life of the stage.

Mirror images, reflections, resemblances, human *fixtures* with which the era of naturalism replaced pumped-up typologies—villains, heroes, eccentrics, fathers, lovers, sufferers, understanders—such is what these "banal living men," actors, have been offering behind the magic circle of illusion. So effort is made to strike at them, at their expectedness, predictability, familiarity, their recapitulations of what we have already experienced, at their presumptuous narrowing of possibility, their fixing of traits, ideas, attitudes, gestures, appearances, human rhythms, moods, emotions—singly or in packages of twos and threes —into incarnations, stiff, presumptuous, *completed* beings. The history of the theater since 1880 is a record of attempts to work free from the morass of illusion.

8. *Three Questions*

Psychology, which works relentlessly to reduce the unknown to the known, to the quotidian and the ordinary, is the cause of the theater's abasement and its fearful loss of energy.—ANTONIN ARTAUD

. . . the theater often does not portray the changes of man and of the world but rather gives an image of an unchanging man in an unchanging universe. Yet we all know that the world changes, that it changes man and that man changes the world. And if this is not what ought to be the profound subject of any play, then the theater no longer has a subject.—JEAN-PAUL SARTRE

The aim of the theater as a whole is to restore its art, and it should commence by banishing . . . this idea of impersonation, this idea of reproducing nature . . . that frantic desire to put "life" into their work . . . no longer would there be a living figure to confuse us into connecting actuality and art; no longer a living figure in which the weaknesses and tremors of the flesh were perceptible. The actor must go and in his place comes the inanimate figure—the ueber-marionette we may call him.—EDWARD GORDON CRAIG

9. On Theaters of Non-Actors

Gordon Craig's idea has been tried, but masks, puppets, marionettes, inanimate figures of many kinds, haven't proved the answer to the problem of the stage. Belief is always possible to reawaken, and in some ways it's easier to believe in marionettes, who don't try to convince us that they're flesh and blood, easier to believe in their task—to create artificial, *aesthetic* life—than in actors, who have to try to *be* the thing whose existence has come about by fiat of the imagination. But marionettes and puppets remove only one dimension of the problem, deprived inevitably from human models, they can ultimately repeat only human gestures and attitudes, even though they've stripped away the tight sheathings of personality and character as we have been defining them. They are still pretenses, whereas the problem is more and more how to make real occasions.

Etienne Gilson writes: "There is no point in adding to reality images of natural beings, which, precisely because they are but its images, add nothing to reality. What matters is to turn out, not an image, but a thing; not to add an image to reality, but a reality to reality." The central procedures of contemporary poetry, fiction, music, dance, painting and sculpture are obedient to this dictum; the theater has struggled in the grip of image making.

In America, where we've produced no significant body of formal dramatic works, there is an increasing interest in theaters of improvisation and games, testimony to the dissatisfaction with the stage as a place for the conjuring up of images. The desire that it become an arena for new, original gestures, performed by actors who are no longer executors, *stand-ins*, but instigators and makers, lies behind the growing repudiation of formal texts as well as the increasing currency of words like "ritual," "myth" and "play" (the verb). A vocabulary with a potential for self-deception and indulgence of adolescent ambitions, it nevertheless also expresses an appetite for theater as an actuality rather than a reflection, an original gesture rather than an interpretive one—for theater, in other words, to stop being illusion.

The movement away from formal, pre-existing texts has been gathering speed for some time. "Why not conceive of a play composed directly on the stage, realized on the stage?" Artaud asked more than thirty years ago. Though he would most likely consider happenings to be not quite the thing he had in mind, Artaud doubtless would have been sympathetic to their intention. The great decrier of psychology and rationalism in the theater saw the supremacy of language as drama's widest curse, and happenings reduce verbal elements to a minimum. He hated the use of drama as a means of giving "information," ideas, or even perceptions about the world, since its proper function, he felt, was to provide visions—new and "terrible" myths. And happenings, while entirely scorning the "artistic" implications of words like "vision" and "myth" and having no traffic with emotions, terrible or otherwise, are theatrical actions rooted in a refusal to impart information and in a wish to be "about" nothing but themselves.

The central point about happenings, environments, mixed-media events and the like is that they've emerged out of an impulse to blot out as much as possible of the remaining distance between theater and life, to destroy the artificiality of drama, its inherent tendency to fix human actions and qualities and its reign as illusion. For there is nothing illusory about these new works; they are real events, distinguishable from the events of ordinary life only by a thin line (there will always be some line of demarcation; as long as we have a word like "happening," we are in the presence of something different from what takes place in our everyday lives, an increment and an analogy to it). Happenings and their successors are meant to indicate by their having been instituted at all that things do occur, that the world is to be looked at and seen freshly again and again.

A remark of John Cage, the philosopher of new theater if anyone is, illustrates what I mean to say: "Theater takes place all the time wherever one is, and art simply facilitates persuading one this is the case." The central implication here for the crisis of the theater is that as long as we think of drama as something to *go to* rather than as something that's a sign of everything else, as long as we regard it as illusion instead of a form of reality, we will go on being bored with it as we are bored, ultimately, with all illusions. The new movement to replace formal, textual, illusionist drama may not triumph soon or ever, but it isn't likely to fade quietly away.

10. Meanwhile, Back at the Art Theaters . . .

The notion that film is a rival and alternative to theater arose with the movies' origins and is to this day a commonplace idea. Whole eras of film history would seem to buttress such thinking; in the archives are thousands of movies that are nothing but filmed plays. Yet even when movies go outdoors, away from sets and props and walls, they clearly employ many of the materials of plays: actors, scripts, dramatic conflict, etc. It was André Malraux who I think first pointed out that only a misuse and misunderstanding of film art could lead to the conclusion that it was an art resembling that of drama; it resembled more nearly, he said, that of fiction. Yet while this is surely true aesthetically, film remains linked in a great many minds—and properly so—with drama: as alternative fields of practice, as alternative magnets for energies, as alternative ways of looking at and dealing with the world.

11. An Anthology of Comments on Film by Students of Drama at Yale

It's a more clandestine experience, darker than the theater.

Actors *perform* on a stage; that's very different from people *living* on a screen.

The camera can give a sense of greater reality than the stage, even in highly "unrealistic" movies.

Films are more responsive to the world around them than theater.

Movies add a new dimension by being open-ended; their techniques expand the imagination . . . they are a great jumping-off point for stimulating immediate thought: they present ideas visually which trigger emotional and intellectual responses much more rapidly than in the theater.

Film transcends reality much more easily than theater.

Movies are technical poetry. You have the potential of a totally controlled environment as opposed to the live quality of the theater.

Movies have the same advantage as the mind has—not being limited in space. There's an immediacy of transition that can't be achieved on the stage.

Films are inhuman, though they pretend not to be; that's a great attraction.

They concentrate and focus for you. It's easier to be involved and also not involved, depending on which you want to be.

Movies handle internals better than any other medium because they have a total range of vision.

Films always give the illusion of the First Time.

Movies have the possibility of all the speed of living without the time wasted—in the bathroom or sitting in a doctor's office. Godard can edit out the three or four frames it takes Belmondo to go from opening the car door in *Breathless* to stepping out.

Anything can happen in the movies.

Anything can happen in the movies. Like theater or any art, film, from one point of view, is also an illusion, but an illusion which doesn't pretend to be anything else. This is its source and ground of freedom: that unlike the theater it has no need to solicit our belief against the evidence of our senses. People "living" in that strange new habitat, a screen; actors "performing" on a stage—the difference is that a reality is being created in the former but in the latter merely an imitation. By being physically "unreal," something that doesn't exist except through an imaginative fiat, the aesthetic reality of film is all the more convincing, all the more supple and responsive. The traditional theater is locked into the physical world, wedded to bodies and language, and has to struggle perpetually against their clichés, against the inexorable exhaustion of possibility; film, on the other hand, extends possibility by being, in the most liberating sense, *abstract,* a series of planes, an arrangement of visual modalities, a juxtaposition and continuity of images which together do not mount up to a new image but a new thing. This is what the theater has found so hard to achieve and this is why its future, far from being a matter of local, contingent considerations, or a question of gaining a new redoubtableness or revived élan, is, in this era of the death of sacred cows, an absolute issue of survival.

MacBird!
and its Audience

The question of whether Barbara Garson's *MacBird!* is a good or bad work of art, or whether it is any kind of art at all, might by now seem irrelevant in the face of the extraordinary public awareness of it as a solid fact, a potent presence. Winds of praise and censure have blown mightily around the play ever since it moved from its origins as a West Coast underground document to infect a segment of the impressionable East with its young, anarchic virulence. A year or so later its status as an object of extreme provocation, of blissful fulfillment for some among us and pained revulsion for others, is fixed and ripe.

There is nothing remarkable about the revulsion, at least not on its broadest and most strident levels: to J. Edgar Hoover, for example, *MacBird!* is quite naturally and without the slightest reflection an appalling thing to have in our midst. Nor is it surprising that a good many genteel observers, prepared to give a welcome to most expressions of dissent—in theory if not right under their noses—should find their libertarian sentiments pushed to the breaking point by the play's undisputed vulgarity and coarse aggression. And finally it is not surprising either that *MacBird!* should have alienated, through its imputation of the assassination of President Kennedy to Lyndon Johnson, a good number of persons who cannot be said to be tainted with either jingoism or excessive gentility, although perhaps with excessive literal-mindedness.

But have the thumbs gone down for these reasons alone? Is to repudiate *MacBird!* going to be the emblem of an alliance with fascists, prudes and squares? Aren't there any grounds for such a repudiation (which will in any case cost you as a minimum penalty your ticket to the fashion show) other than those that have to do with taste, political attitude, or notions of fair play? I think there are, but they are not to be discovered internally, within any rounded, self-describing contours of the play, until there has first been an examination into the nature of the affirmation which has surrounded it like a praetorian guard. *MacBird!* has become much more than the sum of its own parts.

There is something extremely disconcerting about the quality of the endorsement the play has received, as though a man you might have been prepared to accept as a midget were to be recommended to you as a giant. Once it has moved past the level of "it's a free society, isn't it?" that endorsement swells into an ecstasy of response which attaches to Mrs. Garson's fable as though it were a redemption. At this point a kind of quasi-religious atmosphere has indeed formed, in which affirmation and negation are held together the way notions of good and evil are, to adore *MacBird!* being very much the theological complement of the wish to exorcise it. What we can be sure of is that from neither position have we received a true report of the piece's actual appearance, let alone its nature and significance. Like the elephant in the fable which was felt at different points by half a dozen blind men, *MacBird!* has been described—by enemies and adherents alike—in the most fragmentary, inaccurate and thoroughly misleading ways.

The matter is of a kind that forces back into debate just those questions of aesthetic reality and its counterfeits (or its supplanters) which the play's booming career might seem to have rendered idle. Such forms of unseeing, such literal blindnesses as have affected the majority of the commentators on *MacBird!*, seem to afflict the intellectual community at certain times of tension and frustration when a work of art, or a work in the guise and tradition of an art, makes its appearance behind an especially bold and aggressive political or social intention. At these times ordinarily judicious men begin grinding axes with a fury difficult to comprehend, and the spirit of criticism undergoes a radical change from an ideal of inquiry to an actuality of ferocious tendentiousness, the work itself being thrust like a battering ram against a social or political or even moral situation against which all other pressures seem to have failed. Thus does the heyday of the notion of art as a weapon return, *mutatis mutandis,* to suit the spirit of the age.

The last play to instigate a full-scale condition of this kind (for the theater, that mostly supine institution, moments of furor and incitement are rare) was Rolf Hochhuth's *The Deputy.* From the first rumor about its theme— Pope Pius XII's silence in the face of the Nazi extermination of the Jews—aesthetic considerations and even routine theatrical ones were swept aside by a different pressure of opinion and response, one grounded not in an experience or expectation of dramatic forms, but in history, in everything that had been in existence, awaiting reanimation as it were, *before* the play presented itself to view: personal anguish, political hatred, religious antipathy. The play itself became the occasion for a release and exercise of feeling that could hardly be accounted for by its clumsy, tendentious, not wholly convincing political assertions and, more importantly, by its fearfully deficient dramaturgy. The latter was either literally blotted out so as not to impede the free flow of a feeling that would have seized on any pretext, or else, in certain other minds, weary of the base "fictions" of theater, was made to provide the basis for an unsettling new thing, a work whose significance and strange moral beauty were said to lie precisely in its not being art at all, but fact, history, anti-art. The so-called Theater of Fact began when Rolf Hochhuth brushed aside, although with great awkwardness, the claims of the imagination to have the last word, or for that matter the first.

But *The Deputy* was a far less complex phenomenon than *MacBird!* In Hochhuth's play the issues, however grave, were relatively few and circumscribed; the history it dealt with, however atrocious, was completed; the emotions it released, however agonizing, were clear and decisive. Even more crucially, the central material of the play *was* factual, whatever the interpretation of those facts might have been: the Germans did kill millions of Jews, Pope Pius did fail to speak out publicly against the slaughter. In *MacBird!* on the other hand, nothing central is factual (unless LBJ's crudity and intolerable folksiness are to be regarded as "facts," a strange point we will have to return to): John F. Kennedy was not killed by Lyndon Johnson, Earl Warren did not accept his commission as a sinister assignment to cover up the truth. At least whatever one might privately think about these things, they do not have the finished, assured, implacable and irreversible conditions of facts, of demonstrated history, and therefore cannot be expected to yield the same effects on the stage as if they had. (That large segments of the audiences at *MacBird!* do stretch out to meet them as facts, yearn to meet them that way, is, as we shall see, an element of its undeniable effectiveness for just those spectators.)

Beyond this the two plays would seem to present widely different propositions about their aesthetic reality or lack of it. To admire or at any rate to be stirred by *The Deputy* did not mean, as I have said, that one had to admire its techniques and theatrical procedures; one could simply not see them, not see their blatant sentimentality and derivativeness (these defects were in part the fault of the wretched New York production). Or else one could find in the text's heavy, graceless, documentarylike movements the outlines of an exciting counterdemonstration to the aloof, polished, *ineffective* gestures of art. Nobody intelligent, so far as I am aware, ever praised Hochhuth for his artfulness. But the evidence seems to suggest that to admire *MacBird!* is in most cases to see it as high drama, or rather, much more interestingly, to see it as replenishing and revivifying the erstwhile high art of drama by its deliberately "low" and inelegant capers. The jubilation over the play's political and social *démarche* is fused in the minds of its most ardent supporters with gratefulness for an almost revolutionary act of theater.

And yet for all their internal differences and the differences in the responses made to them, *The Deputy* and *MacBird!* share a common impulse and participate together in a new and expanding development of culture. In a crucial sense they are both outside culture, at any rate outside the culture that has always been spelled with a capital C. And although all new works of art always step outside previous culture, their aim is to reconstitute it in a new shape, whereas for these two playwrights there is no such intention. Their hostility or indifference to art means that their works exist without any interest in aesthetic justification or in being added to the stock of aesthetic objects; they have not been created to please the imagination or even, as innovation has perennially sought, to change it, but to change life, to intervene in it. And for their adherents, however much they might cling to aesthetic notions, the impulse to intervene in life, to have such interventions as these made in their behalf, is just as strong.

One of the most unpleasant aspects of the whole *Mac-Bird!* efflorescence is the way critics and other writers of stature have sung hosannas—vague, orotund ones—to its reputed literary achievements. Only Peter Brook among the play's rhapsodizers has admitted that its literary value is nil, although to him this is in fact a source of its strength. As for the others, nothing could be clearer than that they have felt compelled to dignify their raw social motive, their craving for a borrowed potency, by placing the enterprise under a literary star, so that there is something grimly amusing in the spectacle of Mrs. Garson standing off in bewilderment at the literary tributes and protesting, with complete honesty, "I'm not a playwright at all."

In this community of interest, this merging, at least temporarily, of the high-minded and the low, of the literary and the antiliterary, of certain kinds of despair, aggression, impatience and animus (not otherwise likely to be compatible), of conflicting and even contradictory attitudes toward art and intellect reconciled here by a provisional agreement about life—in all this may be discerned the lineaments of a new, barbaric pragmatism.

No other words can do justice to the alarming sense one has, after reading *MacBird!* and seeing it performed, of the gulf between what one has encountered and what other minds, some of them among those one most esteems, seem to have experienced. As a text the play has flashes of wit (a good percentage of them set off before the action ever gets rolling, as in the devising of the dramatis personae itself: the MacBirds, the Ken O'Duncs, the Earl of Warren, the Egg of Head, the Wayne of Morse) and an occasional aptness of paraphrase from Shakespeare, more of the best strokes, incidentally, being from *Hamlet* than from *Macbeth*—"To see, or not to see," "Neither a burrower from within nor a leader be," and so on. And there are sporadic hits on Mrs. Garson's own, as when she has the Egg of Head and Robert Ken O'Dunc say, respectively, as exemplary expressions of political fence-straddling, "I know you think I'm acting like a toad/But still I choose the middle of the road" and "I basically agree with both positions."

But there is also a pervasive clashing of vocabularies— the truest mark of the play's origin in a prep-school mental-ity—which issues less in comic effect than in ugly, pointless incongruity: "Hark, hark! His helicopter o'er the range!" or "Aye, here my liege, the output's based upon/A partial computation of the data." More damaging, there is a per-sistent straining to keep up with the chosen plot, a backing and filling, a pressure to include long stretches of unper-tinent and internally arid material, a continual arriving at the necessity, to quote the key line of *Macbeth* itself, of "outrunning the pauser, reason," at the center of which latter movement lies the ultimate necessity of including the murder of his leader by the protagonist.

Worst of all, the writing frequently descends, when-ever Mrs. Garson is thrown wholly on her own resources and her own poetic and moral spirit shines unimpededly through, to a level of sensibility that is truly appalling. The witches are stirring their brew:

> Taylor's tongue and Goldberg's slime,
> McNamara's bloody crime
> Sizzling skin of napalmed child,
> Roasted eyeballs, sweet and mild.
> Now we add a fiery chunk
> From a burning Buddhist monk.
> Flaming field and blazing hut,
> Infant fingers cooked and cut,
> Young man's heart and old man's gut,
> Groin and gall and gore of gook
> In our caldron churn and cook.

The English critic Nicholas Tomalin, writing in *The New Statesman*, has tersely said everything about this that needs saying: "Why Goldberg's *slime*? Clearly, because it rhymes with crime. Who is seriously concerned with self-immolating Buddhists? Not someone who writes of chunks of monks."

And yet the play "works," we are told; it exhilarates, it liberates, freeing us as by some alchemical action from the congealed, impotent political and social stances, the postures of frustration we have for so long been held in, the inarticulateness which has prevented us from making ourselves known vis-à-vis our public and communal fate. At last the inexpressible has been expressed, the whispered infamies uttered loudly. All the play's justification lies in this liberating and purgative action, which marks, it would seem, not only the rebirth of effective protest but of effective theater as well.

But *does* it work, even through some miracle by which the flagrant insufficiencies and outright barbarisms of the text are overcome, does it really work the way its proponents say it does? Does it work as psychic liberation, social release, political rejuvenation, or as any of those agencies of change which people have perennially wanted from art but which there is no clear evidence that it has ever really provided? Does it work as non-art? Are the energies it is supposed to release authentic? Do they have any permanence? Can they be translated into any kind of effective action? And finally, if it does work in some manner, does it do so at the cost of other values? Is the price of its effects too high?

A good many readers who found themselves repelled by the text of *MacBird!* have testified to one degree or another of seduction by the play on stage. There is nothing to surprise us in this. In an atmosphere of expectation it takes an enormous effort of detachment not to expect something yourself. A community has been formed and you are part of it; social and political passions are in the air, and it is the air you, too, breathe. Beyond that you find yourself succumbing to that mysterious and shameful Pavlovian response, independent of any moral or aesthetic considerations or indeed of judgment of any kind, which takes place whenever certain names and words—the names of the mighty and the words of the underlife—are uttered in new contexts of apparent risk. To hear the names of the eminent tossed about as though in a living gossip column, to hear four-letter words said *right out in public*, seem still to be, for the adolescence few of us ever wholly throw off, sources of a gratification that has its own source in an illusion of sophistication.

But *MacBird!* goes a good deal deeper than that. Writing in the magazine *New Politics*, the novelist Harvey Swados describes his own painful experience at a performance last winter. He tells how he sat at his tiny table in the Village Gate—a nightclub turned theater—among an audience composed of the youthful but also of a greater number of well-dressed thirtyish and fortyish persons than he had expected. The crowd was clearly well disposed toward the proceedings, if not rapturous at first. It had to ride through the play's frequent longueurs, those stretches of barren physical and verbal event which are integumentary in nature, designed to keep the creaky borrowed plot going (and which Swados is the only observer to have remarked on). But it was patient and it was rewarded when what it was really waiting for came at rhythmic intervals. "What a shit!" a recorded voice says of President MacBird, and as Swados notes, "the crowd comes to life with a roar . . . this is what it came for."

Swados goes on to argue that the source of this response lies in the fact that the political figures in the play are not only "in no way superior to us ordinary people, they are far worse. And from this the audience takes its pleasure." The insight is one key to the entire phenomenon of *MacBird!* Only an excessively crude commentary, and there have been many of them, can fail to see that Mrs. Garson's little bomb is not aimed exclusively at Lyndon Johnson (who in fact has a certain large, hideous charm, at least as Stacy Keach plays him in the New York production) or at LBJ together with the Kennedys, but at all politicians and indeed at politics itself. The point has been confirmed, with an entirely different value put upon it, by Robert Brustein, a first-rate critic whose usual taste and intelligence seem utterly to have deserted him in his fanatic sponsorship of *MacBird!*: "it is a work in which all political leaders are seen as calculating, power-hungry and bloody, and nobody comes off well."

What rises into question at this point is not the truth or falseness of this view; whether or not *all* political leaders are as Mrs. Garson depicts them is scarcely the issue—she could not be expected to know. But she has been expected, as a radical activist at the college level, to think, to have attitudes, and the apotheosis of *MacBird!* may be accounted for in one way by the converging of her attitudes with those of many others for whom she has become impresario, spokesman and anthem writer. At the heart of these attitudes, residing there with more or less well-defined shape, more or less consistency, is a nihilism more profound and sweeping, although also more shoddy and literally insincere, than any we have ever known before in our public life.

This nihilism is scarcely of Dostoevskian proportions. There is nothing black about it; it touches no metaphysical depths—or surfaces for that matter; it does not see existence as containing a hole which no amount of human organization or enterprise can fill; it wholly lacks that basis in self-loathing which implied a certain moral stature and which distinguished the nineteenth-century Russian movement beneath its political manifestations. A phenomenon essentially of the young, it makes a virtue of shunning thought and discovers itself instead in action of a kind which requires no antecedents and looks forward to no culminations. Mrs. Garson, as she has repeatedly insisted, has no desire to replace the political figures she is mocking with others; her whole purpose is to try to discredit the institution of politics itself.

That this is irresponsible is not to be established by a rejoinder to the effect that she offers nothing to replace what she is attempting to destroy; Mrs. Garson is not obliged to give us an alternative vision to the one she has of present politics. But she *is* under an obligation to make the present vision accurate, to make her play true, to give it true wit, true fantasy, true feeling. And since *MacBird!* deals with actuality, its whole apparatus of Shakespearean burlesque being designed to get a purchase on contemporary political and social data and the attitudes they give rise to, those facts have to be true, too. Yet it is not "true," not established, that Lyndon Johnson killed President Kennedy; Mrs. Garson admits that she doesn't believe it, which makes her irresponsibility in presenting it as true that much more contemptible. But what is even more contemptible is the defense she and her admirers have made, its central plank being the proposition that having chosen *Macbeth* she was consequently stuck with the plot. As Lionel Abel has written, in one of the most intelligent critiques of the play, "Imagine being stuck with the plot of *Macbeth!*" And even so, one can get unstuck, the simplest way being not to write the play at all.

But the atmosphere of irresponsibility that rises like a smog from *MacBird!* is not fully accounted for by its particularities—Johnson and the murder of Kennedy, the implication that Johnson also caused the death of Adlai Stevenson and Teddy Kennedy's plane crash. These are details and inevitable products of a broader and more disturbing species of irresponsibility, one that is best expressed in remarks Mrs. Garson has made about her own attitude toward her play. "I can assure you," she told an interviewer, "I didn't write a play that made me suffer . . . I didn't disturb myself in the least. It was easy."

It was easy. What a cool antidote to all our notions about the pain and difficulty of moral protest—Swift's lacerated breast, Blake's going dotty as he sang. Out of the suffering and moral horror of the Vietnamese war and the interracial situation in America, out of the crisis in democratic institutions and the particular personal crisis we all feel in relation to our sense of social being, out of universal sorrow and dilemma, this little nihilist from Berkeley, wrapped in her terrifying innocence and science-fictionlike freedom from past or future, sits down and without disturbing herself in the least proceeds to fashion a piece about which the most frequent admiring description is that it is "fun."

"Laughter comes as a reprieve," Ionesco has written; "we laugh so as not to cry." But we laugh at ourselves or at our potential selves or at our doubles—or else we are monsters. A new suffering is added to the world and a new indignity when in the name of moral protest a feeling of moral and psychic well-being steals over men who wish only to laugh at others. "This audience, this sensitive minority of Americans," writes Harvey Swados, "can find an outlet for its impotence only by yielding up to the pleasures of a nihilism which exempts them from any responsibility for the deeds which are being done, or any human indentification with the men who are committing enormities in their name."

The enormities will remain enormities; to despise *MacBird!* is not to endorse Lyndon Johnson—it is a mark of our corrupted atmosphere that one has to make the point. And the enormities will not be changed by bad art, or good art for that matter, or by non-art in the guise of art. If artists and intellectuals are so frustrated that they join up with activists to use *their* battering ram, they would be far better off if they would see that they cannot have it both ways and that it is they who have sold out. Then they could at least learn the price. And they would be in a far better position to recover from the realization, if they ever come to it, that the work they have backed has had no effect whatsoever, except a dry, sterile, incestuous stirring among the already converted, the self-righteous, the exempt.

For the most devastating irony about *MacBird!* is that it converts nobody and cannot even change the converted. In the mocking laughter it arouses there is no true release, no regenerative force, nothing but animus and impotence temporarily worked off and sent rising steamily into the upper air. Nobody who sits roaring at those antics by which a hated figure is made to look foolish—thus depriving even the hatred of its basis—or, so much more shameful, by which a previously admired figure is brought down to the same level, is likely to charge out of the theater and do a single thing to change the state of America or the world. If anything, it is possible to imagine a new and more thoroughgoing sense of impotence taking hold of the spirit once the atmosphere of fantasy is gone, once the play's spell, compounded of wish-fulfillment and the adolescent thrill of name-calling, is broken.

Two other things remain to be said. The hatred of Lyndon Johnson and the frustration that grips all of us who abhor the war in Vietnam have reached a point where, as Lionel Abel says, "no stick is apparently too dirty to beat our president with." Very well, no stick may be too dirty if you feel that you can accomplish something by wielding it. But what you have to accept is that by this pragmatic decision you are undermining the values which, presumably, your hatred of the President is at least partly inspired by. A dirty stick leaves dirt everywhere, not, least on your own hands.

Mrs. Garson, the young nihilist, cannot be expected to mind. But perhaps the most shameful aspect of the deification of *MacBird!* is the way men of other traditions and other values have thrown themselves at her feet. One might like to believe, as these fascinated elders apparently do, that *MacBird!* is the inspiriting creation of a new young breed liberated from outworn subtleties of conscience, pitched on a psychic plane above intimidation by authority, walking clear-eyed through a world of infinite man-made distortions, setting things right, cutting through the knots we have all been tied in with its keen, cold, bright new edge. It may be; but that edge may also be cutting through our lifelines—to the past, to our moral bases and the bases of our judgment, to our possibilities of acting, whatever the deadly pressures against it may seem to be, as responsible men and not as children.

*Our end is to arouse compassion
and then to change it into paradise.*
—JUDITH MALINA

The Living Theatre:
Materials for a Portrait of the Professional as Amateur

1. Background to Apocalypse

The Living Theatre began life nearly twenty years ago in a loft near Columbia, the creation of a young couple named Julian and Judith (Malina) Beck, who were, and are, very passionately involved with questions of social justice, pacifism, anarchism, the fate of human love and the destructions of technological civilization. They also were, and are, vegetarians, believers in astrology and, one is entitled to suspect, addicts of various other ready forms of mystic news. They are communitarians, utopians and advocates of a socialism that is primitive in its emphasis on shared property and goods (with a minimum of both) and wholly contemporary in its revivalist belief in the sharing of passions, ideals, destinies and secrets of the soul.

Julian Beck, now in his middle forties, is tall, thin, pale, high-domed, with a shelf of frizzy gray-brown hair canting down from the back of his head to his shoulders. He has a thin mouth, a large bony nose and eyes that are strangely light, intent and what is usually called piercing. His chief theatrical skill has always been as a stage designer, although he has done considerable acting and directing, too. His wife is a tiny woman, intensely black-haired, with a small round nose and mouth and large brilliant eyes, an elf with enormous energy, a gamin made of steel. Primarily and most successfully a director, she has done some literary work as an adapter of classic dramas and tinkerer with new texts, and has also acted a good deal. Like her husband, she has never been more than a gross amateur as a performer.

Being amateurish at some particular thing was never of much concern to the Living Theatre, which combined this quality with professionalism, skill with ineptitude, originality with cliché and coolness with frenzy in an invisible act of *making theater*, one that was at the same time a way of making a life. As part of that, the Becks were intent from the beginning on fashioning a public attitude toward what they had found mattered to them, and to their constituency, as social beings. What mattered, at least as much as dramatic art, was political reality, especially the reality of atomic weapons and, later, of the war in Vietnam. The Becks were ferocious activists who while managing to keep their productions mostly free of blatant *Tendenz* or explicit ideology were forever throwing out hints of their extra-aesthetic sympathies, most unmistakably by the aggressive, *épater le bourgeois* spirit in which they put on their plays.

It was often a painful and embarrassing experience to go to a Living Theatre production as a spectator full of good will and a readiness to shelve technical and even aesthetic objections in the interests of giving support to experiment and imaginative valor. In your seat, among an audience whose average age was certainly less than thirty and whose dress was as casual and even scruffy as any proletarian impresario could want, you were subjected to continual abuse for your bourgeois origins and presumed sympathies. It came directly at times in the form of harangues before the curtain went up or at intermissions, but most generally and subtly through the atmosphere of bare tolerance, the rugged hauteur, with which the whole enterprise took you in. The Living Theatre was forever trying to shame and convert the people who already believed in them and were manfully trying to go along.

But for us it was a case of *faute de mieux*. What sustained and propelled the Becks as people of the theater was the conviction, not especially widespread at the time, that drama should be arresting, difficult, fiercely contemporary, full of revelation and unrest, a personal encounter. This conviction, translating itself into a flawed, erratic but fervid spirit and methodology, came to recommend itself to a small but steadily growing number of intelligent persons for whom theater had become the emptiest of arts and a social occasion of stupefying inanity. The Living Theatre's productions were jagged, nervous, almost always technically deficient and sometimes wholly inept, but they were full of idiosyncratic zeal and intensity. Through these productions—stagings of classics, neglected and otherwise, modern works (often by poets such as Yeats, Cummings, W. C. Williams, Jeffers) and texts by unknowns—the Theatre offered for the greater part of its first existence the only stage enterprise in New York that could be said to have a soul. And in the last years before it closed its doors (on Fourteenth Street, where it had moved in the early fifties) it gave the American theater two of its most remarkable and vivifying recent works, *The Connection* and *The Brig*.

That the Theatre, apart from its predictable financial difficulties, should have been in crisis almost from the beginning was not a question of any inevitable conflict between aesthetic disinterestedness or professionalism on the one hand and political commitment on the other, not a question of the group's subject or theme but, in the first place, of the allocation of energies and loyalties. The Becks were forever dropping their theatrical activ-

ities to go off on a peace march or participate in a demonstration, occasionally winding up in jail and at these times
leaving playwrights, stagehands, actors ready to go on and
audiences with tickets in hand to get the news at the last
minute that the show was off. More than that, a painful
toll was taken in the company's morale by their leaders'
absolute indifference to any consistency and rigor in training or artistic preparedness, so that the invigorating ideas
about the stage—Artaudian emphases on ritual, violence
and the unconscious; their own vision of a community of
actors with a unified, coherent style and a rooted capacity for ensemble playing—flourished always under siege by
forgetfulness, disjunction and a sense of *other things to do*.

In time the procedural chaos and lack of quotidian
principles (large, overarching ideals and eschatologies were
always available for consolation) came down to a confrontation with pressures of ordinary citizenship. The Becks
were charged in 1964 with owing the United States government some $25,000 in admission taxes collected over the
years and never turned in, and upon their refusal to pay
(on the impassioned but naïve and ill-articulated grounds
that government ought not tax but should instead preserve
the life of so valuable and precarious a cultural endeavor)
had their theater closed down and were themselves sent
to jail for a few weeks. At the trial a certain quality of the
Becks, something we might call pushy martyrdom, was
more than ever on display. A sympathetic judge, prepared to tender the defendants the benefit of every doubt
and the fullest imaginative grasp of their predicament,
was obliged to give them minimal sentences in the face
of their refusal to admit even technical guilt and of Miss
Malina's strident, tearful, expertly staged denunciations
of him and of the social order that had had them hauled in.

Plot-sniffing critics were quick to assert that they had
been the victims of government suppression of art and
ideas, but it was clear that nothing so sinister was at work.

(The situation was reminiscent of the earlier one of Edmund Wilson, who had not filed an income-tax report for years and when called on it by the government proceeded to denounce Washington for its war against culture.) The Becks, in their beautiful primitivism or dangerous innocence, had blundered across a line dividing realms and were paying the penalty for not being able to distinguish them.

If it was a penalty; in fact it turned out to be a blessing. Artistically and psychologically the Living Theatre had been building toward the necessity for radical change, for a departure that might somehow lead to the resolution of a number of contradictions and contrarieties: their growing dislike and suspicion of formal, fixed dramatic texts, and their technical inadequacy thus far for creating, as Artaud had asked, works directly on the stage; their activist desire to change the world, and their recognition that theater, as they had been practicing it, promised no such alteration; their hunger for community, and their inability up to now to maintain intact the community they had organized; their quest for personal salvation, and their wish to be exemplary, effective, to be instigations to the salvation of others. America having come to an end for them, the Becks and a small band of the faithful set off for Europe in the summer of 1964 to find out what they might become.

2. A Scene Before the Sailing

The Village Gate on Bleecker Street. An afternoon in late spring. The annual Obie awards for off-Broadway theater are being presented before an audience of more than five hundred—theater people, fans, Village swingers—who sit with pitchers of beer in front of them and make loud chatter. Judith Malina is to be given an award for her direction of *The Brig*, and her husband one for having designed it. But they are involved with their trial and

have not been able to appear. As the afternoon draws on
and all the other winners have been given their scrolls by
a smiling famous actress, word comes that the Becks are
on their way. Everyone waits, watching the clock, for
the nightclub has been rented only until five.

A few minutes before the hour, the Becks sweep in,
as though from a motorcade with sirens screaming, and
rush to the podium to embrace the judges and other notables. Miss Malina, her hair flying and her eyes on fire,
blows kiss after kiss to the spectators, many of whom shout
back loving things. Beck stands with arms spread wide
to enfold the room. Then Judith takes the microphone and
in a voice breaking with passion thanks all those present for
their love, their faith, their support of the theater against
tyranny. This is our vindication, she sobs, this is our triumph.
Everybody rushes up then and in a swirl of embraces and
back-pounding the Becks are ushered toward their new life.

3. Judith Malina

"We're a group of people gathered together to go through
certain actions, experiences, words, sounds, movements,
whatever, maybe far more than that, I don't know, in
which one person, or all of the people, or several of the
people are in some way changed, helped, raised, or some
event occurs in the life of the participants, or one or
all, which then makes some actual change in the life
situation . . . we are saying essentially the same things that the
early Christians did . . . the very simple, so simplistic that it
becomes terribly complex because of its simplicity, the statement that we can live with each other in peace without violence, that we can supply each other's needs, that there is
enough and we have some way of making it go round . . . we
can do better, simpler, just love one another."

4. Wanderjahre

Reports came back to America about what was happening to them. Snaking through Europe, a practicing, striving, peripatetic utopia, they picked up new members along the way, some of them temporary; young American actors, or would-be ones, would hear the news, go to Europe to live and work with the company for a while and then come home. They spread further word: the group had changed drastically, having become wholly, furiously evangelical, political beyond politics, and for the first time a true collectivity which lived together and built its repertory around its own visions and imaginative creations instead of relying, as it had in the past, on the works of others. The four years of wandering, during which they shaped their new nature before European audiences whose own theaters apparently possessed nothing so far-out or so *self-willed*, brought the Living Theatre back to America in the fall of 1968 as something unified, millennial and giving off a hard, continuous pressure to take sides.

5. Judith Malina

"There is no need to sit and admire someone speaking a line of poetry in a beautiful voice."

6. An Evening in Brooklyn

The Living Theatre has opened its run in New York after having inaugurated its return to America with a series of performances at the Yale School of Drama. The Brooklyn Academy of Music, a courtly, undistinguished building, redolent of the atmosphere of modern dance concerts, recitals by visiting Russians and fall seasons of lectures by outstanding speakers, is aware of having something rather more questionable on its hands. Seven or eight policemen stand around the entrances and a squad car with its lights on is parked across the street. There had been a wild evening in New Haven during which the Becks had been arrested (and later fined), and it had come very close to cutting off their would-be triumphal tour at the start.

But inside the atmosphere is calm if not exactly decorous. The ambience strikes you as not radically different from that of a good many other occasions of the not strictly commercial off-Broadway theater. The audience is an amalgam of well-dressed, "higher-type" theatergoers in their late twenties and thirties, a scattering of older, in some cases grizzled, followers of culture, and a fair number of hippies, or, doubtless more accurately, hippy-style youths. They give off as a group a sense of mild superiority to the business of attending the theater (having instead just shown up), an implication of being prepared to judge something and not merely consume it. If they are not precisely Brecht's ideal audience, they are a long way from being Belasco's.

But the main reason for their moderate political and class composition and the restrained quality of their expectations is probably the fact that tonight the Living Theatre is doing the only "play" in its current repertoire. It is *Antigone,* Judith Malina's translation (and rewriting) of Brecht's adaptation of Holderlin's German version of Sophocles, and it has been directed by Miss Malina and her husband, who also take its leading roles.

It is a play, but it does its best to keep from being any kind of straightforward one. The Becks, it soon becomes apparent, are involved here with that animus toward the classics which is only in part a matter of anti-intellectualism (and theoretically does not have to include it at all), its other basis being a justified boredom with the way plays like this are perpetually being presented, that is, according to someone's received idea of how Greek "dignity" or "majesty" must have exhibited themselves histrionically in their time.

Thus there is nothing artificially dignified and certainly nothing majestic about this production. It proceeds with the feeling of an experiment, not so much one of techniques as of spirit. What seems to be wanted is a sense of liberty from the text itself in the interests of the people doing it. There is no hesitation in skewing the plot around to point up the most contemporary (and obvious) issues and in fiddling with the texture to release an up-to-the-minute aroma, and the very pace and movement—spasmodic, febrile, continually backing up on themselves—reveal a wish to interrupt and sabotage the stately, solemn, boring measures of Greek tragedy as a cultural inheritance.

One is sympathetic to this ambition, as one is to the occasionally purely physical éclat which the Becks have always proposed as their chief theatrical virtue. This takes the form here of inventive groupings, movements off the stage and into the theater-building-as-the-world, communal sounds and gestures of despair, anguish, frenzy and so on, explosions, silences, palpable declensions of feeling, in all of which the chorus becomes the body of the emotion and the action instead of being their commentator.

But the play is nearly intolerable whenever it has to be acted, whenever lines have to be spoken and consciousness invoked. It is evident from the beginning that whatever else it has become, the Living Theatre has lost almost all its never more than marginal abilities for the rudimentary processes of acting: speech, characterization, the assumption of new, invented life. Miss Malina and Mr. Beck are the worst offenders. As Antigone she is alternately wild-eyed, coy, neurotic and impish, a hippy heroine, while he plays a preposterous Creon, monstrous and swollen, a portrait modeled largely on Lyndon Johnson as MacBird. Heavy-handed, amateurish in the full pejorative sense, making its grotesquely predictable political points about freedom and tyranny with the utmost sneering self-righteousness, this *Antigone* reveals, wherever it "speaks," that the group's strength must surely lie somewhere else.

7. *Stephen Ben Israel, a Member of the Living Theatre*

"At first they're antagonistic and hostile and then they kiss your hand. At the end they have the opportunity to come on the stage and do anything they want."

8. Paradise Now

The group's strength lies theoretically in its rituals and games, its processes of antitheater and attempt to break down what has always separated theater from life. It lies in its raids on the expectations of certain audiences and on the preparations other audiences make for being changed or for being made to feel *alive*; and this possible strength derives from its proposition that reality is in need of new morale and that society, sick and loathsome now, demands regeneration through "honesty," "openness" and "sincerity." "You're presenting your real self," one of the company has said, "as real as you can get, as close as you can get to your authentic self."

Thus to place itself before audiences as colleagues and fellow sufferers, to gather spectators in community with them or, alternatively, to do battle with them, to provoke, needle, exhort, preach, shame, cajole and caress, to lay itself bare, to be sacrificial and incorruptible and redemptive *in the middle of society*—this is what the Theatre organizes itself so strenuously to do. A serious undertaking, an ambition having nothing to do with entertainment or feats of skill or coldly formal art served up from a distance. Something new, a way out of all the separate bags?

Paradise Now is the group's latest and most ambitious production, the work that best exhibits what the Becks are about, what they dream of and hunger after, and how they see themselves. The audience on this night is considerably younger and farther out, although the contingent of more rooted and more nearly patrician spectators is still visible, indeed in a way that makes you think of loosening your tie and mussing up your hair as you walk into the theater, where what greets you is the rumor and aspiration of "life" itself.

You are a few minutes late or, more likely, the show has started before its announced time. On the stage sit, stand or mill about some seventy-five or a hundred persons, almost all of them young; interspersed with members of the audience are some twenty or thirty Living Theatre people, distinguishable by their near nudity. People keep coming up to join in, and you, remaining in your place, try to overcome the desire to ask what exactly is happening, since you know this is the kind of question, out of an old, discredited habit of mind and culture, that the event is designed to eliminate.

What is taking place, in the purely ontological sense, is that the separation between audience and stage, spectator and performer, is being broken down, or at least that is the intention. The scene breaks up, to be resumed later in the evening. People drift back to their seats and the production, or phenomenon, resumes its course, structured and laid out, though appearing not to be. Rituals, games, group embraces, "spontaneous" exercises (among them something the company calls a "trans-flip," in which energy is passed from one to another) and—most centrally, violently and dangerously—colloquies, shouting matches and other intimacies with the audience.

Every so often a truly affecting, even lovely image is shaped; the company, which unfailingly responds as a trained organism in the group exercises and is clear and disciplined in its submission of the parts to the whole, arranges itself silently as an anguished exemplary body of victims or moves around the theater with the rediscovered gravity of a religious procession. And at these times, moments of silence in every case, you feel it possible to move out in love toward the sheer beleaguered, impracticable hope that some kind of community is really forming, and toward the group and the Becks themselves, remembering all the hard times, wanting the thing to be redemptive, purgative and new.

But it is all brought down, the whole enterprise, the myth and the possibilities, by an unforgivable naïveté (if it is merely that) and a self-love that undercuts any pretense of love for us. As they did in the past, but much more violently and apocalyptically now, the Becks are castigating the bourgeoisie, the American social order, the world all around. The hatred and the fury may be tactical at some points, but it overwhelms that to become its own fulfillment; aspiring to prophetic thunder, it reaches you as dementia. Once the ritual gestures stop, once the pure physicality gives way to a resumption of social being, the Living Theatre openly reveals its spiritual and psychological bases. They are in tyranny—the special despotism of the weak—in loss and despair, in resentment and impotence, and a profound neurosis masquerading as redemptive zeal.

The theater is filled with talk at every other moment, and it is pure cant, pompous, self-righteous jargon, a feast of cliché and shibboleth. It is speech that reinforces complacency at the very instant it is trying to prod and unsettle, that brings the darkness nearer through its utter innocence about social and political reality, that says what we already know and have found useless *as words*. "This theater is owned by pigs," an actor shouts. "To reinvent love," they all chant, "to do useful work," "to get rid of central control," "to spell out paradise." "The day we stop using money" will be the day of paradise, we are told. "Be the black, be the poor," we are enjoined, and someone unfriendly in the audience yells back, "Why are you charging admission?"

"Fuck the Arabs, fuck the Jews," the actors bellow in a painful attempt to indicate political impartiality in the interests of human solidarity, an effort made even more embarrassing by their next piece of information: "Fuck means peace." "This theater is yours," we are informed, "this theater is for creating a better world." But except for a very rare moment when something unconscious takes over in you, when the self is forgotten or provisionally overcome (and this accomplished *in spite* of the company and in the face of the rampant egotism), the better world is all rhetorical, all easy, easy statement, the easiest of statements.

"Talk to your neighbor on the right, fascist!" one of the company shouts at a man. And then Julian Beck says that there are 29,000 policemen in this city—"Who will form cells to change their consciences?"—and a printing press is brought on the stage and the company shows members of the audience how to use it for the rhetorical elaboration of the better world. Then in an absolutely flawless cameo of irresponsibility Beck, long lank hair falling back from his great bald dome, biblical and furious, announces that "there are 1,500 prisoners in the Atlantic Avenue jail a few blocks from here, who will free them? . . . we're going to march on the jail and free them later tonight, who will march with us?" Of course no one marches later, of course the prisoners remain. It is all easy, irresponsible, outrageous.

Later, members of the audience drift up to the stage again at the urging of the company. On one occasion they link arms in a big circle and sway back and forth; on another they clap in unison to an actor's low chant. What they want, it is clear, is something physical, to get in out of the cold, to lose themselves; they want community without ideas or articulation, sanction to do something different, to *get out of the rut*. When the call comes to take off their clothes, many obey, with neither alacrity nor self-consciousness for the most part, but, it seems to the fully clothed onlooker, with a sad, temporary freedom, a liberty leading nowhere. ("They have the opportunity to come up on the stage and do anything they want.")

There are exceptions, aggressive egos seizing the day. Among the first to shed his outer clothing (there is never any full nudity; as Eric Bentley has remarked, this is an underwear show) is Richard Scheckner, impresario of the rival Performance Group, who swaggers about in jockey shorts, his huge paunch wabbling, and beckons everybody up to the *breakthrough*.

The audience has its naysayers to everything that is going on, even though the majority seems in at least partial sympathy. Young wits take the opportunity to try to score, in some cases for the benefit of wives or girl friends, but more for the excitement of being someone for a brief public moment; their heckling is inevitably sexual and they clearly do not understand *love*—the love that fills the theater air. Some spectators attempt to argue, debate, ask for practicalities in this sea of revolutionary assertion. But this is an occasion of the *spirit*, and they are violently abused by the actors for not being with it. A member of the company rushes through the aisles and screams, "Stop thinking about yourself and think of the dying!" to which a young man, spokesman for a pained and silent minority, returns, "What have you ever done for the dying?"

9. *Julian Beck*

"We are looking for ways to love you. Make it easier for us."

10. Mysteries and Smaller Pieces

The Living Theatre is still involving the audience in fiercely adolescent and rhetorical insurrection—"stop the

war," "don't vote," "abolish the state," "abolish money"
—offering news that is no news. But this production is on
the whole less verbal and declamatory. The group turns
to what it does best, theatrical games and exercises, having
fun with precisely the kinds of actions serious theater anath-
ematizes. They blow their noses over and over, an action
as important as any other; they march around the stage
in marvelous, useless precision; they "pass" one another
emotions and gestures as if in a warm-up for an athletic
event (it is something they have learned from the exercises
of the Open Theatre). Through much of the proceedings
a little girl of perhaps two wanders, the daughter of a
company member no doubt, and she is allowed to do her
thing, to be there with the same rights as everybody else.

The last piece of action, a long mimesis of social despair and the horrors of impersonality, in which members
of the company "die" in agony at various points in the
theater and are carried stiff and strangely remote by
other actors to the stage, where they are piled in a pyr-
amid, is solemn and affecting. What is more, it's a true
theatrical action, a new one. Yet you leave the theater
pondering the mystery of what this skilled, professional
job of image making has to do with the Living Theatre's
platform and posture, its claim of being *real*.

11.

"This theater is for creating a better world . . . not to tell
you lies. This theater is yours."

12.

Reality, truth, are what the Living Theatre is supposed to
be about. Apocalyptic, tendentious to the point of violence,

a self-generated and self-validated juggernaut of renewed humanism and revised sensibility, the company comes at its audiences charged with mission. This is what it hopes you will experience: not performance, presentation, an active shaping for passive onlookers, but action itself in which everyone participates, boundaries break down, and company and audience enter into a new and mystic collectivity, germ center of a coming better world.

At the center of its sensibility and operations, as these concern theater, is the recognition that the stage up until now has rested on the principle of illusion, from which follows the fact that it can be and mostly has been used for confirmation of existing experience or for dream and solace. If you wish to use it for something else, for change, upheaval, Artaud's "plague" which brings about actions of recovered health through homeopathic treatment and leads to action outside the theater, then the illusory nature of the stage has to be overthrown. The problem is whether art really is or has to be an illusion; and the fact that there is a problem stems from our confusion in America between what art and life are like as realms. Art can only be considered an illusion if it is not considered a fiction, which is to say something made up, something whose point is to be made up. An illusion is what is not true about life, it is life misleading us; art is not life misleading us but being reinvented, made up for, given increments.

The stage, in all its modern travail, has grappled with the necessity to be an additional reality, an increment, when every pressure from society asks it to be a complement, a procedure which reproduces life or somehow "enhances" it or gives it "meaning." The popular stage has continued to be illusory, which is to say a matter of life misleading us; we can only say about a work of drama that "life is not like that" when the play is not a work of art, a true fiction. From the late Ibsen to our own moment, serious theater has attempted to become fictional while throwing off illusion; the erosion of traditional plot and character since Ibsen and Strindberg is one process of drama's throwing off its resemblance to life in order precisely to become more alive.

But there is another recent tradition, that of breaking down illusion and imitation in the theater by trying to be "real" through presenting the selves of the performers instead of imaginary ones. The tradition is really one in the line of anti-art: no fictions, nothing "made up," only what is decided on here and now in the place of performance—a theater, a garage or the outdoors, as in the case of happenings and the like. This is what the Living Theatre is ostensibly trying to do in an action designed to change life and not merely to add to it, above all not to confirm it in illusions.

If this is so, and if the theater has to renew itself by dealing with the question of illusion, with the at least partly discredited tradition of impersonation, of pretending to be *someone else* (which the film, for one thing, gets around through its very abstraction, its mythic reality), then what is the point of miming dead men or any other kinds of actual being? If you are to rouse and change audiences, for political purposes or for more general humanistic ones, by putting yourselves in front of them as your own selves, exemplary but also familiar, doing the things the spectator would presumably do if he were not a spectator, and soliciting him to do them, to come up on stage, to sing along, to take off his clothes—then why impersonate anything, why pretend? If the point is to break down the artificial distinctions, then why "act" at all? Is it theater or is it life?

13. Judith Malina

"I think that every situation in which people can break through social restrictions is very good."

14. A Night in the Quaker Meeting House

The Theatre for Ideas is an organization that began by
presenting experimental and offbeat drama, music and
dance in a small West Side studio and has turned more
and more to sponsoring symposiums and panel discussions
on subjects like Vietnam, American democracy, the irrational, and the future of the various arts. Its audiences
generally include nearly everybody who is anybody in the
New York intellectual world, many of whom come to
give support or quarrel with their colleagues on the platform, and others in order to avoid not putting in an appearance. Lately the discussions have attracted overflow
crowds, necessitating larger auditoriums. Even so, on a
Friday evening in March people are being turned away
from a former Quaker meeting house in Gramercy Park
while inside some five hundred others prepare to listen to
a discussion of the Living Theatre.

The official subject is "Theater or Therapy?" and the
panel is composed of Robert Brustein, dean of the Yale
School of Drama, who is to represent the negative, which
is to say to be against the Living Theatre; the writer
Paul Goodman, who is to speak in favor of it; and Judith
and Julian Beck. The moderator is the social commentator
and author Nat Hentoff.

Brustein begins by wondering what the discussion topic
might mean, and then tells the audience that since theater
is never therapy, never heals anyone, he will talk about
whether the Living Theatre has been offering anything useful or revivifying for the stage. It hasn't, he says in a matter-
of-fact voice, since it has repudiated everything central to
the practice of drama as an art, having renounced structure,
ideas, language and the histrionic imagination in favor of a
deadly illiterate amateurism based on acting out. Then he
goes on to describe the group as fascist in temperament and

methods, a manifestation of the new anti-intellectualism and impatience with culture, a sign of the new anarchy.

Before he is halfway through, the heckling begins, a voice shouting something unintelligible from the balcony. Though he manages to finish, the interruptions increase; their gist, and in some cases their explicit content, is that he is "full of shit." The audience, so heavily loaded with literary notables, full of minds used to responding to phenomena and drawing social implications, begins to stir; people look about, question one another. But there is not yet any shape to the disturbance. Paul Goodman, who has been sitting on the floor of the podium with his back to the audience in a gesture of either relaxed intimacy or supreme arrogance, is asked to speak, and after announcing that he has not seen the Theatre since before they went to Europe but believes that he's for it, delivers a rambling disquisition, full of patronizing, smiling "see?"s and "you know"s, on the parallels between the Protestant Reformation and what is going on now among the young disaffiliated like the Living Theatre.

There is some further exchange on the stage, when the heckling suddenly breaks out much more violently. All over the auditorium people leap to their feet hollering or run shouting and gesticulating through the aisles. They are immediately identifiable as members of the Living Theatre, some twenty or twenty-five of them dressed in hippy outfits or various kinds of "colorful" costumes. They keep up their screaming, the import of what they are saying being that the proceedings are foolish. "Go home, go home!" one of them keeps screaming. "Don't listen to this bullshit!"

But the debate on the stage manages spasmodically to go on. Miss Malina tells Brustein that "we're banking on the fact that if the people are given freedom, they'll choose freedom, not fascism . . . we give the stage to the audience in the belief that every single one of them is capable of being a sublime creative artist . . . it's the premise of the work we're doing." Brustein, still calm, remarks that what's taking place is evidence of something else, to which Miss Malina, her eyes dancing, retorts, "It's beautiful!" and Beck, standing there like a noble old savage in sleeveless silver vest and a band pulling back his hair, says, "Better get used to it, it's coming attractions."

Now the meeting house is a scene of near chaos. The Living Theatre members, scrambling down from the balcony, racing through the aisles, scream imprecations at the audience. "Fuck you, liberals!" one yells over and over, while another grabs a woman's purse, runs in front of the podium and empties the contents of the purse over the auditorium floor. The learned and talented audience is registering shock, dismay, or anger; shouting matches take place everywhere. The stage is in milling confusion, its only still points being the figures of the Becks standing there in icy serenity, like field marshals looking down on a battle going as they had planned.

The moderator, Hentoff, huddles with Shirley Broughton, the head of the Theatre for Ideas, who in turn huddles with a large, bewildered security guard. Now, her face white, fighting to be heard, she declares the meeting adjourned, apologizing to the audience and promising them their money back. But though a few persons have already left, almost everyone waits, nobody sitting now, while the uproar and the skirmishing—very close to actual violence now—continue in the hall. For most of those present, what is happening has an almost unimaginable quality of the underlife, irrationality and anarchic aggression bursting through all the civilized arrangements and traditions.

At this point Richard Scheckner seizes a microphone and in a confidential, this-is-my-scene voice tells the audience to be calm, to enjoy themselves, to *go with it*. But nobody pays attention to him, and he is suddenly thrust from the limelight by a far more grandiose ego.

Norman Mailer, who arrived forty minutes late in a dramatic entrance and has been sitting down front with arms folded on his chest, abruptly barrels his way to the podium, takes another microphone and barks in a peculiar Southern accent, a new persona, "Now listen, everybody, I'm Norman Mailer, this is a tough town, there's always someone tougher than you. I'm Norman Mailer."

"Who?" someone calls from the balcony. Mailer, grim, tight, a threatened institution (this is a big occasion for egos, a *test of leadership*), snaps back "Norman Mailer" and goes on to harangue the crowd, trying in some gross and unfathomable way to take command, to bring his own order to the chaos. But he is an absolute failure (later he will remark to Hentoff, "How does it feel to be as ineffectual as me?") and the wild, extravagant, half-ludicrous and half-terrifying scene continues to unfold.

Now Miss Malina addresses the crowd again. Do you see what you've done, she yells, you can't go along, you can't let yourself go! Be free, she tells them, experience it! Everything that I've just seen happen is beautiful and good, it's so beautiful and you won't go along with it! You've ruined it and it's so good! There is amazement and disbelief in the audience. A few who recover first shout accusations that the Becks have planned the whole thing. Jumping up and down, her arms flung wide, Miss Malina screams, "This is a holy place and I'm a religious woman and I swear to you that we knew nothing about it, I swear to you I'm as surprised as you are. But it's so wonderful!" A few minutes later Rufus Collins, one of the evening's chief nihilists, admits to an onlooker that he had told the Becks that afternoon what the company was going to do.

And now the evening settles down to fitful flurries of violent talk and near-physical encounters between members of the Living Theatre, others of whom pose on the stage as Indians, fag queens and lady vampires, and members of the audience, others of whom stand around talking about the events, a common sense being that of some acute and unappeasable sickness having been uncovered. Rufus Collins keeps screaming, "Stop analyzing and start living, that's what this is all about, you fucking liberals!" A heavy-set middle-aged woman goes up to him and says in a flat, even voice, "The things you have been saying are stupid, narrow, ugly, bullying, you are a stupid bully," while Collins goes on chanting in her face, "Fuck you! Fuck you! Fuck you!" It is not until two-thirty in the morning that the last noises die away and the gestures stop being made in the old Quaker meeting house in Gramercy Square.

15. Jonathan Coppleman, a Former Student at the Yale Drama School

"It seems to me that the trouble with the Living Theatre is that they've gotten totally implicated in the society they hate. They stare the legal structure in the face and the legal structure stares [back] and they're frozen in that position and can't move and can't conceive of anything outside those terms. And I think the LT is quintessentially American in the assumption of their own innocence in looking at society and responding to it and [being] paralyzed by the horror which they say is in society but which is really in themselves. And that's why they continually get involved in their opposite; whenever they talk freedom, it's totalitarian. It's an incredible circle, something like the reflection of a Medusa's head. Their eyes are locked into it."

16. Julian Beck

"I'm raging . . . we're going to make it together some-how . . . but you're not getting across to me."

17.

The Living Theatre returned to Europe in April, leaving behind an extraordinary legacy of clashing opinion and violent response. In some places on their tour they seemed to bring news to naïve and experientially starved audiences, to come on as pied pipers of an alternative to present existence; in others, campuses like Berkeley, they were left far behind by spectators much tougher and more sophisticated than they. For the critics of *The Village Voice* their visit proved to be an incentive to an orgy of the self-indulgent, pseudophilosophical and lugubriously personal journalism, full of dreams and confessions, that is usually kept somewhat in check. For the critics of *The New York Times* the occasion was one inspiring the desire not to be left out.

As they moved in sparse and equivocal triumph through America, the group clearly became more and more resentful and dangerous, a wounded animal trying to break out. Many of the members went increasingly on drugs. At the Quaker meeting house one knew that everything inherently irrational and demented in the Theatre's postures and ideology was at its peak, shamelessly and nakedly on display. And one saw because of this how at the basis of the company and its appropriated mission and of the Becks' mythical and wizardlike status as their leaders exists an amazing lie, perhaps the most representative lie of our time.

For the Living Theatre, apart from some circumscribed theatrical gestures and practices, has no status as an achiever of true, uncoerced, felt community or of the regeneration of political possibilities through accurate and hitherto unknown movements and utterances of indictment, repudiation, alternate morale. The claim of love, the claim to be a sacrificial agency for its audiences' resurrection, is the basis of the lie. "Do you think Julian Beck loves you?" a student asked adherents of the group at a discussion, and when she heard cries of "Yes, yes!" replied, "Well, I don't love Julian Beck. And I don't love you. And love is something that has to be earned."

The Becks are fundamentally ignorant of what is happening in the world, nor do they wish to be informed: Self-pity and self-love always crowd out knowledge. If the Living Theatre were truly interested in others or even in peace and human beauty, they would *see what they are doing* instead of plunging forth unappeasably in the fixed conviction of their own righteousness and of the guilt or inadequacy of the people they appear before. (One is continually surprised at how uncomfortable they are in the face of the many members of the audience who are clearly in sympathy, as though something precious in their self-consideration as noble outcasts, unique critics, were being threatened.)

Having made certain moves in the direction of a theater freer of artificiality and closer to the realities, they continually move off into their own astonishing artifices and unrealities. Their arrogation to themselves of peace, love and freedom, unsupported by anything earned, anything achieved or newly discovered about those conditions of humanity ("What have you ever done for the dying?"—a nurse does more), their wanting it both ways—to be a theater of public and political use and at the same time to be an apocalyptic community in search of its own salvation, their clear, hard, unwavering *résentement*—all this is painful to see and experience as it announces itself as rebirth. We are all waiting for the future to take hold in the theater, for politics to be cleansed and revivified by art or any other means; nothing like that is going to come from people who cannot see beyond the mirror.

"It's not a show, it's the real thing!" a member of the Living Theatre shrieked during *Paradise Now*. No, it's not the real thing, it's a show.

ABOUT THE AUTHOR

RICHARD GILMAN is Professor of Playwriting and Criticism at the Yale Drama School. He has been Literary Editor of *Commonweal* and *The New Republic* and Drama Editor of *Commonweal* and *Newsweek*. Mr. Gilman has also taught at Columbia and Stanford universities, and was on the faculty of the Salzburg Seminar.

VINTAGE POLITICAL SCIENCE
AND SOCIAL CRITICISM

A free catalogue of VINTAGE BOOKS *will be sent at your request. Write to* Vintage Books, 457 Madison Avenue, New York, New York 10022.